Penguin Handbook
Friends of the Earth

Friends of the Earth is an environmental pressure group
funded by voluntary contributions. It has over 200 local
groups in the United Kingdom and is part of a world-wide
federation of similar organizations.
Friends of the Earth actively pursues campaigns on energy
strategy, transport policy, land use, the protection of
endangered species and the use of material resources. It is
associated with the environmental research charity Earth
Resources Research.
The organization's address is: Friends of the Earth Ltd,
9 Poland Street, London W1V 3DG (01-434 1684).
Veronica Sekules was Administrator for Friends of the Earth
from 1975 to 1976.

Friends of the Earth Cookbook

Veronica Sekules

Illustrated by Donna Muir

Penguin Books

Penguin Books Ltd, Harmondsworth, Middlesex, England
Penguin Books, 40 West 23rd Street, New York, New York 10010, U.S.A.
Penguin Books Australia Ltd, Ringwood, Victoria, Australia
Penguin Books Canada Ltd, 2801 John Street, Markham, Ontario, Canada L3R 1B4
Penguin Books (N.Z.) Ltd, 182–190 Wairau Road, Auckland 10, New Zealand

First published by Penguin Books 1980
Reprinted 1981, 1984

Made and printed in Great Britain by
Butler & Tanner Ltd, Frome & London

Set in Monophoto Photina

To friends of the earth, everywhere

Contents

Preface

Britain is a wealthy and civilized nation. Its wealth and civilization are the product of a vigorous pursuit of an Elizabethan world view. This aggressive age saw itself in a limitless world full of vacant spaces (we tended not to count the original inhabitants) and unexploited resources. The purpose of life was the creation of wealth by the transformation of raw materials into useful products. Only failure of the imagination or lack of determination were perceived as limits to human achievement. This world view found its culmination in the euphoric growth mania of the post-war decades – the era of conspicuous consumption and the throw-away society.

In recent years this world view has begun to change, widely and fundamentally. The quick and continuing succession of population explosion followed by environmental crisis followed by economic recession, together with the increasingly apparent failure of economic growth to relieve poverty or guarantee happiness, has shaken confidence in such a view. We now live in a limited world which we share with increasing numbers of people. There are limits to the availability of food and raw materials, to energy supplies, limits to how many trees can be cut or how much pollution a river can absorb. The awareness that we live in a world which is changing fundamentally has grown with unparalleled speed.

These changes will affect the way each one of us lives our life at every level and in every aspect. This will be as true of the way we eat as it will be of the way we travel or work or use our leisure. Our old world view led us to create waste as fast as we created wealth. The satisfaction of basic needs for warmth, food, shelter and health for the whole of mankind is an essential condition for future global stability. If we are to achieve this goal without the destruction of the ecological basis of life we must eliminate waste.

There can be few images quite as powerful for illustrating the extraordinary wastefulness of our current habits than the fact that in a world in which hundreds of millions of people cannot get enough to eat, overeating is among the fastest growing causes of death in industrialized countries like Britain. If we are to maintain a civilized society in a changing world our eating habits must be formed in an awareness of the real needs of both the world as a whole and of our own bodies. This book has been written with such an awareness in mind.

Tom Burke
Director,
Friends of the Earth
18.1.79

Introduction

The real power in the future will not be nuclear power, or even energy, but will belong to whoever possesses the sources of food.

Mr Ismail Sabri Abdulla, Egyptian Minister of State

Since the world food crisis of 1974, the likelihood of food being used as a political weapon in international affairs has become increasingly real. In that year, the chaos created by two successive crop failures in the major grain-producing areas of the world reached a peak. The power of the wealthy and the helplessness of the hungry became apparent as never before.

If the panic reached Surbiton, Sunderland or Southampton, it was quickly forgotten. Harvests in the years following 1974 were at record levels. There is now a world grain surplus. Although a welcome reprieve in the short term, it has inhibited the immediate actions that would have been forced upon us had the crisis continued.

As early as 1798, Thomas Malthus predicted that world population would grow in geometrical progression until it outstripped its means of subsistence. So far, advances in technology, which he could not foresee, have delayed a collision between population size and world resources. It is now widely believed that such a collision is inevitable. Present trends show world population to be rising at an annual rate of nearly 2 per cent, with a higher annual rise in the developing world. If this trend were to continue steadily, there would be nearly 2000 million more people in the world by the year 2000. In effect this would mean that every forty days until then, a city the size of London would be born, needing to be housed, clothed, educated and employed, let alone fed. There is, of course, another school of thought. The American ecologist, Paul Erlich, holds the neo-Malthusian view that this figure is unattainable. He believes that gradual environmental collapse will increase, exercising a natural control over the population.

It is, however, clear that speculations about our prospects for survival are by no means in the realms of fantasy. Even if Erlich is eventually proved right, it is still immoral not to plan for the millions of people who will try to survive. The world's population, always finely balanced on the available resources, will have to find more food from somewhere for the foreseeable future.

There are two obvious ways of increasing food production. The cheaper and more attractive way, for the time being, is intensified production on land already in cultivation. But the constant passage of heavy machinery, the prolonged application of chemicals, the systematic removal of hedgerows and the relentless double-cropping all take their toll of the land. In some areas, the soil is being eroded and exhausted with over-use. According to the law of diminishing returns, it is just not possible in highly developed areas to intensify production any further. Much can be done with selective plant breeding, so that crops need be grown less intensively, requiring fewer chemicals to produce optimum yields. Only time will tell whether this can achieve successful results. In the meantime, we simply have to hope that any damage that is being done is not irrevocable.

The alternative solution is to find more land. It has been estimated that between 20 per cent and 30 per cent of the globe's surface is suitable for food production. Inevitably all the best land is being used already. What remains for future exploitation is of marginal value and will be prodigiously expensive to develop. Where substandard soil, or deforested land, are being cultivated, there is a constant danger of wind erosion and gradual desertification, as the plant cover is insufficient to bind the soil particles together. For this very reason, the intensively cultivated, overgrazed and increasingly treeless regions bordering the Sahara are rapidly being absorbed into the desert.

Land loss through careless cultivation or development may equal or even exceed the new land which is being brought into cultivation. In Britain, we have a problem equivalent to that of the Sahara borders. Here, it is not sand that is encroaching on agricultural land, but concrete. Early settlers farmed the lush and fertile river valleys. Around them grew towns and cities, roads and motorways. These rob Britain of 70,000 acres of prime agricultural land every year, an area the size of the county of Berkshire. No amount of reclamation of polar regions or irrigation of desert lands could compensate for that.

Even now, half the world's population is starving. But the problems of feeding the world are not only caused by a scarcity of resources. They have as much to do with the distribution of these resources. On the whole, the developed world does not take food directly from the developing countries, but it does so indirectly, by dominating world markets for food. In 1974, the Central Intelligence Agency in the U.S.A. issued a statement which brought this sharply into focus:

It seems clear that the world of the poor at least will experience continued food shortages and occasional famines over the coming decades . . . the US near monopoly position as a food exporter could give the US a measure of power it never had before . . . Washington would acquire virtual life and death power over the fate of multitudes of the needy.

In Britain, we too could have life and death power over multitudes of the needy. Our motives are not as sinister as those of the C.I.A., but we are just as guilty of dominating world markets for food. Eight million acres are used overseas to grow 50 per cent of our food. The reason is simple. We eat too much meat. Our entire agricultural system is devoted to growing food for animals, which convert it very inefficiently into food for us. Meat, live animals and animal feedstuffs account for nearly 50 per cent of our food import bill. Overall, one third of the world's grain is destined, not for people, but for animals; to feed, not the needy, but developed countries like ours.

An immediate solution to the world food problem is obvious. We could make more land and food available, even for an increased population, by raising fewer animals. Every one of us can help. It would involve a shift in our dietary patterns: less meat and more vegetables. That shift is already beginning. The aim of this cookbook is to push it farther.

Acknowledgements

This book would never have been written had it not been for the unfailing encouragement of many friends and colleagues. Above all, I must thank Angela King and Angela Potter who were deeply involved with the book in its early stages and helped to make it what it is now. Tom Burke diverted some of his boundless energy and enthusiasm towards helping with the original idea and the editing of the manuscript. Colin Blyth, David Baldock, Colin Hines, Richard Sandbrook and John Denham patiently read through my work and made valuable suggestions. I am grateful to Christopher Wardle and Dr Robin Roy for their careful work for Earth Resources Research, which made many aspects of my task very much easier, and to Sue Steward who researched the chapter on pulses. I must also thank Anthony Tucker of the *Guardian* for his section on metals in food, and Mick Hamer for the beer recipes and many samples. I am indebted to Sandy Heslop for being critical and long-suffering, and for writing the section on wine. Bill Roberts, of the Consumers' Association, and Virginia Evans answered many queries. My mother, Marianne Sekules, who first taught me how to cook, also contributed many recipes, as did Angela Potter, John Pudduck, Ingrid Hull and Alma Giersch. My thanks to Shirley Bennet and Sue Steward, who typed the manuscript with great speed, and last, but by no means least, to all those friends who tested recipes, and to Jill Norman and Felicia Pheasant of Penguin Books, with whom it has been a real pleasure to work.

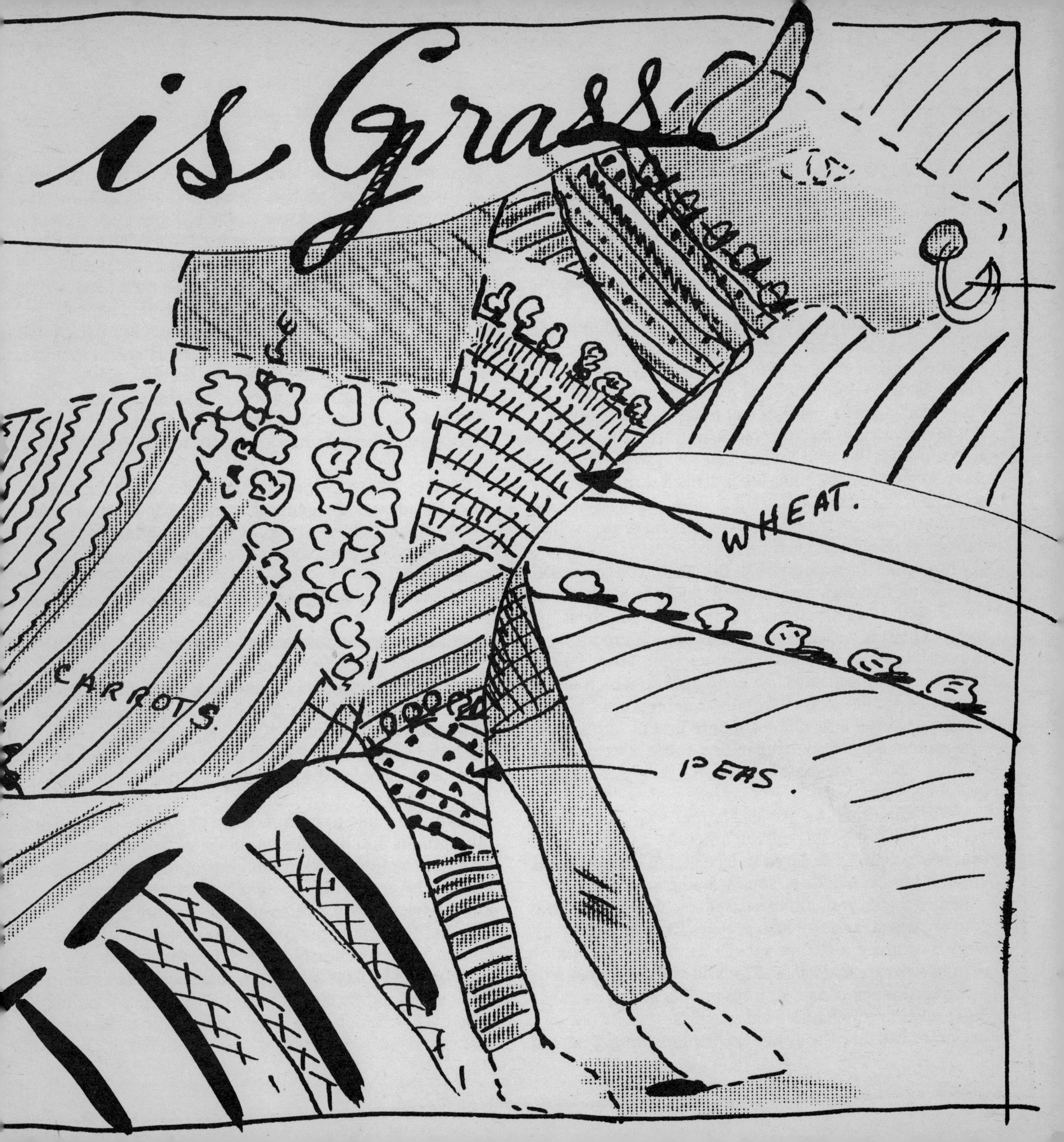

is Grass
WHEAT.
CARROTS.
PEAS.

Not so long ago, 'foreign foods' were regarded in Britain with great suspicion. Now, Chinese, Indian, Italian, French and Greek grocers and restaurants are common in many towns, and many English people can recognize and cook a pepper, an aubergine or a clove of garlic. For a nation of supposedly conservative eaters, this change has been remarkable.

Still, the tradition of the 'Roast Beef of Old England' dies hard. Meat always features as the centrepiece of a traditional British meal, with vegetables taking second place. Many people would be reluctant to see the disappearance of roast beef, yet meat may already be gradually pricing itself out of the market. If we are all to have enough to eat in future, meat will almost certainly have to give way to other foods. This is a dramatic statement, but few people realize how many resources are ploughed into the production of meat and just how expensive the process is.

More than three quarters of British farmland is used for rearing livestock and for growing its feed. This is still insufficient and more feedstuffs, livestock and meat have to be imported, adding some £2000 million to an import bill which is already high enough. From the 15 million tons of feedstuffs, excluding grass, which are given to animals each year, only 4 million tons of meat, poultry, eggs, cheese and butter are produced in return. The protein conversion rate of beef cattle is the poorest of all: 22 lb of protein feed yields only 1 lb of edible beef protein.

In Britain alone, we are feeding not only 56 million people, but nearly 200 million animals as well. The fact that few people have dared to face is that there just isn't enough land available to supply food for both.

Before the days of intensive feeding, sheep and cattle converted poor pasture into protein. Only in winter were they given a dietary supplement consisting mainly of home-grown root crops. Pigs and chickens were fed on crop residues, kitchen scraps and factory wastes. Such meat production was more efficient in its use of resources because the animals were not competing with humans for the same land and food. If we were to revert to levels of animal protein production compatible with this method of feeding, we would still have some meat and we would also have more land available on which to grow vegetables, cereals and beans for ourselves.

The medical profession has for some time been adding weight to the arguments against meat. It is almost certain that a diet of too much meat and animal fat and too few vegetables and cereals makes us vulnerable to an early death from heart failure. The average consumption of animal protein in Britain exceeds the minimum level recommended by the Food and Agriculture Organization of the United Nations by nearly 50 per cent.

It takes a long time for the opinions of nutritionists to filter through to the general consciousness, let alone to governments which negotiate butter subsidies, whilst recommending a reduction in the consumption of animal fats.

At one time the importance of protein in the diet was overemphasized. Protein is a source of energy and is essential for the maintenance of growth and the renewal of tissues. However, only 5 per cent of the energy in a diet needs to come from protein, as opposed to the 10 to 15 per cent that most people receive. In other words, if a healthy full-grown adult needs 3000 calories per day, only 150 of these need to be from protein and could be supplied by as little as two cheese sandwiches.

Plants are able to manufacture protein from sunlight, but animals and humans cannot and therefore have to take in protein from food. Millions of different proteins exist. They are all composed of selections from the known twenty-two amino acids which are linked together in varying proportions and sequences in an endless variety of combinations. During digestion, proteins are broken down into their constituent amino acids and are then recombined to form the particular proteins essential to the body. These have quite specific functions – one may carry vitamin A in the bloodstream, another may be a digestive enzyme, another the hormone insulin. It is possible for the body to convert some amino acids it does not need into those it does, but there are eight, called the essential amino acids, which the body cannot manufacture. These must be supplied by food.

An ideal way of providing all the essential amino acids in the right proportions would be to eat other human beings. Given that this would be unlawful, impolite and distasteful, the next best way would be to eat a variety of proteins from different sources. By combining, say, milk with cereals, bread or pulses (dried beans, peas and lentils) with cheese, fish with potatoes or pulses with grains, the proteins in each food will complement one another – one food will provide the essential amino acids which may be lacking in the other. This is not as complicated as it sounds. In many cases, foods which complement each other's proteins also complement each other's tastes and are eaten together anyway.

A reduction in meat production and an increase in the production of cereals, vegetables and beans will be impossible to achieve as long as the present Common Agricultural Policy of the European Economic Community continues to operate in its present fashion.

The Common Agricultural Policy seems unable to ensure that supply meets demand, nor does it encourage a rational use of the land. Prices for agricultural produce are recommended annually by the E.E.C. Commission and are modified by the ministers of the member countries.

A function of the Common Agricultural Policy is to intervene in the market for agricultural produce, to prevent fluctuations in the supply of various products, and also to maintain the level of rural income. Clearly, farmers will be unwilling to grow more cereals unless there is some incentive for them to do so. The Common Agricultural Policy is a framework within which such incentives can be provided. By a more selective intervention in the market, the E.E.C. could, if it so wished, alter the pattern of agricultural production in Europe, so that more plant protein and less animal protein was produced.

But E.E.C. agricultural policy has to be approved by the agricultural ministers of the member countries before it takes effect. Government ministers are very conscious of the demands of the consumers. Thus it is up to us to create the demand for more vegetable protein. If we do not, nothing will change.

waste not
ETIQUETTE SAYS →
BE SURE TO LEAVE A LITTLE OF YOUR FOOD ON YOUR PLATE WHEN FINISHED
SOME LEEKS.
A FEW PEAS.
A FEW POTATOES
a bit of meat
2.

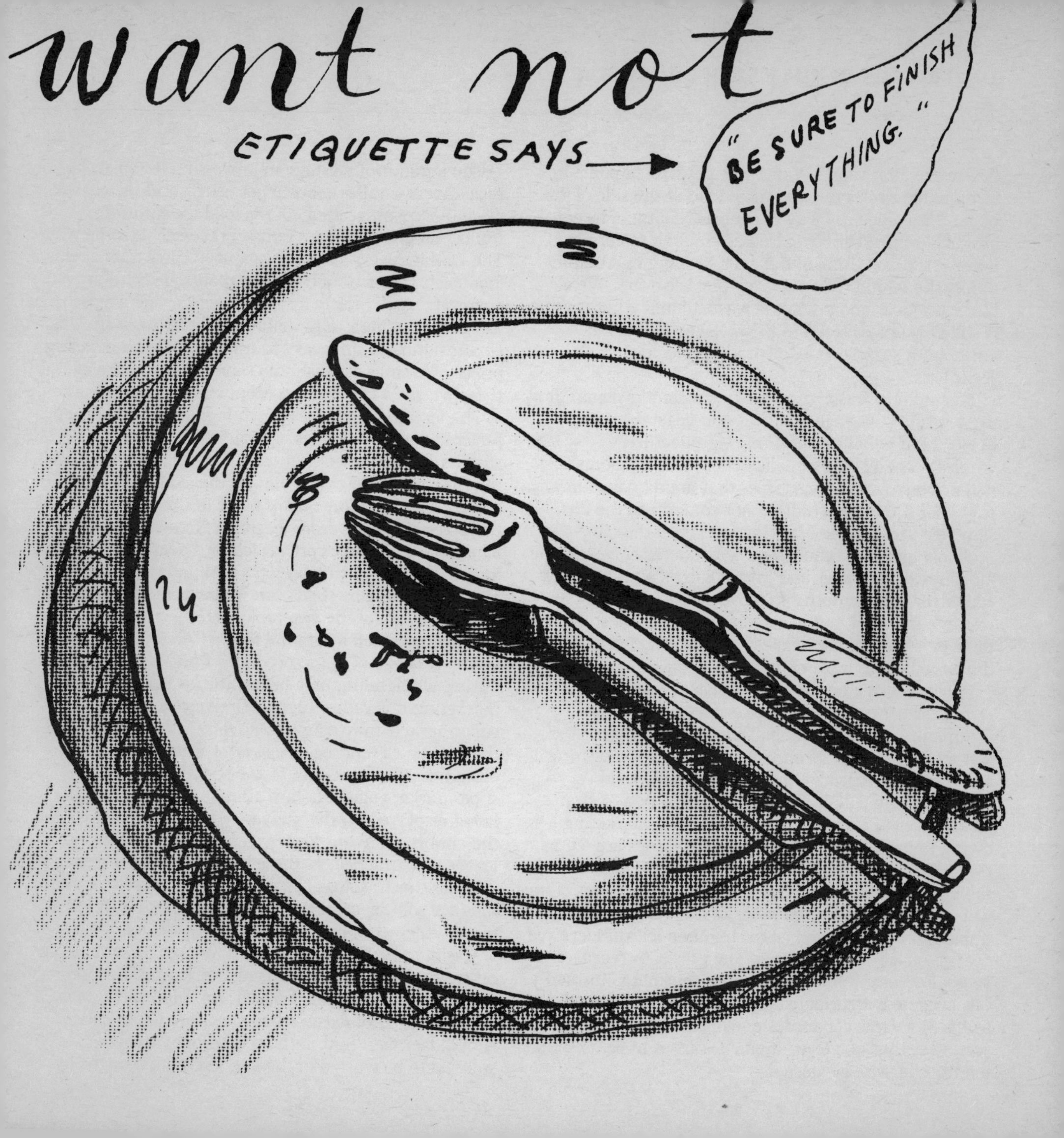
want not
ETIQUETTE SAYS
"BE SURE TO FINISH EVERYTHING."

Before the First World War it was considered polite in fashionable circles to leave some food at the side of the plate, untouched. By way of contrast, many of us can probably remember being told as children to eat up every scrap and think of the poor starving children in India who would welcome even our left-overs. We all have our ideas about what is wasteful and what isn't. It is still thought wasteful to throw away good food although a surprising number of people do so regardless.

The indirect waste incurred by consumers demanding unblemished, damage-free fruit and vegetables is less obvious but equally important. Manufacturers, wholesalers and retailers alike claim that consumers will not buy fruit or vegetables that are damaged in any way. Thus, the foods that do not conform to the top standard are not harvested, even though they are probably quite acceptable and would at least be suitable for soups, fruit purées and juices. Eating with our eyes rather than our mouths is a costly business. The wastage incurred in the form of rejected foods still has to be paid for and can make a significant contribution to the already high price of food.

Much wastage occurs in all stages of production. About 20 per cent of wastage occurs before a food commodity leaves the farm. This is due to a variety of factors including pests and diseases, weeds, bad storage and damage caused by inefficient and unskilled harvesters. (In 1973, 21 per cent of our potato crop failed to reach the required standards for marketing owing to inefficient harvesting.) Some crops are left in the field because they are either overripe or underripe at the time of harvesting. In some years, 25 per cent of the pea crop intended for the fresh market may be left unpicked. Furthermore, crops are often left unharvested owing to lack of demand and low prices. In recent years, harvesting by the customer ('picking your own') has become increasingly common, especially for soft fruits. Since this eliminates one of the major costs to the producer, that of labour, it enables crops to be used that might otherwise be wasted.

The amount of wastage in processing and distribution is relatively small – about 9 per cent – and mostly takes place during processing. Of the food we eat in the United Kingdom, 70 per cent is processed in some way. The food industry generates about 80,000 tons of waste food each year and of this only about one third is currently used, mostly for animal feeds. The wastes used are generally high in protein, have little moisture content and are thus easy to transport. The increasing prices of animal foods should soon make the use of these wastes a much more economic proposition.

The food industry does much to encourage a preference for vegetables and fruits of a perfectly standard appearance. Almost a quarter (by weight) of the fruit and vegetables eaten in this country are tinned. Much wastage takes place in the preparation of these vegetables in order to give them a standard appearance. Potatoes are peeled into neat, oval shapes and one U.S. firm trims carrots on a lathe into perfect cylinders. These methods can waste as much as half of the edible part of the vegetable, and this waste is only occasionally used as animal food.

The wastage of home-produced fruit and vegetables during wholesaling may be as little as 1 per cent, but in marketing it is rather higher. Greengrocers and supermarkets may trim and discard 5 to 8 per cent of their stock. Greengrocers *appear* to waste more as they often trim the vegetables in the shop whereas supermarket vegetables are already trimmed before being displayed on the shelves. Many people would like the option of buying fresh vegetables with their outer leaves still attached, as these can be used as a separate vegetable or in soups. Turnip tops and Brussels sprout tops are sold separately in some markets and this is a trend which certainly should be encouraged.

It is difficult for the individual to have any influence on waste on the farm or during marketing. But Mrs Beeton recognized how households could solve their own problems of waste when she said: 'Great care should be taken that nothing is thrown away, or suffered to be wasted in the kitchen, which might by proper management be turned to good account.' Once foods have been distributed, the highest overall waste occurs in restaurants, canteens, schools, hospitals and, most surprisingly, in the home. An average British family throws away a tenth of all the food it buys in the form of uneaten, cooked food, trimmings, peel and outer leaves of vegetables. In single person households the wastage is even greater.

The pods and outer leaves of vegetables are often discarded by the consumer, generally because it is not realized that they are edible and because they look less attractive than the parts normally eaten. Such rejects can constitute more than half the weight of a vegetable. In the case of peas, the pods make up 60 per cent of the total weight, broad bean pods 75 per cent and the green tops of leeks 64 per cent. All these can be used in soup or stock or can be made into dishes in their own right (see Broad Bean Pod Pâté, page 68, and Pea-pod and Cucumber Soup, page 48). Other foods thrown away in the home are the meat bones, scraps and gravy left on plates and serving dishes at the end of a meal. Such leftovers might sound unappetizing but they could easily be incorporated into soups and stocks as there is still goodness and flavour left in them.

Food is too expensive and valuable to waste. By exercising a little ingenuity we can all follow Mrs Beeton's advice. It has been great fun compiling a selection of recipes using ingredients which are normally wasted. It is very satisfying to create meals out of nothing. I hope that you will find it as enjoyable.

onsequeNCES

and that's
NOT ALL.

← CORRUGATED.

...IS BE TRUE?

Walking down any busy shopping street in Britain, it is hard to believe that there is a world food problem. The colourful array of fruit and vegetables of every conceivable variety, from all over the world, is strangely reassuring. How can the starving outnumber the well fed in the face of such abundance?

Feeding the world's population is a complicated undertaking and its difficulty is enormously compounded by the great number of conflicting interests involved. Farmers are concerned to get the highest price for their produce. Governments are anxious to reduce import bills, at the same time making sure that the population is well fed. The food industry wants to maximize its profits. Consumers want low prices.

These different interests are bound together by a world-wide network of trading relationships, such that events in one part of the system affect the entire network. And all of these interests are dependent on the weather and the environment.

A natural disaster in Manitoba can wipe out the wheat harvest for a whole year. The Manitoba farmers lose substantial amounts of income and have to raise their prices. Consequently, the price of grain rises on world markets, which means that developing countries are unable to pay for their much needed imports. At the other end of the chain, the flour-milling and baking industries are forced to raise their prices, passing on their increased costs to the consumer. The repercussions of an apparently remote occurrence reverberates all over the world.

Disasters of this kind are documented frequently in the newspapers, but there are also disasters of a potentially more controllable kind which can have profound effects on the environment and no less of an effect on the quality and availability of food. The overriding aim of all producers of food, no matter what their other motives are, is to produce more food from less land at the lowest possible cost. The methods of production which result have often had, to say the least, unfortunate results. The practice of growing huge acreages of a single crop encourages an abundance of pests, and consequently the heavy use of pesticides, some of which have already proved harmful. The removal of hedgerows from mechanized farms, in the interests of increasing acreage, not only displaces valuable habitats for wildlife and plants, but is a cause of soil erosion. Intensive livestock farms exacerbate pollution problems by generating vast quantities of slurry which are often difficult to dispose of. It is not only the land that suffers: many fish stocks have been severely depleted and irreparably damaged as a result of excessive trawling by large factory ships.

Many of these problems have to be tackled at source but, in the meantime, there is plenty that we, as consumers, can do to help. We are, after all, at liberty to choose what we buy, and just as the effects of a natural disaster can reverberate around the world, so can the effects of our daily purchases reverberate in a smaller, but ultimately quite significant, way.

Shopping Around

Over the last ten years, several surveys have been conducted into people's shopping habits. The surveys have shown that the majority of people make more than one shopping expedition per week, and that they like to have a wide range of shops within easy walking distance of their homes. The surveys showed, furthermore, that only 27 per cent of shopping journeys are made by car.

Despite these findings, some of the largest food retailers are planning a revolution that will be to the exclusive benefit of the car-based shopper. They intend eventually to open giant hypermarkets on the edge of every town, where access will be difficult without motorized transport. There are already about 150 hypermarkets and superstores in operation. Not only food, but everything from lavatory paper to the sitting-room carpet, can be brought under one roof. The idea is that the customer will spend a great deal of money in the hypermarket rather than little bits here and there in a variety of shops. Because of their size and siting (usually on the edge, but possibly, in the future, in the centre, of towns), the catchment area for hypermarkets is, or will be, very large.

The advantages of hypermarket shopping are far outweighed by the dangers. For one thing, it is senseless to extend the facilities for the car-based shopper in an age when energy is in short supply and when only slightly more than 50 per cent of the population owns cars anyway. Local authorities are on the whole opposed to hypermarkets. Many are providing pedestrianized shopping precincts in an attempt to reduce and control the amount of traffic in town centres, to make local shopping a pleasanter and more relaxed activity. With a hypermarket on the edge or in the centre of the town, traffic is bound to increase, and the amount of traffic will be in the control of the hypermarket owners, not the local authority.

Inevitably, the convenience and competitive prices offered by hypermarkets tempt many shoppers who would otherwise use local shopping centres. This can only be to the detriment of the local shopkeepers, many of whom will be forced to close down. In the United States, where hypermarkets are much more widespread than they are here, the closure of local shops within the hypermarket catchment areas has accelerated in recent years. Those shops that have remained have been forced to alter the range of goods they offer, selling exclusively packaged convenience items, with a few fresh foods for immediate sale. Hypermarkets, no matter how large, cannot possibly offer the wide range of goods that are now available in most town shopping centres. In the hypermarket world, everything is standardized. The marketing is all done through central depots. If any of the produce on sale happens to be local, it will first have travelled back and forth from the depot, will no longer be fresh, and will invariably be packed with

added preservatives, for the ease of transport and storage. From the shoppers' point of view, this can only be a regression, particularly for the shopper who wants choice, high quality and freshness as well as low prices. Ideally, local authorities should ensure that everyone has a good shopping centre within walking distance of their home.

Vegetables' Lib

The recipes in this book were originally arranged seasonally. There was a summer/autumn section and a winter/spring section, with a chapter for all-the-year-round foods. Up to a point this worked quite well. Root vegetables and greens, apples and pears are appropriate winter foods and tend to disappear from the shops around May, to be replaced by summer salad vegetables and soft fruits. But it quickly became apparent that technology had advanced to such an extent in the food industry that the seasonal grouping of a great many foods was no longer relevant. It is many years since the availability of meat and fish has varied with the seasons and the same is beginning to be true of fruit and vegetables. Hardier strains of seeds, the wide use of glasshouses and improved methods of storage mean that the season for a great many varieties has been considerably extended. Brussels sprouts are available well into the spring, green beans well into the autumn, cauliflowers, onions, potatoes, carrots, cabbages, mushrooms, cucumbers, tomatoes and lettuces are grown practically all the year round. Many more of our seasonal deficiencies are made up with imports from abroad so that we can now eat courgettes, green peppers, aubergines and tomatoes throughout the winter as well as in summer. However strongly one may disapprove of the amount of energy that is used to produce hothouse foods, or to transport vegetables across Europe, these methods of supplying foods are probably here to stay and it is certainly very hard to resist buying Spanish tomatoes or onions when they are cheaper and better than those which are home-produced.

Nevertheless, it is very easy to get carried away with that argument. It is probably a good idea for Europe as a whole to become self-sufficient in temperate fruit and vegetables, but it would be better still if Britain could be more independent of imports from Europe than she is at present. The British climate is ideally suited for growing hardy outdoor vegetables, but, although some fifty varieties are grown commercially, less than 1 per cent of the total agricultural area of the United Kingdom is used for growing them. Because of lack of demand and interest, some fruits and vegetables, such as Jerusalem artichokes, salsify, cardoons, rampion, seakale, quinces, medlars and mulberries have all but disappeared or, in some cases, only survive in folk memory.*

Increasingly, green peppers and aubergines are more attractive to the shopper than are the more familiar swedes, parsnips and turnips. The tendency has been, and will continue to be, for the E.E.C. to standardize varieties of fruits and vegetables throughout Europe. We almost lost the Bramley apple in favour of the insipid and oversweet French Golden Delicious and, if we don't learn to treasure what varieties of fruits and vegetables we have left, they too will suffer the sad fate of the cardoon and the rampion.

However, the food industry is probably more to blame than any other body for diverting the attention of the public away from the wide variety of fresh fruits and vegetables and towards its canned and frozen products. Despite the fact that the growers are developing hardy varieties that will withstand the harshest frosts and the heaviest downpours, the industry continues trying to persuade us that it is only through their preservation techniques that our range of fresh produce is extended to last throughout the year. When we take a look at what the industry has done with the pea crop, it becomes clear what they mean.

In 1965, 18,000 acres of land were devoted to growing peas for marketing fresh, while 83,000 acres were given over to peas for processing. In 1975, the acreage devoted to fresh peas had dropped to 11,000, whereas the acreage of peas intended for processing had risen to 146,000. The chairman of Unilever, whose subsidiary, Birds Eye, is one of the largest pea processors, when asked what attracted him most about his job, replied: 'The power to change things, the power not to have to accept things as they are. You can alter things. For instance, the agriculture of East Anglia has been altered by the operations of Birds Eye.' It is not really surprising that he can make this claim. Frozen and canned peas are a perennial and convenient alternative, not only to fresh peas, but to any other vegetable, and the more widely they are accepted as such, the more so will other vegetables be ousted.

There are probably plenty of people around who have never even tasted a fresh pea, let alone a delicious pea-pod soup, and who could blame them, when, because of the processors, the appearance of fresh peas in the shops is more fleeting every year. It is high time that we liberated our vegetables from the doldrums they have been suffering for years and brought them out as competitors to their frozen and foreign cousins. All this requires is a little determination on the part of the shopper, and ingenuity on the part of the cook. By ignoring indigenous fresh vegetables, we are wasting a tremendously valuable, easily produced and potentially delightful source of food.

*Cardoon: resembles a globe artichoke; the blanched leaf stalks are eaten. Once popular here but now commoner abroad.

Rampion: native British plant of Campanula tribe; the long, fleshy, white roots are eaten.

Factory Farming

Factory farms are supposed to be one of the great success stories of the last twenty years. It is because of them that we are provided with an abundance of eggs and cheap chicken, lean pork, pure white veal and Christmas turkey; and eventually, there will be fatless ducks and geese as well. A distinct advantage to the producers is that the farms require far fewer staff than do conventional livestock farms. The animals or birds are kept indoors in small cages or enclosures restricting their movement to a minimum, which makes them very easy to manage. Their high protein diet enables them to reach the required weight very quickly – calves are ready within twelve to fourteen weeks – so the turnover and the profit margins are relatively high.

The major inefficiency of factory farming is that the protein conversion rate is very low. Thus, every 100 lb of crude protein feed produces only 17 lb of edible protein from chicken, 13 lb from pigs and 5 lb from cattle. Seen in these terms, it is a fantastically wasteful method of food production. On the land required to feed a cow for a year, enough food could be grown to provide a balanced diet for two human beings, whereas the cow would provide the human beings with an unbalanced diet for less than three months. This would never be contemplated in any but the wealthiest countries. The greatest irony is that some of the poorest developing countries make a meagre living by selling animal feed ingredients to the West, while their populations live on diets with practically no meat content.

The conditions in which animals are kept in battery farms are not exactly conducive to a happy life. Chickens are allowed only one square foot of space each, in which to live. As many as a million birds can be stacked in their cages in a single shed where they never see the light of day. Often they are debeaked to prevent them from attacking one another. They are literally live factories for producing eggs and meat.

The farming of veal can be even more cruel than this. Calves are often kept in quite unnatural conditions in order that their flesh may remain lean and white. They are denied the roughage and exercise that young animals need and enjoy. For the duration of their lives they are tethered in minute pens and fed only on skimmed milk. They quickly become anaemic and develop a craving for iron which, again, is denied them. They are not allowed any straw in their pens in case they eat it, and they are even prevented from licking the wooden slats on which they stand in case they get iron from their urine in that way. It seems incredible that a nation of animal lovers should be content to imprison animals for the whole of their lives in such hostile conditions. We lavish attention on some animals while condemning others to a life of misery.

It is easy to forget that factory farming is a recent innovation. It suits the agricultural industry to persuade the public that it is the only way of producing enough meat for our needs, but before the advent of the factory farm, we also had enough meat for our needs. Meat consumption has risen considerably in the last twenty years simply because meat has become cheaper. In 1973 it was estimated that the average person in Britain purchased 35 per cent more protein (mainly from meat) than the D.H.S.S. minimum recommended requirements, and D.H.S.S. requirements are high by international standards.

It has been estimated that without factory farming – that is, if all livestock were free range and were fed a dietary supplement of root crops, crop residues and the wastes from food processing factories – we would have enough meat for approximately 2 oz per person per day, which would be less than we are used to now, but nutritionally adequate.

At the moment, it is exceedingly difficult to buy free-range meat, especially in large towns and cities. One shop in London – Wholefood, Paddington Street, W1 – sells nothing but free-range meat. The Organic Food Service, Ashe, Churston Ferrers, Birkham, S. Devon, publishes a list of farms selling free-range produce. It would also be a good idea to check with local butchers and farms. Free-range eggs and poultry are easier to come by, but it is worth checking whether those claiming to be so, really are. Eggs that are sold as 'farm fresh' will most probably be from battery farms.

The greater the demand for free-range produce, the more likely it is that production will increase and the extra few pence per pound is a cheap price to pay for the knowledge that the animals have been fed economically and reared humanely.

Convenience Foods

Although tinned, frozen and packaged foods were sold in the 1930s, the market for factory-prepared foods did not really expand until well after the Second World War. In the 1950s, there were some 1500 lines of processed foods available; now there are more than 10,000.

Convenience or processed foods range from quick-frozen and tinned foods, cake mixes and prepared puddings, to complete dehydrated and frozen meals. They are heavily advertised and attractively packaged. The whole method of selling is supposed to encourage impulse buying. Surveys over the whole country have shown that households spend about a quarter of their housekeeping money on processed foods.

Convenience foods have become popular largely because they have a 'built-in maid service' – all the work in assembling and preparing the ingredients has been done by the manufacturer. They add variety to the diet and enable people to present whole meals in an instant. The range of tempting foods prepared by the manufacturers is constantly growing; dishes are becoming more complicated and exotic ingredients are gradually being introduced. This is known in the trade as 'value adding'. Food manufacturers know very well that people can only eat so much and that very soon there will come a point at which their market remains static – particularly if the population stops growing. 'Value adding' is literally increasing the sales potential of a raw food by subjecting it to a manufacturing process. It is a calculated attempt to appeal to a more sophisticated market: to 'Tomorrow's Women' (to use the unctuous phrase chosen by one manufacturer in a report on market trends) who have little time but plenty of money to spend. The foods are expensive to buy, even though they cost much less to prepare in the factory than they would in the home. This is partly because the foods are cooked in bulk, but also because the manufacturers normally use short cuts: substituting cheap chemical ingredients for more expensive fresh ones. This is the most worrying aspect of convenience foods. Some care is taken to replace nutrients which are lost during preparation, but nearly all factory-prepared foods contain high levels of carbohydrates (sugar and flour) and chemical additives.

Of the additives which are not used as preservatives or nutrients, many are used purely for cosmetic purposes: to restore colours lost in preparation, to enhance or create flavour, to prevent lumps from forming during storage or to enable canned foods to slip easily out of the tin. Some 230 chemical substances are currently permitted for use in foods. All additives have to be tested by technologists employed by the food industry, who submit evidence of their safety to a government agency: the Food Additives and Contaminants Committee. The F.A.C.C. scientists either accept this evidence, or conduct independent trials and prevent the use of the additives until they are satisfied as to their safety. The F.A.C.C.'s policy does not permit a proliferation of additives, but the toxicity tests which are conducted for chemicals are not always adequate. Some are out of date and need re-examination; other tests have used too small a sample and have produced misleading results. In some cases, chemicals have been rigorously tested and banned in some countries, but are still in use in Britain, pending further trials by British scientists.

What is most alarming is that hardly anything is known about the compound effects of all the chemicals in preserved foods. It is well known that convenience foods are more fattening than the equivalent foods freshly prepared, but research is badly needed to discover whether the effects are even more insidious than that. We should perhaps take a warning from research that has been carried out in the United States of America. It has been found that as people get richer, they become lazier in their eating habits. Rather than eating fresh fruit, vegetables and eggs, they consume large amounts of ready-prepared 'garbage' foods and are showing the effects of malnutrition. The manufacturers have obviously been successful with their 'value adding' sales techniques, but we must make sure that we are not as gullible over here.

Overpackaging

Food packaging has a number of legitimate purposes: to protect goods from damage; to maintain hygiene; and to supply goods in convenient quantities.

It is quite obvious, though, from a glance in any supermarket, that packaging is not only used for practical purposes. Brightly coloured packets in hundreds of different shapes and sizes shout their brand names at the customer from every shelf. Packaging is often used mainly for its persuasive powers of advertising. The most conspicuous overpackaging is that of novelty foods – usually quite ordinary items in elaborate layers of wrapping to make the quantities look larger and the contents more inviting than they really are. In many supermarkets, fruit and vegetables are unnecessarily overpackaged to suit the requirements of distribution methods that are themselves questionable. Oranges have an adequate natural wrapping but are put into cardboard trays and covered with plastic film. Root vegetables, tomatoes and onions are sold in set weights in polythene bags which make them go slimy and mean that they cannot be properly examined. Cucumbers, despite having a tough outer skin, are squeezed into plastic tubes. Drinks are sold, not in returnable bottles, but in cans, cardboard cartons and plastic or glass non-returnable bottles. What is more, at the cash desk these already overpackaged items are placed in paper bags and plastic carriers.

All this packaging has to be paid for, and it is paid for by us, in more ways than we think. We pay not only for the raw materials and the advertising, but also for the energy that has been used to make the packet, and for the eventual disposal. For instance, it can take about 30,000 British Thermal Units of energy to make 1 lb of aluminium. This is six and a half times the energy required to produce 1 lb of steel. The vegetable canning process can use eleven times more energy than is needed to prepare vegetables for the fresh market. Recycling can alleviate the problems and expense of dumping as well as being quite a profitable enterprise. In 1971–2, Worthing Council made £50,000 on the recovery of 6500 tons of discarded material. This is only possible if the rubbish is properly sorted and the packing is made of a single material. The tendency to increase the use of composite packaging materials has made recovery much more difficult and means that the only destiny for the materials is to contribute to the 18 million tons of non-degradable rubbish which is discarded every year.

Some shops are becoming aware of the necessity to sell foods loose. Most whole-food shops set a shining example by using the minimum of wrappings, and by selling liquids in other shops' 'non-returnable' bottles, brought in by their customers. Many supermarkets have a counter where cheese and bacon can be bought wrapped in paper, which is marginally preferable to plastic cling-wrap. One or two supermarket chains are beginning to follow the example set by their Continental counterparts by selling fruit and vegetables loose – they are chosen and weighed by the customer and checked at the cash desk – which just goes to show that they don't really have to be wrapped at all. A few shops are also beginning to discourage the use of paper bags for reasons of economy. It is worth knowing that a shop is not entitled to insist that you use a paper bag. Once you have paid for your purchase, it is legally yours and they are not allowed to touch it without your permission, and that includes putting it into a paper bag. A receipt is quite sufficient proof of payment.

We, as buyers, can do a great deal to make sure that this awareness grows – by avoiding overpackaged goods, by patronizing shops which sell foods loose, by buying in bulk, by using shopping bags instead of plastic carriers and paper bags and by insisting on buying liquids in returnable bottles, returning them to the shop from which they were bought. The use of packaging will only be acceptable if it is kept to a minimum, is all re-usable and preferably returnable. It is up to us to insist that this happens.

Sweet Teeth

In 1937, cargo ships called in to the remote island of Tristan da Cunha, bringing the inhabitants their first ever supplies of refined white sugar and flour. Within a few years, 50 per cent of the population developed dental caries, with the highest incidence in young children. Five years before the advent of these supply ships, only 13 per cent of the population of the island had any form of dental decay, and caries were totally absent in the children under five years old.

Sugar is not a healthy food, in fact it is a mistake to call it a food at all. It is, as nutritionists put it, a source of empty calories. In other words, it is a source of energy, but virtually nothing else, as it contains no protein and practically no vitamins or minerals. The real danger is that, eaten in large enough quantities, sugar satisfies the appetite, but does not satisfy any physiological requirements of the body. Far from it: it rots our teeth and makes us fat.

Nevertheless, sugar and sweets are enormously popular. Between 1880 and 1973, consumption of sugar in Britain had risen from 64 lb per person per year to 104 lb per person per year. Not all sugar is eaten in the form of confectionery, cakes, puddings and jams. Nowadays, nearly all processed foods contain sugar. It has become a standard ingredient in tinned and frozen vegetables, tinned soups, breakfast foods and bottled sauces and spreads, to name but a few examples. It is also added to processed baby foods, thereby encouraging the babies' first teeth to be sweet – and rotten.

As if that weren't bad enough, European governments are insisting that the E.E.C. makes it a priority to become self-sufficient in sugar. In Europe, sugar has to be produced principally from sugar beet, which requires far more land for its cultivation than does West Indian sugar cane. So, European sugar production can only be increased at the expense of other, more nutritious food crops. If the E.E.C. aims to be self-sufficient in all temperate foods – which it does – then it would do much better to forget about sugar beet altogether and concentrate on more essential foods.

Were the consumption of sugar restricted to the occasional helping of jam, or a slightly sweetened pudding, then that would be no bad thing. Sugar is also a good preservative and is essential for brewing wines and beers. We have included recipes for some sweet things in this book, as a diet consisting of nothing but savoury foods would be, frankly, dull. Sugar should be used with moderation, as should any strong herb or spice, as excessive amounts can kill delicate flavours very easily. Fruit compotes are very much richer in flavour if they are only slightly sweetened. Jams and jellies need no more than 1 lb of sugar to 1 lb of fruit and can often be made very successfully with less. Often the sugar in puddings can be replaced with dried fruits which already contain sugar. Most important of all, the demand for sugar would be very much reduced if children were encouraged from an early age to eat nuts and raisins or fresh fruit instead of sticky boiled sweets and chocolates. They would need, apart from anything else, to make fewer unwelcome visits to the dentist.

Energy and

3 TRANSISTOR
WITH ALTERNATIVE ELECTRIC PLUG

5 ELECTRIC LIGHT

20. BLENDER

1. DISH WASHER.

2. REFRIGERATOR

4. GARBAGE DISPOSAL

21. COFFEE GRINDER.

4.

Equipment

8 air INTAKE

IC
ER
MIX
MASTER

ELEC. LIGHT

15.

16 TOASTER

17.
ELEC.
COFFEE POT.

ELECTRIC
FAN

18.

GRILL
19.

9
ELEC.
CARVING KNIFE

11
DRYER

12.
ELEC.
KETTLE

13.
MICROWAVE
OVEN.

14.
GAS STOVE

HOW MUCH OF THIS IS NECESSARY?

Energy will never again be a cheap and plentiful resource. In Britain we are better off than are the people in many other countries, as, for the time being at least, we are self-sufficient in energy. We have enough North Sea oil to last a few decades, enough coal to last a hundred years or more, and supplies of natural gas to last well into the 1980s. Ultimately, though, we have a serious problem in that our supplies of energy are finite. Until we can develop renewable sources of power such as solar, wind and water, we shall have to use what is available to us with restraint.

A surprisingly large amount of energy – a quarter of total annual consumption – is used in private homes. That is more than that used by air, rail, road and water transport, farming and the public services put together. Most of the domestic energy is used for space heating, lighting and appliances, with about 10 per cent used for cooking. It is quite easy, however, to reduce even that relatively small amount: if every single household in the country did, then the national energy savings would be quite significant.

Which Cooker? Which Fuel?

This is the miner
That dug for coal
That boiled the water
That raised the steam
That drove the turbine
That turned the magnets
That made the current
That flowed in the wires
That came through the meter
That ran down the flex
That entered the kettle
To make the tea
. . . In the house that Jack built.

Electricity powers Jack's house. A wiser person would have found it cheaper and less wasteful to use coal or gas directly to boil the water. 'Thinking Electric' may be good for the Electricity Council, but it is bad for the pocket and for the country to use electricity in the kitchen.

A power station needs four units of primary energy to make one unit of electricity. About 70 per cent of the energy content of the oil or gas used to fuel a power station ends up as waste heat. More is lost in transmitting electricity long distances between the power station and the kitchen. It may be convenient, but it is costly.

The biggest energy saving which any household could make would be to cook with natural gas. Because it is a primary fuel, it only has to be transported before it is usable. A panful of water boiled on a gas stove is ultimately using a fifth of the energy used by the same pan on an electric stove. Moreover, the temperature of a gas flame can be regulated more quickly and easily than an electric hotplate, and most cooks prefer gas for that reason alone.

Solid-fuel cookers are very suitable for long slow cooking. Their great advantage over other cookers is that they can also be used to heat water and radiators. For large households, needing large meals and plenty of hot water and heating, they are very economical. In a household which is empty during the day, or tends to do a lot of fast cooking, they would be very wasteful as they have to be kept constantly alight, at an even temperature.

Saving Energy

The oven

The oven of a gas or electric stove is expensive to heat and, in order to make the best use of the energy, it should be filled to capacity. It is quite possible to cook an entire meal in the oven, instead of using the oven for some dishes and the top of the stove for the rest, but make sure that you have a supply of casseroles of different shapes and sizes so that you can fit several of them into the oven at once. If you just want to cook a casserole and not a three-course meal, it would be worth putting together a stockpot from the vegetable trimmings to cook in the oven at the same time. If you plan to bake bread, bake three loaves rather than just one. The extra effort and time to make two more loaves is very small and the fuel cost will be exactly the same. Bread keeps fresh for quite a while if it is kept in the fridge.

The oven stays warm for at least twenty minutes after it has been turned off. For dishes which don't need careful temperature control, it is possible to turn the oven off towards the end of the allotted time and allow the dish to finish cooking in the left-over heat. Recently some drying cabinets for preserving herbs, vegetables, pulses, etc. have come onto the market. These cabinets, which fit on top of the stove, are filled with wire trays and use no energy other than left-over heat. They are expensive to buy, but anyone can adopt the principle by using left-over heat in the oven, perhaps investing in some extra oven racks so that large quantities can be dried at once. As the process of drying can be spread over several days, there is never any need to turn on the oven specially.

The top of the stove

People often think that it is economical in fuel to use a small saucepan for cooking a small amount of food. This is not necessarily true and it is much more important to make sure that all the heat from the cooker is directed into the pan, rather than into the air around it. With an electric cooker, this means having a set of pans which are the same size as the hotplates; with gas, it means making sure that the flames stay under the base of the pan.

Pasta and pulses need to be cooked in plenty of boiling water, but for anything else to be boiled or steamed, use the absolute minimum, otherwise energy –

and water – will simply go to waste. Bring the water to the boil in a covered pan as it will boil much more quickly that way. Once it has boiled, turn the heat right down to minimum, to keep the liquid at a constant simmer. It is worth remembering that the temperature of boiling water and simmering water is exactly the same, and that the steam is exactly the same temperature as the water underneath and cooks just as efficiently.

Heating the kitchen

Even if all these energy-saving rules are observed, a certain amount of heat loss from the cooker is inevitable. The oven, in particular, is never properly insulated and the temperature of the kitchen always rises when it is in use. In winter this can actually be a bonus. If the kitchen itself is properly insulated, the stove can be a valuable source of space heating for the whole room and other sources of heat can be cut down or dispensed with altogether.

Make sure, if your kitchen contains a refrigerator, that it does not stand right next to the cooker or any other source of heat. A refrigerator works by cooling air drawn in from the atmosphere. If the air is particularly warm, it will have to work extra hard, and it can use up to twice as much energy as it would under normal circumstances.

Energy-Saving Equipment

Segmented pans

These are simply saucepans divided into halves or thirds so that several vegetables can be cooked at once. They thus use the energy of one ring rather than two or three.

Steamers

These are ideal for cooking most vegetables. A steamer can be either a pan with holes in the base to allow the steam to filter through from boiling water in a pan beneath it, or a pierced metal stand with hinged 'petals' attached, designed to sit inside an ordinary saucepan. The vegetables are cooked in one of these, covered, over a very little simmering water. The minimum amount of energy is used, few nutrients are lost and the vegetables retain much more flavour than conventionally boiled ones. Several vegetables can be cooked at once, as with a segmented pan.

A pressure cooker

A pressure cooker seals in the steam that escapes from a normal saucepan. This results in an increase in pressure which forces the super-heated steam through the food. It is much quicker than cooking food in an ordinary saucepan, taking, on the whole, a third of the time. Bringing the food to pressure usually takes a few minutes and the cooking time is not counted till after that, so pressure cookers are not invariably economical: with some vegetables the total time and energy may not be any less than for ordinary methods of cooking. They are invaluable, however, for cooking pulses, soups, stews, steamed puddings and stock and, if they are used for these purposes, considerable savings in energy can be made.

Cooking Methods

Stir-frying

Stir-frying is a method of cooking used by the Chinese. All the ingredients for the dish are sliced very thinly indeed (a *mandoline* is the ideal tool for this, see page 38) and literally stirred and fried for no more than two minutes in very hot oil in a rounded shallow metal pan called a 'wok' (a large metal casserole or saucepan will do). A variety of flavourings and sauces are added to the basic ingredients. This is an excellent fuel-saving method of cooking and, as the food is cooked for such a short time, most of the nutrients are preserved.

Thermos-flask cooking

Wide-necked thermos flasks can be used for cooking pulses and stews or casseroles which would otherwise need long slow cooking in the oven or on top of the stove. To prepare the pulses, first soak them in plenty of cold water for twelve hours. Warm the thermos by rinsing it out with a little water just off the boil, tip in the pulses with more boiling water and replace the thermos top. Leave for twelve hours. Stews and casseroles should be part cooked and put into the thermos at boiling temperature.

Boiling eggs

Bring a small amount of water to the boil in a large, covered saucepan. Cook the eggs for the required amount of time, with the lid kept tightly on the pan. If you like your eggs only just set and rather creamy in texture, try this method: Boil some water in a kettle and pour it, while still boiling, over some eggs in a saucepan. Put the lid on the pan, making sure that it fits well, and leave the pan undisturbed for twelve minutes, by which time the eggs will be ready. This is Eliza Acton's method and uses only the energy required to boil the kettle.

The haybox

The haybox is the ultimate in fuelless cookery for the enthusiastic energy saver. It is a suitable method to use for anything which needs long, slow cooking in liquid. Hayboxes were widely used during both world wars, but the principle is much older and has been adopted in various forms over the centuries.

The box should ideally be made of wood, at least four inches bigger in length, width and height than the casserole to be placed in it. It should have a tightly fitting, hinged lid. Pack the box well with any material that will absorb heat (such as screwed-up newspaper, rags, towels, blankets, hay or straw) leaving a well in the centre for the dish. Cook the stew, or pulses, or whatever, for a quarter of the usual time and then pour at boiling temperature (this is important) into a warmed earthenware casserole into which the food will just fit. Cover the casserole and place it in the well in the box, making sure that it fits tightly. If necessary, add some more wadding around the sides of the dish. Pack some more of the lining material tightly on top of the casserole and close the lid of the box securely. The cooking time will generally be four times as long as the dish would take in a cooker. It is very important to remember to heat the food in the casserole to boiling temperature again before eating it, so that all bacteria, encouraged by the long slow incubation, are killed.

Fuelless Labour-Saving Equipment

Most electrical kitchen gadgets consume negligible amounts of energy, unless they are very heavily used. However, in view of the increasing necessity to cut down on domestic use of energy, it is worth investigating ways in which electrical gadgets can be replaced by manual ones. At least these use only human energy and, incidentally, they don't break down so frequently – the cost of repairing electrical gadgets can be very high.

Knives
The first essential is to have a set of sharp knives of differing sizes. Carbon-steel knives are easier to keep sharp than stainless-steel ones, though they do rust easily and should be regularly oiled (with cooking, not lubricating oil!) to prevent this happening. A knife sharpener is a must. A sharp grater with a variety of different-sized grating surfaces is another worthwhile tool. It must be sharp, not only because it is more efficient, but also because certain nutrients in vegetables, notably vitamin C, can be destroyed if the vegetables are cut or shredded with blunt instruments.

Mouli-légumes
The *mouli-légumes* is one of the most useful utensils ever invented. It is really a sophisticated sieve with a masher for forcing the food through the holes. It has folding feet which can be hooked over saucepans and bowls to hold it steady. It takes most of the work out of sieving and mashing anything from soups to purées. It has three interchangeable blades – fine, medium and coarse – and will do anything that a blender will do, except purée crisp, raw vegetables or make mayonnaise. Its advantage over a blender is that, as it is a sieve, the stringy and hard bits of vegetables will not pass through it and the resulting purée is usually smoother and freer from lumps than an electrically blended one. It should be cleaned immediately after use, otherwise the particles of food will dry onto it and be difficult to remove.

Mouli-julienne
The *mouli-julienne* is rather like a large rotary cheese grater. It grates vegetables much more quickly than the customary upright grater and has five interchangeable bases of varying sizes.

Auto-chop
The auto-chop is a gadget for chopping vegetables and nuts. It consists of a plastic drum, open at the base, containing a sharp, zig-zag blade attached to a plunger which emerges through the top of the drum. The food to be chopped is placed on a board underneath the drum and the plunger is beaten down onto it, with the palm of the hand. The blade inside the drum rotates slightly with each beat of the plunger and can chop the vegetables quite finely and quickly. It is especially efficient for chopping nuts.

Rocking knife
The rocking knife is another simple chopping tool with the advantage that it can be sharpened. It is simply a crescent-shaped blade, attached to one or two handles,

which chops the food as it is rocked backwards and forwards over it. If it is sharpened enough, it can be used for dicing or even mincing meat. These knives are sometimes sold with a matching-sized wooden bowl in which to chop the food. One can occasionally buy multi-bladed rocking knives. These knives may be hard to find in all but the best kitchenware shops. They should be more widely available.

Universal slicer or mandoline
This is a very useful tool which can slice vegetables very thinly in half the usual time. There are several different types, but it is basically a thick wooden frame with one or two blades in the centre, held by screws and wing nuts. The angle of the blade can be adjusted according to the thickness of the slices wanted.

Pestle and mortar
A pestle and mortar can be used for pounding food very finely. It can transform nuts into a powder, or vegetables and fish into pastes; it can be used to pound garlic, herbs and spices. A pestle and mortar is generally made of wood or heavy stoneware.

Hand mincers
Hand mincers are very robust and tend to be more efficient and quite as fast as electric mincers for mincing meat, vegetables, pulses, nuts and dry breadcrumbs. They usually have three grades of blade, which are fastened in place by a wing nut and are easy to clean.

Egg beaters
Egg beaters or rotary whisks are essential for whisking egg whites or cream and will do the job in a matter of minutes. They work on a ratchet principle and there are super-speed ones available which are as quick to use as hand-held electric beaters.

Metals and Cooking*

We are surrounded by metals. They are a natural but varying component of the earth's crust. They are there and hence in our food and water, whether we like it or not. A whole range of metals can be essential ingredients of the diet in very small amounts and potential poisons if the amounts are only slightly increased. Their importance has been increasingly recognized during the last few years.

Of course the *acute* poisonous nature of metals has been known for centuries. The new area being unravelled by laboratory research and epidemiology is concerned with chronic exposure to metals at concentrations which are very low and quite undetectable in the normal course of events. But in general, problems are only likely to arise when, by one route or another, the metals become concentrated at levels higher than are environmentally normal.

Lead, copper or cadmium from plumbing pipes can be sources of metal contamination. In Britain and the U.S.A., relationships have been shown to exist between cadmium and blood pressure, and between high levels of lead in drinking water and mental retardation, elevated blood-lead levels, lowered I.Q. and otherwise unexplained hyperactivity in children.

Metals can become concentrated to high levels in food processing, through air or water pollution, through the application of chemicals to plants or crops (such as mercurials to grain), or as a secondary effect of a technology. Many colourings used in glazes on pottery, or in enamels on ovenware, are made with highly toxic metals such as cadmium, lead or uranium. And many

---

*This section is contributed by Anthony Tucker, Science Correspondent of the *Guardian*.

cooking pans or containers may be made from, or surfaced by, poisonous metals.

In some circumstances, these metals can be released in amounts which could lead to poisoning. The chemical route in the kitchen, as in the consumer protection laboratories which test ovenware for problems of this kind, is by acid leaching. Many foods, such as fruit juices, most soups, stews and oven-prepared dishes involving vegetables, and many sweets including those involving lactic acid, will leach metals from the surface of the containers. You cannot prevent this by covering them internally with foil. For this reason, in Britain, the U.S.A. and – less vigorously – within the E.E.C., there are strict controls on the nature of utensil materials. Pottery glazes are now almost universally based on 'leadless frit', and it is unlikely that there will be a recurrence of the cadmium-rich and uranium-rich table and enamelled ovenware which caused serious alarm in Europe and the U.S.A. in the mid 1970s. Yet there are still many utensils around from earlier times and from areas in which controls are poor. It is wise to observe some simple rules.

Although it may make life dull, beware of colour *inside* a utensil (or its lid), or as a component of plastic articles or wrappings intended for storing food. The coloured articles may be perfectly safe, but unless there is a clear statement of the nature and safety of the colouring material, avoid it.

Never store acidic foods in metal or coloured containers – not even overnight. Some of the most attractive metal containers have, in the past, proved dangerous. Chrome and nickel surfaces, for example, often overlay cadmium. Pewter is a very variable alloy of zinc, copper, antimony and tin, which in small amounts do not matter but which soon build up to toxic levels with leaching.

Beware of old pottery whose creamy-white inner glaze may turn out to be a leaded-frit and deadly for the kids if their summer lemonade is stored in it. In general, choose stoneware in preference to earthenware: its higher firing temperatures produce surfaces which are more resistant to leaching. Enamelled ovenware dishes usually have white interiors and are fine whatever their age. Present-day controls have eliminated many of the highly publicized hazards.

New technologies, such as the production of non-stick surfaces, have brought new, but low-level, problems. Non-stick linings release significant amounts of fluoride when first used, and it is probably wise to do some leaching of your own. That is, before using the pan for cooking, heat some fat in it to a fairly high degree, throw it away, and repeat this process several times.

Old friends in the kitchen remain the best. Copper is an essential trace element in the diet (it plays a crucial role in the production and function of red blood cells) and, although the use of copper cooking utensils may routinely increase the amount of copper in the diet, there are no known hazards in normal use.

Aluminium, although not yet confirmed as an essential trace element, is certainly not toxic at the levels normally accompanying cooking processes. Nor is iron – if you are lucky enough to have a cast-iron pan.

Yet all these materials can be dangerous if foods are left in them for any length of time. When you store, use glass or colour-free plastic. And if you have lead or copper piping in your house, then run the water for a minute or two in the morning before filling the kettle. It is easy and it is wise to take care.

SOUPS

ASPARAGUS STALK SOUP

BREAD SOUP. WITH BREAD SOUP BOWL

5

CARROT

CUCUMBER

AND

YOGHURT

Fennel
and
lemon
SOUP.

Stock

Victorian households always had a stockpot on the boil, stock being an essential ingredient for the soups, gravies and sauces which were such a feature of Victorian cooking. The tradition is still maintained in France where stock forms the basis of the *potage du jour* and many other dishes. Although the soup chapters of most good cookery books contain recipes for stocks, few people make them nowadays. Dried bouillon cubes are sold as a convenient substitute but they are relatively expensive, taste of little other than monosodium glutamate and salt, and cannot replace the rich flavour of a good home-made fresh stock.

For a clear soup, stock should be made with fresh raw ingredients, whether they be vegetables and herbs or meat or fish trimmings and bones. If the stock is to be used as the basis for a thick soup or sauce, then cooked left-overs, bones and peelings which would otherwise be thrown away are ideal ingredients. Either way, the cost is negligible and the amount of effort involved minimal.

The ingredients for stock should be chosen with some care. No amount of boiling will restore old and stale food to life, so left-overs should be used before they dry up and lose their flavour. Also, certain foods are not very suitable: fatty meat, for instance, dressed salads or combinations of meat and fish. Basic ingredients for various kinds of stock are suggested in the following recipes. A recipe for fish stock can be found in Chapter 6, Fish.

Jellied Brown Bone Stock

1 ox foot
1 marrow bone
1 beef shin bone
1 large onion, unpeeled
2 large carrots, scrubbed
2 sticks celery (or leaves and stalks from 1 head)

1 bay leaf
a bunch of parsley and a stalk of thyme
2 tsps salt
6 pints/3 litres water

Have the bones chopped into small pieces by the butcher. Dry fry the bones in a large saucepan until browned. Pour the water over them, bring to the boil and skim until the scum stops rising. Add the remaining ingredients and simmer for 3 hours. Strain the hot stock, leave to cool and skim off the fat. (The fat can be used for cooking.)

To make this stock in a pressure cooker, you would need to halve the quantities unless your cooker is very large. Cook under 15 lb pressure for 45 minutes to 1 hour.

For a light stock, use uncooked chicken pieces and giblets. Butchers who sell uncooked chicken pieces often sell the untidy bits – the beaks, wings and necks – very cheaply. Use 2 lb/1 kg chicken bits to 6 pints/3 litres water and use the same vegetables as above, but peel the onion (the peel colours the stock brown).

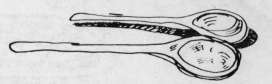

Stock from Cooked Meat and Bones

Use the less fatty meats. Pork and lamb are inclined to make a stock with an unpleasant greasy flavour. Stocks made from cooked meats are not as clear as those made from raw bones, but are useful to enrich the flavour of most thick soups and stews. They are an ideal way of using up left-overs.

Place the left-over meat in a large saucepan – you will need at least ½ lb/250 g meat. A cooked chicken carcass is ideal, and don't forget to use the bones and meat left on plates. Add 1 whole onion; a scrubbed potato or cleaned potato peelings; any outer leaves of vegetables, stalks and pods; any other vegetable peelings and left-over cooked vegetables; a bay leaf; 6 to 8 peppercorns; and 1 teaspoon salt. Cover the contents of the pan with cold water, bring to the boil, skim and simmer for 1½ hours (or 20 minutes in a pressure cooker at 15 lb pressure).

Vegetable Stock

A good strong vegetable stock can be made almost exclusively from scrubbed vegetable peelings, stalks and pods.

To 1 lb/500 g peelings, add 2 whole onions (the peel gives the stock a good rich brown colour), a few dried mushrooms, a handful of soaked pulses (lentils or any dried beans), a handful of peanuts, a bay leaf, a few parsley stalks and thyme sprigs, the leaves and stalks from a head of celery, 6 peppercorns and 1 teaspoon salt.

If you haven't enough peelings, make up the quantity with whole, scrubbed vegetables.

Put all the ingredients in a large saucepan, cover with water (about 3 pints/1½ litres), bring to the boil and simmer for 1½ hours (or cook in a pressure cooker for 20 minutes at 15 lb pressure). Strain and leave to cool.

The water in which vegetables or pulses were cooked makes a very good base for stock and can, in an emergency, be used instead of mixed vegetable stock, although the flavour will not, of course, be as strong.

Vitamin B_1 is highly soluble and as much as 50 per cent can be lost into the water in which vegetables were boiled. For instance, peeled potatoes lose 25 per cent of their vitamin B_1 and 16 per cent of their mineral content into the cooking water, so it is well worth retaining.

Keeping Stock

Stock will keep for 2 to 3 days in a cold larder or refrigerator. It is best kept in a stoneware, glass or clear plastic container as a metal pan will transfer its flavour and possibly harmful deposits to the liquid. Without a refrigerator, or in unusually hot weather, the stock should be brought to the boil once a day. Stock can be enriched and extended with fresh ingredients if it is kept properly, but, as a kitchen constantly generates fresh ingredients suitable for a stock, it is really better to make it fresh each time it is needed.

Asparagus Stalk Soup

Serves 4 to 6

Some types of asparagus have short, succulent green tips and long white fibrous stalks. In this case, it is best to cut off the tips to serve on their own or in a flan (see page 67) and to use the stalks for soup.

thick stalks from 1 lb/500 g asparagus and a few tips for garnish	1 tbs flour
	1½ pints/1 litre water
	¼ pint/150 ml milk
1 oz/25 g butter or margarine	salt and pepper

Cut the stalks into short lengths and plunge them into 1½ pints /1 litre boiling water. Reduce the heat, cover the pan and simmer for 30 minutes, or until they are tender. Melt the butter or margarine in a clean pan, stir in the flour and gradually add the milk, stirring all the time until the mixture is thickened. Cook for 5 minutes, adding a little of the asparagus water if the roux becomes too dry and sticks to the pan. Rub the asparagus stalks through a sieve or a mouli-légumes and add gradually to the roux, with the rest of the cooking water. Season, chop a few tips for a garnish and simmer for 10 minutes.

Bread Soup

Serves 4 to 6

This is a bread soup as the Hungarian peasants used to make it. The recipe is from a pre-First-World-War cookery book by Charles Gundel, proprietor of the St

Gellert hotel in Budapest. He says it tastes like meat soup.

9 oz/250 g dry crusts from a rye loaf	3 eggs
3 oz/75 g finest quality lard or bacon fat	4 oz/125 g onions
1 oz/25 g parsley	1½ pints/850 ml water
	½ oz/15 g paprika
	pinch salt

Cut the bread crusts into small cubes and fry in boiling hot fat, together with the parsley and onions, both chopped very finely. Add the water, salt and paprika and simmer for 10 minutes. Bring the soup to the boil, beat the eggs, and add them gradually to the boiling soup, stirring all the time. Serve immediately.

Brussels Tops Soup

Serves 4

Brussels tops are occasionally sold as greens in markets and greengrocers. They have a sweeter flavour than cabbage greens and are worth looking out for. Serve them steamed or boiled, as you would greens, or make them into soup.

2 lb/1 kg Brussels tops	1 pint/600 ml stock or water
2–3 onions	milk to dilute
1 clove garlic	salt and pepper
oil, butter or margarine for frying	pinch nutmeg

Chop the onions and the garlic and fry gently in a little oil, butter or margarine. Add the Brussels tops. Cook for a minute or two to allow the greens to soften a little and then add the boiling stock or water. Cover the pan and simmer for 10 minutes or so – not too long or the greens will lose their colour and flavour. Press through a *mouli-légumes*, heat through and add milk to thin as required. Season with salt and pepper and a pinch of nutmeg.

This soup can also be made with turnip tops.

Sprout Soup

Serves 4

At the end of the season, Brussels sprouts are often large and overblown. Rather than throwing away the outer leaves, which are usually quite good and fresh, make them into soup.

2 potatoes	1½ pints/850 ml water
1 onion	salt and pepper
¾ lb/350 g outer sprout leaves	

Scrub the potatoes well without peeling them and chop roughly. Peel and chop the onion. Place the chopped vegetables in a pan, pour the water over them and simmer for 10 minutes. Wash and trim the sprout leaves and add to the potato stock. Simmer until the potatoes and onions are soft. The sprouts should still be green. Press through a sieve or *mouli-légumes*, adjust the seasoning and serve.

Carrot and Barley Soup

Serves 6

3 oz/75 g pot barley	salt and pepper
1 lb/500 g carrots	2 pints/1 litre boiling water
2 onions	
1 oz/25 g margarine or butter	

Cook the barley for 40 minutes in the boiling water. Cut the carrots into small pieces, chop the onions and fry gently in margarine or butter until just beginning to soften. Drain the barley water into the pan in which the carrots are cooking and leave to simmer with the lid on until the carrots are very soft. Add the barley and rub everything through a *mouli-légumes*. Stir the mixture as you strain it as the barley is inclined to settle into lumps. Heat through, season well and add more liquid if necessary, though this soup should be very thick.

Cauliflower Leaf Soup

Serves 4 to 6

1 lb/500 g cauliflower leaves and stalks (those left attached to a large cauliflower should be enough)	1½ pints/850 ml water or stock
½ lb/250 g onions	milk to taste
margarine, oil or butter for frying	salt and pepper
	a pinch of nutmeg

Separate the leaves from the stalks and wash both well. Chop the stalks and the onions roughly and fry in a saucepan in a little margarine, oil or butter. Pour over them the water or stock, bring to the boil and simmer with the lid on the pan for 10 to 15 minutes. Add the leaves, after about 5 minutes. Press through a *mouli-légumes* or sieve, season with salt and pepper and a pinch of nutmeg, heat through and add a little milk just before serving.

Chestnut Soup

Serves 4

This soup is so good that it is worth the effort of peeling the chestnuts!

1 lb/500 g chestnuts	1 pint/600 ml water
1 stick celery	1 cup milk
1 carrot	salt and pepper
1 onion	
butter or margarine for frying	

Slit the chestnuts and boil them for 20 minutes or so. Alternatively, grill them until they burst open. Remove the peel and the inner skins. Chop the vegetables and cook them gently, first in the butter or margarine, and then with the water added. When they are soft, add the chestnuts and cook for 5 minutes longer. Rub everything through a sieve or a *mouli-légumes*. Season well, add the milk, heat through and serve.

Chestnut and Apple Soup

Serves 4

1 lb/500 g chestnuts	1½ pints/850 ml water
3 onions	salt and pepper
2 cooking apples	
butter or margarine for frying	

The method for this soup is exactly the same as for the Chestnut Soup, above, but it is better without the milk.

Chinese Chicken and Mushroom Soup

Serves 4

2 wings and neck of a fresh chicken (or two chicken backs)	1 carrot
	1 bay leaf
2 pints/1 litre water	1 tsp thyme
2–3 peppercorns	1 tsp parsley
1 onion	1 tbs soya sauce
	salt and pepper
	2 oz/50 g mushrooms
	green tops from 2 leeks

Place all the ingredients, except the soya sauce, salt and pepper, mushrooms and leeks, in a large pan, bring to the boil and simmer for 2 hours. Strain and add the soya sauce, salt and pepper. Reheat. Slice the mushrooms and the leek tops very thinly. Add these to the soup a minute or two before serving, to heat through.

Cucumber and Yoghurt Soup

Serves 4

This soup is extremely easy to make and is very light and refreshing on a hot day.

1 cucumber	salt and pepper
½ pint/300 ml plain, unsweetened yoghurt	1 tsp paprika mixed with 2 tsps oil
½ pint/300 ml milk	

Peel and dice the cucumber. Place in a large soup tureen or china bowl and stir in the yoghurt and the milk. Season generously with salt and pepper and leave to chill for several hours in the refrigerator. Spoon into bowls and decorate with swirls of paprika mixed with oil.

Any or all of the following ingredients make good additions to the basic mixture: crushed garlic, a few peeled, chopped and de-seeded tomatoes, a handful of chopped raisins.

Fennel and Lemon Soup

Serves 4 to 6

1½ lb/750 g fennel bulbs	2 pints/1 litre water or light vegetable or meat stock
2 large onions (3 oz/75 g)	
2 potatoes (3 oz/75 g)	salt and pepper
1 lemon (grated peel and juice)	1 tsp lightly roasted fennel seeds
1 tbs oil, butter or margarine	top of milk (optional)

Scrub the fennel and the potatoes and peel the onions. Cut them all into thick slices and stew gently in the oil, butter or margarine in a large saucepan. Pour the hot stock or water over the vegetables, cover the pan and simmer for 20 minutes or so, until they are soft. Rub through a sieve or *mouli-légumes*. Heat through slowly, stirring all the time, season and add the juice of 1 lemon, and, if you like, a little top of the milk. Mix the roasted fennel seeds with the lemon peel and sprinkle a little over each bowl of hot soup, as a garnish.

Leek and Potato Soup

Serves 4 to 6

Most leek dishes call only for the white parts (see Devilled Leeks, page 80. The green leaves are more strongly flavoured and make a good soup.

green tops from 1 lb/500 g leeks	a little oil
	1 clove garlic
1 lb/500 g potatoes	1½ pints/850 ml stock
1 onion	salt and pepper

Peel and chop the potatoes and the onion. Fry both lightly in a little oil, add the garlic, crushed, and fry for another few minutes. Pour on the stock, cover the pan and simmer slowly. Meanwhile, wash the leek leaves well, chop them and add to the pan when the potatoes are half cooked. By the time the potatoes are done, the leeks should be soft but still bright green. Press the whole lot through a sieve or *mouli-légumes* and heat through gently for another few minutes. Add more stock or milk, if necessary, season and serve.

Washed young leek leaves can also be used raw, very finely chopped, in place of chives.

Brown Lentil and Ham Soup

Serves 4 to 6

½ lb/250 g brown or green lentils	1 bay leaf
	pinch dried thyme
1 ham bone	6 peppercorns
2 carrots	3 pints/1½ litres water
2 onions	

Bring all the ingredients to the boil in a large saucepan. Reduce the heat, cover and leave the soup barely simmering for 2 hours. Remove the bone and press the soup through a sieve or a *mouli-légumes*, or mash with a potato masher, first removing the herbs and peppercorns. Season and thin with more water, if necessary.

If this soup is to be cooked in a pressure cooker, for which it would be an ideal candidate, then it should take about 40 minutes at 15 lb.

Lettuce Soup

Serves 4

Slightly tired, or bolted, lettuces are ideal for this soup, but make sure that they are not bitter.

1 large lettuce
1 bunch watercress
5–6 sprigs fresh mint and parsley
1 tbs other fresh herbs, finely chopped
milk (optional)

1 clove garlic
1 onion
1½ pints/850 ml stock or water
1 tbs margarine or butter
salt and pepper

Chop the onion, crush the garlic and stew in the margarine or butter. Shred the lettuce, chop watercress and herbs finely and cook for a few minutes with the onion and garlic. Add the stock or water and simmer until the lettuce is limp, but still green. Strain twice through a sieve or *mouli-légumes* (this soup is better if very finely puréed). Adjust seasoning, add a little milk, if liked, and serve.

Meadow Herb Soup

Serves 6

This is a German recipe, given by Frau Alma Giersch.

1 bunch each: young nettles, sorrel, watercress, chives, plantain, parsley, lovage
2 pints/1 litre stock
2 oz/50 g butter or margarine

1½ oz/35 g flour
salt and pepper
1 egg per person

Wash the herbs well and plunge them into a little of the boiling stock. Leave for 1 minute, remove them and chop them very finely. Melt the margarine or butter in a large, clean saucepan, stir in the flour and gradually add all the stock. Simmer for 15 minutes, then add the herbs and seasoning and simmer for 5 minutes more. Warm the soup bowls. Bring the soup to the boil and, when it is scalding hot, dish it into the warmed bowls. Quickly crack 1 egg into each bowl. Serve immediately.

Parsnip and Walnut Soup

Serves 4 to 5

¾ lb/350 g parsnips
2 oz/50 g walnuts, shelled
2 onions
a little margarine

1½ pints/850 ml water
½ pint/300 ml milk
salt and pepper

Grate the walnuts and infuse them in hot milk for half an hour or so. Chop the parsnips and onions and cook gently in a little margarine for a few minutes, then add the water and simmer until soft. Rub through a *mouli-légumes* and add the walnuts and milk. Season and heat through, taking care that the soup does not boil.

Pea-pod and Cucumber Soup

Serves 2 to 3

Those who have tasted a refreshing pea-pod soup will never again feel that shelling peas is an effort. The peas are worth buying for their pods alone!

pods from 1 lb/500 g peas	*1 medium onion*
1 cucumber (unpeeled)	*salt and pepper*
½ pint/300 ml stock	*nutmeg (optional)*

Chop the onion roughly and simmer with the pea-pods in the stock for 20 minutes. Slice the cucumber, add it to the pan and simmer for 10 minutes longer. Press through a sieve or *mouli-légumes*, season and serve hot or chilled, with a sprinkling of nutmeg, if desired.

Iced Whole Pea Soup

Serves 6

1 lb/500 g peas in their pods	*salt and pepper*
1 sprig mint	*arrowroot or cornflour, if*
1 onion	*required*
a little butter	*chopped mint, for garnish*
2 pints/1 litre water	

Wash and pick over the pea-pods carefully and trim off the stalks and any strings. This is not absolutely essential but it makes them easier to sieve later on. Slice the onion and fry lightly in butter. Add the peas, still

whole in their pods, and the mint. Cover with the water and simmer until the pods are tender. Press through a sieve or *mouli-légumes* (it may be necessary to do this twice if the pods were stringy). Heat through slowly and season. Thicken, if necessary, with arrowroot or cornflour. Chill the soup for several hours and serve with chopped mint sprinkled on each bowlful.

Silesian Potato Soup

Serves 6

This recipe was also given by Frau Giersch.

approx. 1 lb/500 g potatoes	*2 oz/50 g lean bacon*
2 carrots	*1 onion*
2 leeks	*fat for frying*
2 sticks celery	*parsley*
1 oz/25 g butter or	*salt and pepper*
margarine	*2 pints/1 litre water*

Peel the potatoes and cut into cubes or slices. Clean and chop the other vegetables (except the onion) and stew all together in a pan with a little butter or margarine. Add the water and cook until soft. Put through a sieve or *mouli-légumes*. Cut the bacon and onion into small cubes or thin slices and brown lightly in fat. Add this and some finely chopped parsley to the soup. Season and serve.

Baked Tomato Soup

Serves 3 to 4

This is an ideal way of using tomatoes that are rather watery when raw, as the baking really intensifies their flavour. It would, however, be expensive on energy unless you were using the oven anyway for another dish.

1½ lb/750 g tomatoes
2 medium onions
1 clove garlic
a little oil
small bunch of leaves and
    stalks from a head of
    celery, finely chopped

2 tbs water
½ tsp dried marjoram
½ tsp dried basil (or double
    the quantity fresh)
1 tsp sugar
salt and pepper

Cut the tomatoes in half, place in a deep ovenproof dish, season with salt, pepper, marjoram and basil and bake in a moderate oven until soft and runny (about 10 to 15 minutes). Chop the onions and simmer in oil with the crushed garlic, and the celery leaves and stalks, in a saucepan with the lid on. Add about 2 tablespoons of water as they start to soften. When both the tomatoes and the onions are soft, mix them and then press through a *mouli-légumes*. Adjust the seasoning, add the sugar and serve piping hot. This soup is good with croûtons.

Iced Tomato Soup

Serves 4

2 lb/1 kg tomatoes
½ cucumber
2 cloves garlic
2 tsps salt

1 tsp sugar
black pepper
chives, for garnish

Stew tomatoes very gently over a low flame with no added fat or liquid, or bake them as in the preceding recipe. Put through a sieve or *mouli-légumes* when soft. Place in a bowl to cool. Chop the cucumber finely, crush the garlic and add, with the seasoning, to the tomato purée. Leave in the refrigerator to chill. Serve with a teaspoonful of snipped chives in each serving.

Turnip Soup

Serves 4

1½ lb/750 g turnips
2 oz/50 g butter or
    margarine
½ pint/300 ml milk
pepper and salt
chopped parsley

grated nutmeg
1 tsp sugar, optional (if
    turnips are slightly bitter,
    this often improves their
    flavour)

Plunge turnips into boiling water for 5 minutes and drain. Chop them into thick slices. Melt the margarine or butter in a pan and add the turnips. Cover and sweat until the turnips are mashable. Stir in the milk and put the mixture through a fine sieve or a *mouli-légumes*, using the finest base. Add a good sprinkling of grated nutmeg and ground pepper, a little salt and, if necessary, sugar. Reheat and serve with chopped parsley on top.

For many years now, fresh fish has been declining in popularity and no one really knows why. It could be that, as meat became cheaper after the war, people switched their loyalties. The growth of the frozen-fish industry undoubtedly had something to do with the change in fashion. Frozen fish fingers and cod cutlets are much easier to prepare than fresh fish and can be bought in the supermarket along with all the other groceries. Even fish and chip shops are facing real competition and many are offering kebabs, chicken and pies as alternatives to fried fish. Now yet another nail has been put into the coffin of the fresh-fish industry. Prices for fish have risen to such an extent that many of the more popular varieties are now as expensive as steak.

The increases are not just due to the rise in wage and fuel costs. According to most expert sources, all but a few of the most important North Atlantic and Mediterranean species have been overfished during the last twenty years. Anyone who reads the Press must be aware of the state of the cod and herring fisheries, where we have been at 'war' with the Icelanders and now the Europeans over conservation measures. Equally threatened are plaice, sole and haddock, and in some areas, mackerel, saithe and whiting will soon be on the critical list.

Britain is a member of the E.E.C. and, as such, has given up an exclusive claim to U.K. waters. This is despite the fact that new international custom allows each state to claim a 200-mile exclusive economic area beyond its coast. Each country within the E.E.C. has a twelve-mile limit within which its own fishing fleets still have exclusive rights. Otherwise, the seas around E.E.C. countries are common ground to the limit of 200 miles, or, where claims overlap with non-E.E.C. states, to where there is a median line.

Inevitably, the European fleets tend to concentrate in the best grounds, which are mainly around the shores of Great Britain. French trawlers, for instance, have in recent years taken 80 per cent of their catch from British waters. Competition between individual fleets is strong and it is crippling the British fishing industry. For this reason, the U.K. Government has fought hard to obtain a large percentage of the allowable European catch.

But it may, even now, be too late. Fierce competition, and the use of large, mainly Soviet, factory ships, have already caused the rapid decline in fish populations. Another problem is regulation. The nets used by foreign industrial trawlers tend to have a smaller mesh than that allowed for British ships, which means that they can catch the tiniest fish, which should be allowed to breed. Furthermore, they can make catches of 100 tons in a single trawl. The fish at the bottom of the net tend to be crushed by the weight of the others, and have to be thrown back into the sea, as are the fish that are of the wrong species. If the entire shoal is of the wrong size or mixture of species, it is released. Most of the discarded fish die.

Fish-meal trawling has also endangered many species. Those fish which are caught intentionally are often an important source of food for the more valuable species which are caught for human consumption. Frequently, the valuable commercial species are caught unintentionally, thus causing an unnecessary depletion of their populations.

Conservation measures imposed by the E.E.C. are intended to go some way towards ensuring that fish populations are maintained at a sustainable level. Equipment for deep-sea fishing is to be supervised. Certain areas are to be closed for long-term fishing, so that fish can breed, and limitations will be imposed on total catches, annual quotas being set for each species. The E.E.C. is also anxious to protect the interests of the inshore industry – employing about 80 per cent of the labour force. Inshoremen work with very small boats, eighty feet or less in length, and they tend to be much more sensitive about fish populations than the industrial trawlers which do most of the damage. British fishermen have always wanted fishing zones exclusive to them to be increased from twelve to fifty miles, and the U.K. Government has consistently been intent on protecting the interests of the British industry, no matter what the E.E.C. wants.

Until the complicated questions of conservation, competition and politics are disentangled, there are still a few familiar and several less well-known fish which are not yet overexploited. Blue whiting, common and blue ling, sprats and dogfish, horse mackerel and salt-water eels (sand eel, conger eel) are not at present in danger. Reasonably plentiful at the moment are most shellfish: crabs, cockles, mussels, whelks and oysters.

Conservation measures are essential for all species, not only those which are in danger, but they are very difficult to enforce. The allocation of quotas and the monitoring of populations is particularly difficult to control. In some cases, population sizes simply aren't known. There have been many experiments in recent years, with both salt-water and freshwater fish farming, which may provide some of the answers. Freshwater fish farming is nothing new. The Egyptians farmed a large carp-like fish called tilapia, more than 4000 years ago, and farming of similar species continues today in some parts of Africa and Asia. Fish farming in Asia is often combined with rice growing. Stocks are introduced into the paddy fields when they are flooded, and the fully grown fish are collected when the fields are drained. This arrangement helps the rice to grow, as the crop benefits from the fish excreta. Freshwater fish farming in Britain is at the moment only considered economic for the luxury fish – salmon and trout – but experiments are in progress with carp, to see if they can be reared commercially on sewage farms.

Salt-water fish farming is still very much at the experimental stage. The young fish are reared in tanks until they are large enough to be released into enclosed coastal areas or large floating cages. Plaice, Dover sole, lemon sole, halibut and turbot have been reared in this way, and so far, turbot have been the most successful.

Fish and Pollution

Oil pollution in the sea and around coastal waters is steadily on the increase. In 1977, over 180 oil spills were reported around the coasts of Great Britain – news of only a fraction of which reached the Press. Oil spills can occur in a variety of ways: when two ships collide, when tanker ships run aground against rocks, from leaks from oil platforms or pipelines, or when tankers deliberately empty cargoes of used oil into the sea. It is generally agreed, however, that the bulk of accidental pollution at sea occurs as a result of human error – either because of inadequately trained crews or because of substandard ships. Substandard ships are frequently chartered by major oil companies, they say, on the grounds of economic necessity. If anyone could afford to overcome that particular problem and charter safe ships, it ought to be the major oil companies!

The extent of the damage to wildlife from oil spills is still not known for sure. The Royal Society for the Protection of Birds noted 3712 oiled birds on their reservoirs in 1977, but many more may have been beached elsewhere. The skin of most pelagic fish is coated with a slimy mucous which in most cases gives them protection, but in heavily contaminated areas, their gills become clogged and then they die of suffocation. The long-term effects of oil pollution, and the effects on their breeding and migration habits, are simply not known. Chemical dispersants for crude oil can do much more damage than the oil itself. This was the case after the Torrey Canyon disaster in 1969, when more deaths occurred after the dispersant was used than before. Spills of refined diesel oil can also do more damage than crude oil, and it appears that the fish have no way of avoiding contaminated areas and are not protected by their skin coating. Shellfish such as mussels and oysters are particularly susceptible as they are static. Experiments have been conducted which show that their populations suffer considerably, even in slightly contaminated waters. In this country, the regulations which are supposed to protect shellfish populations are wholly inadequate.

International organizations which deal with marine pollution, such as the Inter-governmental Maritime Consultative Organization (I.M.C.O.), the Food and Agriculture Organization of the United Nations, U.N.E.S.C.O. and the Advisory Committee on Pollution of the Sea (A.C.O.P.S.), are active in monitoring the occurrences and effects of oil pollution and, sooner or later, effective (one hopes) legislation will follow.

In the meantime, it is unlikely that pollutants will be transferred from the fish to the consumer, as polluted fish pick up a taint in their flesh, which is immediately recognizable – and unpalatable.

The greatest danger from 'polluted' fish is perhaps surprisingly – and sadly – from smoked fish. Smoked fish is about the most potentially carcinogenic food we eat, as all the lethal tars in the wood are concentrated in the fish during the smoking process. This has, however, been recognized and it is to be hoped that steps will be taken to reduce the danger to health.

We have given the most endangered fish – cod, plaice, sole, herring and haddock – a breather by excluding them from this chapter. There are many other fish to take over while their populations are being restored.

A short list of some of the less familiar fish follows. Others are mentioned in the recipes.

Blue Whiting

A deep-sea fish that is similar to whiting and can be used in all recipes as a substitute for it. It has not yet been widely accepted and is only rarely stocked by fishmongers.

Gurnet or Gurnard

A small (about 8 oz/250 g) rosy coloured fish, its body is dominated by a large pronounced head. It is related to the *rascasse*, a Mediterranean fish which is an essential ingredient for *bouillabaisse*. It has a very good, mild flavour and blends well with delicate sauces. It is in season from autumn to spring.

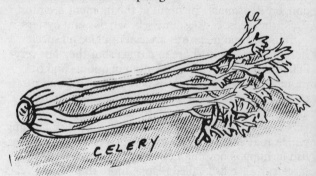

CELERY

Horse Mackerel or Donkey Mackerel

A deep-sea fish and, as its name suggests, the nearest relative to the mackerel, though it is milder in flavour and less oily. It can be used in all mackerel recipes. The fish are small (8 to 12 oz/250 to 350 g), and silver-grey, with large eyes.

Ling

In flavour, this belongs to the whiting and hake family, though it has firmer flesh. It is longer and thinner than whiting, but its appearance is otherwise very similar.

Shad

The nearest relative to the herring, but even bonier and larger in size (1½ to 2 lb/750 to 1 kg). It can be used in place of herring in all recipes, but it is best steamed first and then filleted.

Snapper

These fish vary in size from 2 oz/50 g to about 1 lb/500 g. They are oval in shape and flattish and a pretty rose colour. The flavour is good, although they can be dry and quite bony.

Carp

A large scaly freshwater fish, much esteemed in Germany and Eastern Europe, where it is the traditional fare for Christmas Eve, served with a rich sweet and sour sauce and stuffing. The flesh is moist, but it can be tasteless.

Lasht or Bream

Also a large freshwater fish, similar to carp in appearance, though it is a greyish white. It can be stuffed and baked in the same way as carp, though, again, it tends to be flavourless.

Fish Stock

Head and bones from 1 strongly flavoured fish (e.g. mackerel), or from 2 delicate fish (e.g. whiting or ling). Fishmongers will often sell heads and bones for stock-making. Shellfish bones can also be added.

1 onion	6 peppercorns
1 carrot	1 tsp salt
1 bay leaf	1½ pints/850 ml water

Simmer all the ingredients together in the water (with the lid on the pan, or the whole house will smell of fish) for 20 minutes. Strain and use as a base for soup or sauces. Fish stock must not be cooked for too long as it becomes bitter.

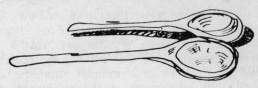

Rich Fish Soup

Serves 6 to 8

½ lb/250 g filleted, white fish (coley, saithe, whiting, ling, gurnard or horse mackerel would be suitable)	1 tsp paprika
	1 strip lemon peel
	1½ pints/850 ml fish stock
	1 tbs olive oil
1 smoked mackerel (about 12 oz/350 g)	2 cloves garlic, crushed
	1 bay leaf
2 onions	salt and pepper
2 carrots	6 whole mussels or shrimps (optional)
1 tbs tomato purée	

Peel and chop the onions and carrots very finely. Fry them in oil until softened and beginning to brown. Add the garlic and bay leaf and then the white fish, skinned and chopped into small pieces. Pour in a little of the stock and simmer for 5 minutes. Skin, bone and flake the smoked mackerel and add with the paprika, lemon peel, tomato purée and the rest of the stock. Cover the pan and simmer slowly for half an hour. Season highly with salt and pepper.

The optional whole mussels or shrimps can be added just before serving.

Shrimp and Tomato Soup

Serves 3

½ pint/100 g shrimps (or
  prawns)
¼ lb/250 g tomatoes
1 pint/600 ml water
½ lb/250 g onions

oil for frying
1 large clove garlic
1 wineglass cider
chopped parsley

Slice the onions and brown them in oil. Add the chopped or crushed garlic and the peeled and chopped tomatoes; stir and remove from the heat. Peel the shrimps or prawns. Cover the shells in a saucepan with the water and simmer for 20 minutes. Strain the liquid and add to the tomatoes and onions and simmer until they are soft. Five minutes before serving, add the cider and the peeled shrimps. Serve with a sprinkling of parsley in each bowl. This makes a very thick soup for three. It can be thinned to serve four people, but the flavour will be less intense.

Choosing and Dressing a Crab

Always buy crabs from a reputable fishmonger and make sure that they are freshly boiled. Inspect the head end of the crab. Some white flesh will be showing between the top shell and the claws. If this is yellow or grey, the crab is not fresh; if it is pure white, the crab will keep for a day or two.

If you buy the crabs live, the most humane way of killing them is *not* to plunge them into boiling water, but to thrust a skewer deep between the eyes. This kills them instantly. They should then be boiled in salted water for 20 to 40 minutes, depending on size.

To remove the meat, crack the crab by holding the top shell firmly in one hand and breaking off the body with the other. The only edible parts are the brown, creamy meat, most of which will be in the main shell, although some will have clung to the body, and the white flaky meat inside the body and the claws. The inedible parts which should be removed are: the gills, or spongy fingers, attached to the body; the small sac and any green matter that lies in the big shell; and the tail. Spoon out all brown meat from the top shell, and any that clings to the body. Crack the top shell along the natural curved markings on each side – they will come away quite easily – and wash the shell thoroughly. Twist off all the claws from the body. The big claws are full of white meat which can be removed with a skewer once the claws have been smashed with a hammer. The small claws have meat in them in the fattest part which is attached to the body. Remove the meat in the same way, keeping the lower part of the claws for decoration. Finally, cut the body in half, or in several pieces, and scrape out all the white meat with a skewer. This is the most fiddly part, but the body can contain quite a lot of white meat, so it is worth doing. Take care in all cases to avoid mixing splinters of shell with the flesh.

If the crab is to be eaten plain, lay the white meat in the centre of the shell, cream the brown meat thoroughly and pile it on either side. You can 'stretch' the brown meat by mixing it with breadcrumbs moistened with cream, sherry or cider and seasoning it with salt, pepper and mustard.

Baked Crab

Quantities are for 1 small crab, enough for 1 person as a main dish

1 dressed crab
1 tbs thick béchamel sauce
  or cream
1 tbs soft breadcrumbs
1 tbs grated dry cheese

1 tsp English mustard
salt and pepper
cider or sherry to moisten if
  necessary

Mix the white and dark meats of the crab in a bowl with the béchamel sauce, breadcrumbs, cheese, mustard, salt and pepper. Moisten with cider or sherry if the mixture is too stiff. Pile the mixture into the cleaned top shell of the crab, stick 3 small claws into each side and bake for 15 to 20 minutes in a hot oven.

Stuffed Grey Mullet

Serves 4 generously

These delicious fish, with firm white flesh, creamy and mild in flavour, are caught off the Cornish coast during the summer and autumn. They can grow to a very large size.

This is a simplified version of a Turkish recipe for mackerel. Mackerel are also good cooked this way, but perhaps a little too rich.

4 small grey mullet (8–12 oz/250–350 g each) or two larger fish (1½ lb/750 g each)	2 oz/50 g raisins, soaked
	2 tbs walnut or olive oil
	2 tbs chopped parsley
	1 tsp allspice
2 large onions, finely chopped	salt and pepper
	2 oz/50 g soft breadcrumbs
2 oz/50 g walnuts, chopped	1 egg

Clean the fish, making a large incision along one side of each fish. Leave on the heads and tails. Heat 1 tablespoon of the oil in a pan and fry the onions lightly, until they are soft. Remove from the heat, and stir in the nuts, raisins, parsley, spice and seasoning. Bind well with the breadcrumbs and the egg. Lay the fish in a casserole or baking tin and press the stuffing into the incisions. Sprinkle them with the remaining oil and bake, covering the dish with a lid or with oiled paper, for 20 minutes in a moderate oven. Remove the cover and bake for 5 minutes more. Serve with boiled potatoes and a fresh green salad.

Mackerel

Traditionally, mackerel has been caught on long line in small open boats off the Cornish coast. Recently, big Scottish trawlers have been 'poaching' the catch and selling to Russian ships moored off the coast. This has serious consequences, as the fish populations can no longer be properly monitored and the inshoremen are being deprived of a large chunk of their livelihood. Very little attention has been drawn to the plight of the mackerel, as it is for some reason generally despised in this country. As cod and herring have become scarce, prices in the shops have soared. Mackerel remains one of the cheapest of fish. It shouldn't be – it should be protected and valued as the delicacy it is.

Grilled Mackerel with Devilled Butter

Serves 4

4 small mackerel (8–12 oz/250–350 g each)	2 tsp Fresh mustard
	2 tsp Worcestershire sauce
oil for basting the fish	2 saltspoons (or large pinches) salt
1 oz/25 g butter or margarine	1 saltspoon cayenne pepper
	2 egg yolks

Clean and gut the mackerel. Make diagonal cuts in the skin of each one and grill on both sides, brushing occasionally with the oil. Allow 10 minutes each side. Meanwhile, make the devilled butter: melt the butter, remove from the heat and mix in the French mustard, the Worcestershire sauce, salt, cayenne pepper and, lastly, the egg yolks. Pour this butter inside the hot mackerel on serving.

This sauce is also good with poached halibut, or with grilled donkey or horse mackerel.

Mackerel and Mushroom Flan

Serves 4

8 oz/225 g shortcrust
  pastry (see page 150)
1 large mackerel (about
  1 lb/500 g); saithe, horse
  mackerel and shad are
  also suitable
1 oz/25 g margarine or
  butter
1 tbs flour
¼ lb/100 g mushrooms

6 capers or pickled
  nasturtium seeds (see
  page 161)
1 tsp mustard
salt and pepper
½ pint/300 ml milk
1 bay leaf
4 slices lemon, peel and pith
  removed
½ tsp paprika

Clean the mackerel, cut into pieces and simmer in the milk with the bay leaf. When it is cooked, remove from the pan, skin and bone the fish and mash the flesh with a fork. Melt the margarine in a clean pan, stir in the flour and gradually add the milk in which the fish was cooked. Stir vigorously until it is smooth, then add the fish, the capers or nasturtium seeds and the mushrooms (both chopped or sliced), the mustard and salt and pepper. Leave to cool a little. Line a 10-inch (25-cm) flan dish with the pastry (which is less likely to stick or go soggy if the dish is *not* greased) and pour in the filling. Lay the lemon slices on top of the fish. Dust with a little paprika and bake for 30 minutes, with the oven at gas mark 5 (375°F, 190°C).

Mussels

Mussels are found all around the coast of Great Britain. They are at their best from October to March. Take care when you buy mussels, as they must be absolutely fresh and tightly closed. If the mussels on sale in the shop are gaping open, don't buy them. If you buy mussels some time before they are to be cooked, leave them covered with cold water, with a handful of oatmeal strewn amongst them. To prepare them for cooking, scrub them well with a stiff brush and remove the barnacles and beards with a knife. Rinse them several times to remove all the sand and grit. Discard any open ones.

One pint of mussels weighs about 1 lb (1 litre weighs about 800 g).

Stuffed Mussels

Serves 4, allowing about a dozen each

2 quarts/2 litres mussels
2 heaped tbs soft
  breadcrumbs, soaked in
  water and squeezed dry
2 tbs chopped parsley

2 oz/50 g butter or
  margarine
1 large clove garlic, crushed
salt and pepper

Mash the breadcrumbs with the butter or margarine, parsley, garlic, salt and pepper to a smooth purée. Cook the mussels in a little boiling water in a large, covered pan for 2 minutes. Remove them from the pan and discard any that have not opened in cooking. Take off one shell from each and spread a little of the stuffing over the mussel. Lay the stuffed mussels on flat baking sheets and bake in a very hot oven for 5 minutes.

The stuffing can be varied considerably, using different mixtures of herbs or chopped spinach, finely chopped ham, or bacon, chopped mushrooms, capers or anchovies with the basic breadcrumb and garlic mixture.

Mussel and Eel Stew

Serves 6

1 quart/1 litre mussels
1 lb/500 g conger eel – cut
  from the middle as the
  tail end is extremely bony
  and best for stock
  (alternatively, use rock
  eel, i.e. catfish)
½ lb/250 g baby onions
¼ lb/125 g mushrooms
1 bay leaf
1 tbs flour

½ pint/300 ml water or fish
  stock
¼ pint/150 ml milk
1 oz/25 g margarine or
  butter
1 glass white wine or cider
1 tbs chopped parsley
2 egg yolks
2 cloves garlic
salt and pepper

Clean the mussels thoroughly. Bring the water or fish stock to the boil in a large pan and cook the mussels, with the lid on the pan, for 2 minutes. Remove them from the stock, discard any unopened ones and shell them, leaving a few unshelled for a garnish. Simmer the eel in the stock for 15 minutes or so, until it is soft. Remove from the pan, skin and bone it, and cut it into small pieces. Melt the butter or margarine in a clean saucepan or metal casserole and add the onions and the bay leaf. Brown them over a fairly high heat, then cover the pan and simmer gently for 10 minutes, shaking the pan occasionally. Stir in the flour, then gradually add the stock, and then the milk. Simmer for 15 minutes. Add the shelled mussels, the eel, the mushrooms and the wine or cider and keep the pan at a simmer for 5 minutes longer. Pound the garlic to a paste with the egg yolks, spoon in a little of the fish sauce, then stir the mixture carefully into the stew. Add salt and pepper to taste and heat through very gently, stirring all the time until it has thickened. Do not allow the stew to boil.

Just before serving, distribute the remaining mussels and the chopped parsley over the top and cover the pan for a minute or two to allow the mussels to heat through.

Shad with Celeriac and Anchovy* Sauce

Serves 2

1 shad (about 1 lb/500 g),
  lightly steamed and
  filleted
8 salt anchovy fillets, soaked
  in water for ½ hour

1 small celeriac root
  (4 oz/125 g)
2 potatoes (4 oz/125 g)
a little milk or cream
black pepper and a little salt

Scrub the celeriac root thoroughly and cook it in boiling water for about 30 minutes, adding the scrubbed potatoes after 10 minutes. Peel the vegetables while they are still hot and rub them through a sieve or *mouli-légumes*. Season the purée lightly and thin to the consistency of a sauce with a little milk or cream. Lay the shad fillets in a flat casserole, pour the sauce over them and decorate the top with the anchovy fillets. Bake for 20 minutes in a moderate oven.

*Beginning in the late 1950s, Peru became the world's leading exporter of anchovies for fishmeal intended for poultry and livestock. Their market was huge. By the early 1960s, they were supplying two thirds of the world's fishmeal, which accounted for one fifth of the total fish catch. Unfortunately, the anchovies stopped cooperating. In 1972, they began to disappear from offshore fishing areas, and the catch has since been reduced from a peak of 12 million tons per annum to less than 5 million tons. Most of the anchovies on sale here come from the Mediterranean.

Shrimp or Prawn Butter

Shrimps and prawns are both expensive, but this recipe turns them into a fairly economical dish by extracting every scrap of flavour from their shells.

½ pint/125 g shrimps or
   prawns

3 oz/75 g butter or
   margarine

Peel the shrimps or prawns and set the flesh aside. Remove the eyes from the shells with tweezers, and pound the shells in a mortar, together with the butter or margarine. Pass the mixture through a fine sieve, pressing well against the sides with a wooden spoon to extract all the moisture from the shells. Either mix the shrimps or prawns back into the butter and use as a spread, or use the butter as the base for a sauce, soup or soufflé, with the shrimps as garnish.

Shrimp or Prawn Sauce

½ pint/125 g shrimps or
   prawns
3 oz/75 g butter or
  margarine

2 tbs flour
¾ pint/450 ml milk
salt and pepper

Make a shrimp or prawn butter as in the previous recipe. Melt half of it in a saucepan and stir in the flour. Gradually add the milk and simmer gently for 15 minutes. Add the rest of the butter and the reserved shrimps or prawns, and a little more milk, cider or white wine if necessary. Season and serve as a sauce for poached turbot, whiting or hake.

Fried Sprats

Serves 4

Sprats are small fish, the size of sardines. They are similar to herring, though stronger in flavour. Smelts are similar to sprats and can also be cooked this way.

1 lb/500 g sprats
1 egg, beaten
flour for coating

3 tbs oil
lemon wedges

Clean and fillet the sprats. The easiest way to do this is to cut off the heads, slit carefully along the belly and remove the guts. Expose and remove the backbone by working away the flesh with a knife. It should come away very easily. Dip the fillets first in the beaten egg and then in the flour. Fry them in hot oil until they are golden on both sides. Serve immediately, with wedges of lemon.

Sprat and Potato Casserole

Serves 4 to 6

This is based on a Swedish recipe which uses anchovies instead of sprats. The mixture sounds odd, but is very good.

½ lb/250 g sprats, filleted
   and marinated for a day
   in 2 tbs salt
2 large onions, chopped
2 oz/50 g butter or
   margarine

1 lb/500 g floury potatoes
½ pint/300 ml creamy milk
½ lb/250 g cheese, grated
pepper

Slice the onions and fry them until they are brown in half the butter or margarine. Scrub the potatoes and cut them into matchsticks or very thin slices (a *mandoline* is useful for this; use either the crinkle blade for matchsticks, or the ordinary blade for slices). Rub a casserole dish with butter or margarine and layer the potatoes with the sprats, drained of excess salt, the onions, cheese and pepper, starting and finishing with potatoes. Pour in the milk, which should not cover the mixture. Bake in a low oven (gas mark 3, 325°F, 170°C) for 2 hours. The potatoes should be soft, and should have absorbed all the liquid.

Squid

Squid are eaten a lot in Spain, Italy and the South of France. They swim near the surface in shallow waters and one can often see them being caught by local fishermen in the Mediterranean, who kill them by beating them against the rocks. Squid are caught off the coast of Britain in the North Sea. They are not yet popular here, perhaps because they look unattractive and people do seem to be squeamish about preparing them. They can be tough when undercooked but, well cooked, they are delicious, with a strong fishy flavour. They are not difficult to clean. Hold the tentacles firmly in one hand and the body in the other and pull them apart. Remove the spine from the body – it looks like a piece of clear plastic and is easily detached. Rinse out the body. Cut the tentacles away from the guts, being careful not to pierce the dark green ink sac (the ink is sometimes incorporated into squid dishes, but is very bitter). Discard the guts. It is only the tentacles and the body which are eaten.

Squid bodies are often served stuffed with mixtures of rice or breadcrumbs, herbs, ham or anchovies, olives and capers and the chopped tentacles, and simmered in a tomato and wine sauce. Another popular method of serving them is to chop the tentacles and slice the bodies into rings, dip them in batter and deep fry them until they are crisp.

The following recipe is a very simple one, which should appeal even to conservative palates.

Squid with Tomatoes and Garlic

Serves 4

1 lb/500 g North Sea squid
1 lb/500 g tomatoes
2 onions
2 cloves garlic
salt and pepper

1 glass red or white wine, or cider
1 coffee-cupful oil
$\frac{1}{2}$ tsp marjoram, oregano or basil

Clean the squid. Chop the tentacles and slice the body into rings. Slice the onions and simmer in the oil. When they are soft, add the squid. Fry gently for a few minutes and transfer to a casserole dish. Add the rest of the ingredients. Season and bake for $1\frac{1}{2}$ hours in a slow oven. Serve with rice or potatoes.

Grilled Trout

Trout are usually served plainly grilled or fried in butter or with almonds. This way of grilling the trout with garlic and onions is Italian and greatly enhances the delicate flavour of the fish.

1 trout per person

FOR EACH FISH:

1 sprig parsley
few slivers sliced garlic

3–4 slices onion
salt and pepper
oil

Clean and gut the trout. Insert the slivers of garlic, onion slices and sprig of parsley into each one. Season and brush inside and out with oil. Grill until the skin is crisp and brown, brushing occasionally with more oil. Allow 10 minutes per side. Serve herbs, garlic and all.

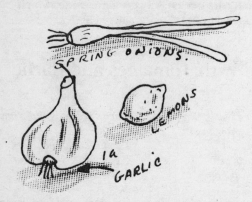

Whiting with Cucumber Sauce

Serves 4

Whiting is a delicately flavoured fish with soft and flaky flesh. Blue whiting, pouting, hake or ling can be used instead.

2 whiting	1 tbs parsley, chopped
1 medium-sized cucumber	1 tsp fennel, chopped
2 small onions	2–3 fennel stalks
¾ pint/450 ml water	1 hard-boiled egg

Clean and fillet the whiting. Simmer the fish until cooked, but not falling apart, in a little boiling water with the fennel stalks.

For the sauce, dice the cucumber, chop the onions and simmer them together (reserving a tablespoonful of the cucumber) in ¾ pint/450 ml water. When they are soft, rub through a sieve or a *mouli-légumes*. Add the chopped fennel, parsley, hard-boiled egg and the reserved cucumber. Pour over the fish, heat through and serve.

Whiting with Courgettes

Serves 4

This recipe is also suitable for hake, ling, mullet or bream.

2 whiting, filleted	juice ½ lemon
1 lb/500 g courgettes, sliced lengthwise	1 tbs oil
½ lb/250 g tomatoes, quartered	1 clove garlic, chopped or crushed
1 dsp chopped fresh basil or marjoram	salt and pepper

Rub a little of the oil around a shallow ovenproof dish. Lay a few of the courgettes in the dish with the fish fillets on top. Place the rest of the courgettes and the tomatoes over them; sprinkle with the herbs, garlic, salt and pepper, lemon juice and more oil. Cover with oiled paper and bake for half an hour in a moderate oven.

Fish and Tarragon Soufflés

Serves 6

This recipe makes a small amount of fish go a long way. The soufflés are nicest served in individual ramekin or cocotte dishes, but the mixture can equally well be baked in one large soufflé dish.

1 lb/500 g white fish (whiting or ling are ideal)	3 large eggs, separated
¾ pint/450 ml milk	1 bay leaf
2 tbs flour	2 tsp chopped fresh tarragon (or 1 tsp dried)
1½ oz/35 g butter or margarine	salt and pepper
	2 tbs dry breadcrumbs

Gut the fish and place whole in a large saucepan with the milk and bay leaf. Simmer until the fish is cooked. Remove the fish from the pan, rub off the skin, take out all the bones and flake the fish. Melt the butter or margarine in a clean saucepan, stir in the flour and then, gradually, the strained milk in which the fish was cooked. Beat over a low heat until smooth. Leave to cool, then stir in the egg yolks, the flaked fish, the tarragon and the seasoning. Whip the egg whites and fold in gently. Grease six individual dishes and divide the mixture between them. Sprinkle with breadcrumbs and bake for 20 minutes with the oven at gas mark 6 (400°F, 200°C). Serve immediately.

VITAMIN "C" LOSS

VIT. "C"

A GRATER.

GRATER

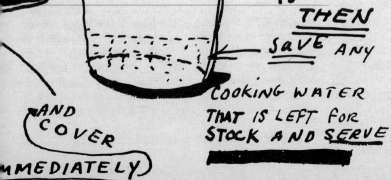

AND COVER IMMEDIATELY

4. THEN SAVE ANY COOKING WATER THAT IS LEFT FOR STOCK AND SERVE

5. SERVE IMMEDIATELY.

Sad to say, in this country we have no tradition of vegetable cookery. In fact, English cooks, even in some of the best restaurants, are renowned for producing mush. Whether boiled, baked or in a white sauce, the ingredients are often so carelessly prepared and overcooked as to be unrecognizable.

Prolonged cooking and reheating of vegetables destroys not only their flavour and texture, but also their nutrients. Vitamin C and vitamin B_1, which are present in many vegetables, are both water soluble, and leach easily into the cooking water. Vitamin C is particularly sensitive to heat and can be completely destroyed if vegetables are kept lukewarm for any length of time. School and hospital canteens are often the worst offenders, particularly as they aim to produce nutritious food. Tests on hospital patients have shown that old people, especially, actually suffer vitamin deficiencies as a result of eating vegetables that are consistently overcooked by the canteens.

During the Second World War, greens and root vegetables were major sources of vitamin C, as citrus fruits were virtually unobtainable. It was the R.A.F. canteens (modern canteens please take note!) which perfected a method of cooking vegetables in such a way as to preserve as much of the flavour as possible. Their instructions have largely been forgotten, but are repeated here as a reminder to anyone who is in the habit of overcooking vegetables.

1. Use the vegetables while they are absolutely fresh. If they have to sit around before they are cooked, leave them in a cold damp place and handle them as little as possible.
2. If vegetables are cut with a blunt knife or grater, they lose a considerable portion of their vitamin C within about five minutes. If they are cut with sharp implements, there is little loss, even after three hours or so.
3. As soon as possible after cutting the vegetables, cook them in a covered pan in a very little *boiling* water until they are just tender. If the quantities are large, cook them a few at a time, using the same water for each batch.
4. Save any cooking water that is left for stock, and serve the vegetables immediately while they are at their best.

The beauty of vegetable cookery is that there is endless scope for experimenting with different combinations of flavours, textures and colours. Faced with a table laden with dishes filled with aromatic mixtures ranging from deep red beetroot, creamy white potatoes and dark green cabbage to glowing red tomatoes, no one could possibly yearn instead for a dish of stringy brown meat floating in a greasy grey sauce.

The recipes in this chapter can be served as main or as side dishes, and many make good hot or cold starters to a meal. Although the selection of vegetables and vegetable dishes is as large and as varied as possible, there is plenty of scope for new discoveries and many more experiments.

Artichokes, Globe

The globe artichoke is the flowerbud of the *Cynara scolymus*, a member of the thistle family. It was introduced from France in the sixteenth century and quickly became a popular delicacy in this country, where it grows very easily in a sunny and well-drained position. The flower heads are cut before they are fully opened. Only the flesh at the base of the larger leaves, the tender inner leaves and the fleshy heart, which is hidden under the 'choke' (aptly named, as that is what it makes you do if you eat it) at the centre of the plant, are eaten. Globe artichokes are sometimes stuffed before cooking, but they are then very messy to eat. They are delicious – and best – served quite simply, as outlined below.

To prepare: Allow one artichoke per person. Cut off

the woody stalks and plunge the artichokes into boiling salted water. Cook for 20 to 35 minutes, depending on age and size. Test them by pulling away one of the lower leaves. If there is no resistance, the artichokes are cooked. Serve them hot with melted seasoned butter, or cold with French dressing or mayonnaise.

Asparagus

Asparagus is in season for six to eight weeks in early summer. It grows easily in this country, but is often imported out of season from the United States. Asparagus is quite rich in vitamins A, B_1 and C and in protein. It is best served simply, as its delicate flavour is easily drowned by elaborate sauces. Wash the spears and trim the white stalks (keep the trimmings for stock). Tie the spears into a bundle and place in a panful of boiling water, keeping the tips free, as they cook more quickly than the stalks. Cook for 25 to 40 minutes. Asparagus can, alternatively, be cooked over boiling water in a steamer. Serve the spears hot with melted butter, a bland margarine, olive oil or a vinaigrette dressing.

At the end of the season, when the stalks are tough and woody, the tips can be trimmed off completely and used for flans or as a filling for omelettes, or baked in a little béchamel or cheese sauce. Keep the stalks and a few of the tips for soup (see page 43).

Asparagus Flan

Serves 4

6 oz/175 g shortcrust
   pastry (see page 150)
tips from 1 lb/500 g
   asparagus, lightly cooked

3 eggs
¼ pint/150 ml milk
salt and pepper

Line a flan tin with the pastry. Beat the eggs with the milk and stir in the asparagus tips and seasoning. Pour into the flan case and bake for 30 minutes at gas mark 5 (375°F, 190°C).

Mixed Spring Vegetables

Serves 3 to 4

tips from 1 lb/500 g
   asparagus, cooked
1 bunch spring onions
salt and pepper
½ lb/250 g shelled broad
   beans

1 small lettuce, shredded
1 oz/25 g butter or
   margarine

Chop the spring onions, including the green parts, very finely. Cook them quickly in the melted butter. Add the asparagus, the broad beans (pre-cooked if they are floury) and the lettuce and stir until heated through. Season and serve immediately.

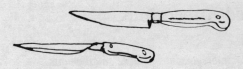

Aubergines

Aubergines were first grown in southern Europe in the thirteenth century as an ornamental plant and very beautiful they are too. They can be grown successfully in England indoors or under glass and even outdoors in hot summers like that of 1976. Aubergines can be unpleasantly bitter, especially if the fruits are old, so it is best always to slice them half an hour before they are to be cooked and sprinkle them generously with salt. The bitter juices will be extracted by the salt and can then be rinsed off.

Aubergine au Gratin

Serves 3 to 4

1 aubergine	*1 level tsp fresh chopped*
½ cucumber	*thyme (or ½ tsp dried)*
¼ lb/125 g mushrooms	*1–2 tbs oil*
3 heaped tbs soft	*1 medium onion*
breadcrumbs	*1 tomato, sliced*
1 clove garlic	*salt and pepper*

Slice the onion and dice the cucumber, mushrooms and aubergine. Fry the onion lightly in a little oil and, when it is beginning to soften, add the salted and drained aubergine. Remove from the heat and stir in the mushrooms, cucumber, thyme, salt and pepper. Put the mixture in an oiled ovenproof dish and sprinkle with the breadcrumbs, seasoned and mixed with the chopped or crushed garlic. Arrange tomato slices on the top, sprinkle with more oil and bake for 45 to 50 minutes at gas mark 6 (400°F, 200°C).

Stuffed Aubergines

Serves 4

2 medium aubergines	*2 small onions*
2 tbs bulgur wheat or	*2 tbs peas*
medium oatmeal	*½ tsp dried herbs*
4 mushrooms, chopped	*1 tbs chopped parsley*
1 tbs oil	*2 tbs water or cider*
salt and pepper	

Cut the aubergines in half lengthwise, sprinkle salt on the cut sides and leave them to drain in a colander for half an hour. Wash them and then scoop most of the pulp out of the middles. Fry the onions lightly in oil; add the wheat or oatmeal, herbs, salt and pepper and a tablespoon or two of water. Simmer until the water has been absorbed and then add the chopped mushrooms, peas and the chopped pulp from the aubergines. Stew for a minute or two longer and then pile the stuffing into the aubergine halves. Pour a thin layer of oil and 2 tablespoons water or cider into a shallow casserole, lay the aubergines in this and bake in a moderate oven for ¾ hour.

Broad Beans

Broad beans can be enjoyed at their very best when they are home grown, picked when they are young and tender, and eaten pods and all with a little butter or oil or raw in salads. Broad beans are high in protein, calcium, vitamin B_1 and vitamin C and so need careful R.A.F.-style cooking (see page 66) to preserve all their nutrients. The older beans are good plainly boiled, and can also be added to stews and casseroles, or sieved and served as a purée. The old pods, puréed, make a good pâté or dip. See also Tomatoes Stuffed with Broad Beans on page 93.

Broad Bean Pod Pâté

Serves 3 to 4

Young broad bean pods are delicious steamed or boiled and served on their own with butter or margarine and black pepper. This recipe makes use of older stringy pods.

1 lb/500 g broad bean pods	*2 tbs olive oil*
1–2 cloves garlic	*salt and pepper*
chopped parsley (optional)	

String both sides of the pods and steam them until they are soft. Press them through a *mouli-légumes*. Mix in the crushed garlic and then gradually add the oil, stirring constantly until the purée is thick and the oil thoroughly amalgamated. Season with salt and pepper, and some chopped parsley, and chill. Serve with bread or toast.

Green Beans

There are many varieties of green beans: runner beans, French beans, mottled beans, purple beans which turn bright green on cooking (called Blue Lake) and the many new varieties of stringless beans and heavy-cropping dwarf beans. They are all rich in calcium, vitamin A, vitamin B_1 and vitamin C.

French beans and the stringless varieties are at their best when boiled or steamed until barely tender and served quite plain with just a little butter, margarine or oil, and salt and pepper.

Green Bean and Pasta Ragout

Serves 4

$\frac{1}{2}$ lb/250 g green beans, lightly cooked
1 red pepper, sliced
3 oz/75 g black olives
1 tsp green peppercorns or plenty of freshly ground black pepper

1 large onion, sliced
3 oz/75 g cooked macaroni (weighed when raw)
2 tbs good fruity vegetable oil
salt

Stew the onion gently in the oil and, when a little softened, add the red pepper. Cut the beans and macaroni into short lengths and add with the olives, green peppercorns (or black pepper) and salt to the pan. Continue to stew gently until the pasta has absorbed some of the oil.

Serve hot with wedges of fresh crusty brown bread. Makes a good first course.

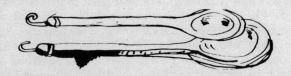

Green Beans Provençale

Serves 3 to 4

1 lb/500 g runner beans
4–5 tomatoes, peeled and sliced
2 tbs oil

1 large onion, sliced
1 clove garlic, crushed
salt and pepper

String the beans and cut them into halves. Stew the onion and garlic in the oil for 5 minutes, then add the beans and the tomatoes. Cover the pan and simmer for about 15 minutes, or until the beans are tender. Serve hot or cold.

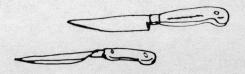

Beetroot

The most famous beetroot dish is the Russian borshch, a soup made with fermented beetroot juice, and often cabbage as well. In England beetroots are invariably served cold in salads or pickled, but they make good hot dishes, and are particularly good baked in their skins, peeled while hot and served immediately with salt, pepper and butter or yoghurt. Beetroots are hardly worth buying ready cooked, as the flavour is always boiled out of them. Average-sized roots take about $\frac{3}{4}$ hour to boil or steam (in their skins, or the juice will run out), or $1\frac{1}{2}$ hours to bake in a moderate oven. Beetroot leaves, if you can get them (probably only if you grow the beets yourself), are very rich in iron and are delicious lightly steamed and served with butter, oil or margarine. If you do grow beets yourself, try the golden variety for a change – they are almost better than the common red ones and it is a great pity that they are so rare in the shops.

Beetroot and Celery Purée

Serves 4

This is a very good combination, with a strong celery taste and the deep rich colour of the beetroot.

¾ lb/350 g beetroots
1 tbs margarine or butter

¾ lb/350 g celery (1 large head)
salt and pepper

Boil or steam the beets until soft. Slice the celery very thinly and cook gently in half the margarine. When the celery is soft, peel and mash the beets and mix the two together. Season and serve with the rest of the margarine or butter on top.

Broccoli

Broccoli is, along with cabbages and cauliflowers, a member of the Brassica family. There are several types: purple sprouting – with little purple flowerets and lots of dark green leaves; ordinary sprouting – similar, but with green, not purple, flowerets; and the large broccoli, looking like a purple cauliflower, which turns green when cooked. The first recipe calls for sprouting broccoli, the second for the purple cauliflower kind.

Broccoli with Almonds

Serves 3 to 4

1 lb/500 g sprouting broccoli
1 tbs oil

2 oz/50 g almonds, shelled
salt and pepper

Wash the broccoli and cut up roughly. Steam or boil in a very little water until tender. Meanwhile, skin the almonds by pouring boiling water over them and squeezing them so that the kernels pop out. Sauté the almonds in the oil until they are browned and crisp and pour them over the drained broccoli. Season with salt and pepper and stir to distribute the almonds.

Broccoli with Mushroom Sauce

Serves 3 to 4

1 head purple broccoli
¼ lb/125 g mushrooms
½–¾ pint/300–450 ml stock (if in a hurry, make with boiling water and yeast extract)

1 green pepper
1 heaped tsp cornflour
salt and pepper
1 tbs oil, butter or margarine

Separate the broccoli into flowerets, slice the green pepper and simmer gently in the oil, butter or margarine in a covered pan until soft (about 15 to 20 minutes). Add the sliced mushrooms and the cornflour mixed with the stock. Season, bring to the boil and pour into a warmed dish for serving.

Brussels Sprouts

Sprouts tend to be ruined by overcooking more often than any other vegetable, which is a pity as they are perhaps the best of the winter vegetables if carefully cooked. They are also rich in nutrients: calcium, vitamin C and protein. The following method ensures that they stay green and fresh-tasting and they will take no more than 10 minutes to cook.

Wash them well and cut away the ends of the stalks and any mushy outer leaves. Make a slit in the thickest stalks. Place them in a large saucepan, in a single layer if possible, and pour in a little boiling water, barely enough to cover the stalks. Sprinkle salt over them, add a knob of butter or margarine, cover the pan and boil them briskly until the water is absorbed. Keep an eye on them, as they burn easily in the last stages. It takes a bit of practice to judge the amount of water exactly, but once mastered, the method never fails and the sprouts taste very special indeed.

At the end of the season, when sprouts tend to be large and overblown, trim away the outer leaves to the tight centre, but don't throw them away. They make an excellent soup. See page 44 for a recipe.

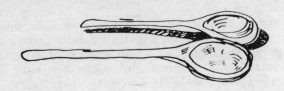

Cabbage

Just as there are many varieties of bean, so there are even more varieties of cabbage: the Dutch white, which is best for salads; red cabbage, which is best after long, slow cooking; Savoy cabbage; the scaly looking Primo cabbage; spring cabbage, or greens; and a newcomer to this country, Chinese cabbage. Kale, Brussels sprouts, cauliflower and broccoli are members of the same family. Cabbages are among the oldest established of the vegetables grown in this country. They became especially popular in the eighteenth century and a favourite taunt of the Thames boatmen to the poorest amongst their numbers was 'You who can't afford butter to your cabbage, or bacon to your sprouts...!' Cabbage is very rich in calcium, vitamin C and vitamin A, which unfortunately are often boiled out of existence.

One of the best ways of cooking Dutch, Savoy, Primo or spring cabbage plain is to slice it and throw it into a saucepan with a knob of butter or margarine, salt, and no water except that clinging to the leaves after washing. It can then be cooked very gently in its own steam, with the lid on the pan. It should emerge tender but still slightly crisp and rich and buttery in flavour.

Green Cabbage with Rice

Serves 4

1 lb/500 g Savoy, Primo or spring cabbage
1 large onion
1 tbs chopped green herbs or 1 tsp dried
dash tabasco sauce
½ lb/250 g rice, cooked
1 clove garlic
2 eggs, beaten
salt and pepper
margarine, butter or oil

Wash, chop and steam the cabbage until tender. Slice and fry the onion and the garlic. Mix the onion, garlic, rice, cabbage, herbs, tabasco sauce and seasoning and bind with the eggs. Place in an ovenproof dish, dot with margarine or butter, or sprinkle with oil, and bake for 20 minutes in a moderate oven.

Stuffed Cabbage Leaves

Serves 4

1 leafy green cabbage

FOR STUFFING:
½ lb/250 g potatoes
2 small onions
oil for frying

salt and pepper
grated rind ½ lemon
¼ pint/150 ml stock
1 large carrot
1 tsp mixed herbs
1 tsp lemon juice

Separate the cabbage leaves, cut off the thickest ribs and steam until the leaves are pliable. For the stuffing: Cook and mash the potatoes, without peeling them. Slice and fry the onions lightly in oil until soft; grate the carrot and the lemon rind. Mix all these ingredients together in a bowl, adding lemon juice, salt and pepper and herbs. Place a little stuffing in the centre of each leaf (the amount depends on the size of the leaf). Fold the stem end over the stuffing, then the sides inwards and the top towards the centre to make a cigar-shaped parcel. Lay the cabbage rolls side by side in a flat ovenproof dish, spoon the stock over them and bake for 20 minutes in a moderate oven, basting every now and then.

Spiced Spring Greens

Serves 4

1 lb/500 g spring greens	1 onion
1 tbs sultanas	2 tbs walnuts or roasted
1 tsp allspice or mixed spice	hazelnuts
salt and pepper	1 tbs oil

Chop the onion and fry it gently in oil. Add the nuts and sultanas when the onion is starting to soften, and simmer for 5 minutes. Wash and chop the greens and add to the onion mixture with the mixed spice or allspice, salt and pepper. Add 1 tablespoon water, cover the pan and leave to simmer until the water is absorbed – not longer than 10 minutes.

Chinese Cabbage

It goes without saying that this type of cabbage comes from China, where it has been known since the fifth century. It is only in the last couple of years that it has been grown commercially in this country. It is long and narrow in shape, each cabbage weighing about 2 to 3 lb. The leaves consist mainly of a large white midrib, looking a bit like the midrib of spinach beet, and are tightly packed around the heart. Chinese cabbage is very light and crisp and delicately flavoured; it is best for salads, but is also good, not boiled, but lightly fried in the Chinese manner. Chinese cabbage could be substituted for the cauliflower stalks in the recipe on page 75.

Red Cabbage with Fennel and Garlic

Serves 4 to 6

1 small red cabbage	oil for frying
(1–1½ lb/500–750 g)	½ lb/250 g fennel bulb
strip orange peel, chopped	4 onions (about ½ lb/250 g)
3 cloves garlic	salt and pepper

Slice the red cabbage, the onions and fennel and fry in a little oil. Add the crushed garlic, the seasoning and the orange peel and simmer for 1 hour with the lid on the pan, or transfer to a casserole and cook in the oven.

This can also be cooked in a pressure cooker for 20 minutes at 15 lb pressure.

Spiced Red Cabbage

Serves 6

1 red cabbage (about	oil for frying
2 lb/1 kg)	1 tbs sugar
2 large cooking apples	2 cloves
1 stick cinnamon	½ tsp caraway or cumin
1 bay leaf	seeds
1 tbs vinegar or red wine	salt and pepper
2 large onions	

Slice the cabbage, apples and onions thinly and fry lightly in a little oil in a large saucepan. Add the sugar, spices, bay leaf and vinegar or wine, season and simmer, covered, for at least 1 hour. (Alternatively cook in a pressure cooker for 20 minutes, or cook in the oven.) At the end of cooking the cabbage should be deep purple in colour and the apples and onions should no longer be visible. Remove the bay leaf and cinnamon tick, adjust the seasoning and serve. This is delicious all on its own, and it also goes well with pork, game, sausages or baked potatoes.

Cardoons

A member of the globe artichoke/thistle family and grown for its crisp, succulent leaf stalks. Cardoons were introduced to England in the seventeenth century but, although they grow well, they have never been as popular here as they are in France. Seeds should be sown in April in rich moist soil. In August, when the plants are about 4 feet/120 cm tall, they should be staked and the leaf stalks earthed up, like celery, for blanching.

Mrs Beeton's Recipe for Cardoons

Cut the stalks into 3-inch [7-cm] lengths, remove the prickles, cover with salted boiling water, boil gently for about 15 minutes, and drain well. Rub off the skins with a cloth, replace the cardoons in the saucepan, cover them with cold water, add a little salt, and boil until tender. Serve with white sauce.'

They can also be served with butter or margarine or parsley, or baked in a béchamel or cheese sauce.

Allow 1 lb/500 g for every two or three people.

Carrots

According to the seventeenth- and eighteenth-century herbals, the humble carrot was endowed with quite remarkable properties. William Salmon, writing in 1710, says that carrots are 'Aperitive, Attractive, Digestive, Carminative, Diuretick [increasing the flow of urine], Cephalick [good for brain troubles], Stomatick, Nephitick, Hysterick [operative on the womb], Lithontriptick [capable of breaking up stones in the bladder], Alterative [affecting nutrition and adjusting it to the normal], Alexipharmick [acting as an antidote to poisons] and Spermatogenetick [productive of lust]'.

It need hardly be said that carrots do not possess all these qualities, but it is true that they can help you see in the dark. Carrots are very rich in vitamin A. A deficiency in this vitamin results in poor night vision and, eventually, blindness.

Carrot Soufflé Flan

Serves 4

6 oz/175 g shortcrust pastry (see page 150)
1 medium onion, chopped
1½ oz/35 g margarine or butter
2 eggs, separated
2 oz/50 g grated cheese
½ tsp finely chopped fennel leaves, fresh or dried

6 oz/175 g grated carrots
2 tbs wholemeal flour
⅛ pint/75 ml milk and ⅛ pint/75 ml cider or ¼ pint/150 ml milk
salt and pepper

Fry the onion in the margarine until it begins to brown. Turn down the heat and add the carrots, stirring them until they soften to a purée. Add the flour, milk and cider and stir until the mixture thickens. Add the grated cheese, salt, pepper and fennel, remove from the heat and beat in the egg yolks. Leave to cool, then fold in the whites, stiffly beaten. Line an 8-inch/20-cm flan tin with the pastry, fill the pastry shell with the mixture and bake in an oven set at gas mark 6 (400°F, 200°C) for ½ hour until the filling is well risen.

Carrots with Lemon, Honey and Dill

Serves 4

1 lb/500 g carrots
juice ½ lemon
2 tsp chopped dill (or fennel
  or parsley, if dill
  unavailable)

2 tsp honey
2 tsp water
salt and pepper

Scrub the carrots and cut them into even-sized lengths. Put in a pan with the lemon juice, honey, chopped dill, water and seasoning. Simmer until tender, then season with a little salt and pepper before serving.

Carrots with Lentils

Serves 4

1 lb/500 g carrots
½ lb/250 g orange lentils
1 tbs margarine

1 medium onion
juice 1 lemon
salt and pepper

Slice the onion and carrots thinly and fry in the margarine until soft. Cook the lentils in about ½ pint/300 ml boiling water until they are soft and mix them with the carrots and onions. Season, add lemon juice and serve. Good with rice or barley.

Carrot Tops

Young carrots are sometimes sold with their ferny leaves still attached. These, as you might expect from their appearance, taste like a carrot-flavoured parsley. Use them as a herb in soups, sauces and stuffings. They are rather too pungent for use in large quantities.

Cauliflower with Garam Masala

Serves 4

This, and the following recipes, are as different as possible from the ubiquitous cauliflower cheese!

1 head cauliflower
1 onion, chopped
salt

1 tbs garam masala
1 tbs oil

Wash the cauliflower and separate into flowerets. Heat the oil in a frying pan and fry the onions and the cauliflower together over quite a high heat, stirring all the time. When softened, add the garam masala and salt to taste, stir and turn the heat down very low. Cover the pan and leave the vegetables to cook through in their own steam. It takes altogether about 10 minutes.

Cauliflower with Hazelnuts and Fennel

Serves 4

1 head cauliflower (or 1
  head purple broccoli)
3 sprigs fennel (herb, or 1
  leaf from fennel bulb,
  finely chopped)

2 oz/50 g roasted hazelnuts
2 tbs margarine or butter,
  melted
salt and pepper

Break the cauliflower into flowerets and steam until just tender. Chop the nuts and fennel and mix with the melted margarine or butter. Place the cauliflower in a shallow dish, pour the sauce over and bake for 20 minutes at gas mark 6 (400°F, 200°C).

Cauliflower and Egg Curry

Serves 2

2 hard-boiled eggs
1 onion, finely chopped
1 oz/25 g butter, margarine
   or oil
¼ pint/150 ml water
1 tbs yoghurt (optional)
salt and pepper
8 oz/250 g cauliflower (½ a
   small one)

½-inch/1-cm piece fresh
   ginger, finely chopped
1 tsp coriander ⎫
½ tsp cumin   ⎪
½ tsp paprika   ⎬ all
½ tsp turmeric ⎪ ground
¼ tsp mustard   ⎭

Steam the cauliflower until tender, then mash or purée through a sieve or *mouli-légumes*. Heat the fat in a saucepan and fry the onion and ginger until browned (if fresh ginger is unobtainable, use 1 teaspoonful powdered ginger with the rest of the spices). Add the other spices and fry, stirring well, for ½ minute. Pour in the cauliflower purée, thin with water and yoghurt, add the eggs, whole or coarsely chopped, season and simmer for 10 minutes. Add more water if the mixture is too dry. Serve with brown rice, barley, millet or buckwheat.

Stir-Fried Cauliflower Stalks

Serves 3 to 4

These are delicious and not unlike beanshoots. Sliced cabbage stalks and Chinese cabbage can be cooked the same way. The whole process of cooking should take about 2 minutes. The vegetables will be slightly softened but still crisp and very hot. Fresh ginger can be bought in Indian, Asian or Chinese shops and is sometimes sold in greengrocers and street markets. If it is impossible to find, add a teaspoonful of powdered ginger to the sauce instead.

10–12 thick cauliflower
   stalks and leaf ribs (1
   large cauliflower should
   have enough still
   attached)
1 clove garlic

1 tbs oil
1 tbs soya sauce
1 tbs water
1-inch/25-mm piece fresh
   ginger root
1 heaped tsp cornflour
1 tsp sherry

Scrub the stalks well, cutting out any bruised patches. Trim away the leaves and shred them; slice the stalks diagonally, very finely. Peel the garlic and the ginger and slice very finely.

For the sauce: mix the cornflour, soya sauce and sherry in a cup or bowl with 1 tablespoon water and set aside. Heat the pan you are going to use – a wok, which is the round-bottomed shallow metal pan used by the Chinese, is best but, failing that, a large shallow saucepan or metal casserole will do. When the pan is hot, pour in the oil and leave that to heat through. Test the temperature by throwing in a small piece of the ginger; it should immediately go brown. First, cook the ginger and the garlic together for a few seconds. Add the cauliflower stalks and, with two wooden spoons, keep stirring and lifting them as they fry so that they cook evenly and don't stick. After a minute or two, add the leaves, stir once or twice and then dribble a very small amount of hot water down the side of the pan. It should immediately evaporate into steam and help cook the vegetables. Pour on the sauce and mix well, adding more water if the mixture is too thick. Serve immediately.

Celeriac

Celeriac is closely related to celery, but the roots are more prized than the stalks, which tend to be rather tough, though they are fine for soups. Celeriac is very good puréed with equal quantities of potatoes and onions, as a vegetable dish, or, thinned, as soup. It can also be diced or cut into strips and used instead of celery in the recipe for Celery and Spinach Crumble (see below). In France, where it is more widely known than here, it is often cut into strips, blanched and served cold in mayonnaise or vinaigrette as a first course.

Celery

Celery was cultivated by the Romans from wild smallage. It belongs to the parsley family and is in season from September to April. It is often imported from the United States during the summer and is hence very expensive. Celery is very rich in calcium.

Celery with Herbs and Lemon

Serves 3 to 4

1 head celery	1 tbs butter or margarine
1 tbs fresh herbs or 1 tsp dried herbs	$\frac{1}{2}$ lemon

Scrub the celery well and cut each stick into 2-inch/5-cm lengths. Melt the butter or margarine and fry the celery gently until softened but not limp (about 20 minutes). Chop the herbs if fresh ones are used and add to the pan with the juice of the $\frac{1}{2}$ lemon. Cook gently for another 5 minutes.

The same method can be used for cooking fennel, but allow less time than for celery.

Celery and Spinach Crumble

Serves 3

4–5 stalks celery	1 medium onion
4–5 tomatoes (bottled if fresh unavailable)	1 dsp oil
$\frac{1}{4}$ tsp caraway seeds	4 large spinach leaves
2 oz/50 g margarine	$\frac{1}{4}$ lemon
4 oz/125 g breadcrumbs	salt and pepper

Slice the onion and chop the celery into $\frac{1}{4}$-inch/6-mm pieces. Sauté together in the oil for a few minutes to soften. Add roughly chopped tomatoes, caraway seeds, salt and pepper, and the juice of the $\frac{1}{4}$ lemon. Cover and simmer for 10 minutes. Meanwhile, prepare the crumble: Chop the spinach as finely as possible and melt the margarine. Mix the margarine, spinach and breadcrumbs and spread on top of the celery mixture in a fireproof dish. Season with salt and pepper and grill until the top is crisp.

Celery Leaves

Save the small stalks and leaves from the top of the celery sticks. Clean them well and hang them in a warm dry place such as an airing cupboard or near a stove. Snip the leaves and use them as a herb or seasoning and keep the dried stalks to use in a *bouquet garni*. Where lovage is required in a recipe, celery leaves can be used instead as the nearest approximation to the flavour. Store them in a screw top jar.

Celery Leaf Fritters

Serves 4

2 oz/50 g wholemeal flour	4 tbs water
1 tbs oil	1 egg white, beaten
4 tbs fresh chopped leaves and stalks from a head of celery	salt and pepper

Beat the flour with the oil and water. Leave to stand for at least $\frac{1}{2}$ hour and then fold in the egg white, the celery leaves and seasoning. Fry in hot oil until golden on both sides.

Chicory

Chicory is not one of the commoner vegetables, despite the fact that it has been known in this country since the seventeenth century. It was first introduced from Belgium and it is known there, and in France, as *witloof* or *endive belge*. In the seventeenth century here, it was called succory and was used raw, for salads. Chicory is not very easy for amateur gardeners to grow. The process was described to me by Dr Amanda Simpson, who, with her husband, runs Chicory Crops Ltd in Gloucestershire, the only farm in England to specialize in chicory. The seeds are planted in the open field in May. By September, the plant looks rather like sugar beet. The roots are then lifted, the leaves trimmed away and the roots transferred to a peat bed in a dark shed. In the dark, damp atmosphere, what is technically the second year's growth appears and, by November, the first tender white chicory plants are ready for cutting. Cropping continues until the following May. It is essential that the plants remain in the dark, otherwise they become green and bitter. At Chicory Crops they are even packed for distribution indoors under a 'safe' green light. Shopkeepers are much less careful and invariably expose chicory to the light, making it acquire the bitterness which many people find distasteful. When you buy chicory, keep it in a dark place and it will remain white and keep its delicious sweet flavour.

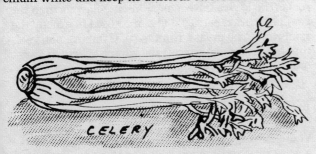

CELERY

Chicory roots can be used to produce a second, smaller crop, but normally they are sold for cattle feed or to be dried and ground as an additive for coffee.

Raw chicory is very good for salads and goes particularly well with tomatoes.

Cooked, it is best braised. Allow 2 whole chicory per person. Trim off the stalks, wash the plants and put them into a well-buttered ovenproof dish. Cover with buttered paper and a lid and bake gently in the oven for about 1 hour, or until tender.

Courgettes

Courgettes are baby marrows, members of the gourd family which includes ornamental gourds, pumpkins, melons and cucumbers. The delicate flavour of courgettes is superior to the even more delicate flavour of large marrows. Some varieties are bright yellow in colour and they are just as good, if not better, than the green ones.

Courgettes with Rosemary

Serves 2 to 4, depending on greed

Cut 1 lb (500 g) courgettes in half lengthwise and fry gently in a tablespoon of oil with a sprig of chopped rosemary. Season and serve.

Courgette Ratatouille

Serves 6

3 lb/1½ kg courgettes, sliced
½ lb/250 g onions, sliced
2 tbs tomato purée
3 tbs oil

2 cloves garlic
1 tsp dried oregano
salt and pepper

Sauté the onions in the oil and, when softened, add the remaining ingredients, with plenty of salt and pepper. Simmer on top of the stove, or in the oven, for ½ hour.

Some water may be necessary if the courgettes dry out in cooking, though the mixture should not be liquid, but rich and thick.

Fennel

Fennel was widely cultivated in Britain from the Middle Ages onwards and was used as a salad herb along with borage, chickweed, onions, garlic and leeks. Its popularity has gradually waned and it is now thought of as a foreign vegetable. It has a mild and pleasant taste of aniseed and has a particular affinity with fish. Any of the celery recipes are suitable for fennel.

Garlic

Garlic was introduced into Britain by the Romans. It remained popular throughout the Middle Ages as an ingredient in salads, soups and sauces. By the sixteenth century it was disparagingly called the 'poor man's physic' and by the seventeenth century its culinary use was quite unacceptable. Garlic did not really come back into favour here until after the Second World War, when people started to become interested in French cooking. Garlic is easy to grow, requiring little attention, though it needs plenty of sunshine.

The last little piece of garlic is almost impossible to squeeze through the holes of a garlic crusher. Save these pieces and put them in a screw top jar full of oil. After a few days, the oil will be thoroughly impregnated with the pungent flavour. Use this oil in salad dressings, or for cooking. Change the garlic every few weeks as it loses its flavour. This makes a little garlic go a very long way.

1a GARLIC

Good King Henry

Good King Henry is a common garden weed which used to be cultivated for use in the kitchen. It is a rather undistinguished-looking plant, growing to the height of about 2 feet/60 cm, with a straight narrow stem, diamond-shaped bright green leaves and sprays of tiny knobbly greenish flowers. *Fat Hen* is a very similar-looking plant which is also edible and extremely common. It is ironical that gardeners expend much time and effort to grow spinach and to destroy these weeds. They are much richer than spinach in iron and protein and are also good sources of vitamin B_1 and calcium. They can be cooked exactly like spinach.

Hamburg Parsley

Hamburg parsley was introduced into Britain in the early eighteenth century, though it is still not widely known. Its edible roots resemble parsnips and taste like a cross between parsnips and celeriac, and recipes for both these vegetables are suitable for Hamburg parsley roots. The leaves have a more intense flavour than the common curled parsley and can be used in exactly the same way. The great advantage of Hamburg parsley is that the leaves will survive the winter, whereas ordinary parsley tends to die off.

Hop Shoots

Young hop shoots were once quite commonly served as a vegetable, and still are in parts of France. They can be picked in the hedgerows in spring when they are 4 to 5 inches/10 to 12.5 cm long. They should be boiled in a little salted water, drained and served like asparagus, with melted butter.

Jerusalem Artichoke

Jerusalem artichokes are knobbly tubers and not related to the globe artichoke. The name is thought to be a corruption of the Italian name, *girasole*, meaning sunflower, of which the Jerusalem artichoke is a relative. They are quite fiddly to peel, which puts many people off them, but, if they are not too damaged, they can simply be well scrubbed and trimmed before cooking as the peel is quite tender. 'New White' is a variety with fewer knobbles than most. They tend, like cardoons and salsify, to darken quickly if they are not cooked as soon as they are prepared. A little lemon juice or vinegar sprinkled over them helps to prevent this.

They taste best of all, not boiled, but sliced and sautéed in butter or margarine, with a sprinkling of fresh herbs and salt and pepper. Their flavour is enhanced by a little garlic, and they are good with onions and bacon.

Jerusalem Artichoke Casserole

Serves 3 to 4

1 lb/500 g Jerusalem
   artichokes
1 clove garlic
pinch nutmeg
1 wineglass cider
1 dsp oil or margarine

1 large onion
½ tsp dried or 1 tsp fresh
   mixed herbs
salt and pepper
1 wineglass stock

Slice the onion and cook in the oil or margarine until it begins to brown. Quarter the scrubbed artichokes and place these with the onion, herbs, garlic, nutmeg, salt and pepper in the pan. Cover with the stock and cider and simmer until the artichokes are tender.

Kale

Kale is a much richer source of iron than spinach and is also particularly high in vitamins A, C, E and K. It is very hardy and can be picked until April when other vegetables are scarce. Kale leaves are very attractive, and, lightly cooked, they can be used as a garnish in place of parsley sprigs, or used as a 'bed' for salads and first courses.

Kale Roast

Serves 4 to 6

2 tbs minced onion
3 tbs margarine
1 lb/500 g cooked kale,
   chopped
1 egg, beaten
1 tsp salt
3 sticks chopped celery

1 tbs flour
3 tbs liquid in which kale
   was cooked
4 oz/125 g fried wheatflakes
½ tsp pepper

Sauté the onion and celery in the margarine and stir in the flour. Add the kale liquid, stirring well, and then all the remaining ingredients. Allow the mixture to cool and place in a greased baking dish. Bake at gas mark 6 (400°F, 200°C) for 30 minutes.

Kohlrabi

Kohlrabi is a swollen root which grows above the ground and tastes rather like a turnip. The leaves can also be eaten. Sow the seeds from April to June and pull the roots when the size of a cricket ball. Do not peel them but scrub well before boiling or steaming. Alternatively, slice them thinly and fry in a little oil. They are also good very thinly sliced and eaten raw with a little salt. The stuffed turnip recipe on page 94 is also good with kohlrabi.

Leeks

Leeks were cultivated by the Greeks and Romans and it is alleged that the Emperor Nero used to eat a combination of leeks and oil in order to improve his voice. No wonder the Welsh chose the leek as their national emblem!

Sautéed Leeks

Serves 3 to 4

1 lb/500 g leeks
1 tsp paprika or ½ tsp
  cayenne pepper

1 chopped tomato
2 tbs oil
salt

Wash the leeks very thoroughly, and cut the white sections into 2-inch/5-cm lengths. Chop the green parts finely. Heat the oil in a large frying pan and fry the leeks over a moderate heat for 5 minutes so that the outsides brown very slightly. Sprinkle with the paprika or cayenne pepper and salt, chop the tomato and add to leeks. Cook slowly until tender.

Devilled Leeks

Serves 4

6 even-sized leeks
1 clove
1 sprig thyme
½ teacupful cider
6 slices toasted bread
1 tbs fresh breadcrumbs
2 sprigs parsley

1 bay leaf
½ oz/10 g butter or
  margarine
½ teacupful stock
2 dsp mild mustard
salt and pepper

Trim the green tops from the leeks. Keep them for salad, for Leek and Potato Soup (page 46) or for Mushroom Stalk and Leek Leaf Sauce (page 83). Cut the white parts into 2-inch/5-cm lengths and wash them well; place them in a saucepan or metal casserole with the herbs, the spices and the butter or margarine. Season with salt and pepper and pour the cider and stock over them. Cover the pan and boil briskly for 1 minute. Transfer the leek mixture to a casserole (unless a metal casserole was used in the first place) and bake for 30 minutes in a moderate oven. Toast 6 slices of bread, cut into triangles and arrange them around the sides of the casserole. Remove the herbs, spread the mustard over the leeks and the toast, sprinkle the top with breadcrumbs and return the dish to the oven for another 10 to 15 minutes.

Mange-Tout

Mange-tout, or sugar peas, are tiny young peas in tender sweet pods which are eaten whole. String both sides of the pods and steam or cook in a little butter for 5 minutes. They need no further treatment and are a delicious vegetable all on their own.

Marrows

There are several kinds of marrow apart from the familiar enormous torpedo-shaped kind. Little Gems are small orange-sized fruits, good for grilling or stuffing. Vegetable Spaghetti – when split open the flesh is in strands like spaghetti – is good boiled whole, opened and served with melted butter, salt and pepper. Custard Marrows, or Custard Apples, are pale green and saucer-shaped and, stuffed, they make a very attractive dish.

Ordinary marrows are good grilled: Cut the marrow (peeled if it is a very large one) into thick slices. Brush with oil, sprinkle with salt and pepper and cook for 10 minutes on each side under a hot grill, brushing frequently with oil. Cooked this way, the marrow slices have an attractive charred appearance and a distinctive flavour.

Stuffed Marrow

Serves 2 to 3

1 marrow, 8–10 inches/20–25 cm long	2 carrots
2 onions	1 green pepper
½ tsp fennel seeds	1 tbs cheese
salt and pepper	oil

Cut the marrow into 2-inch/5-cm slices and scoop out the seeds from the centre. Chop the carrots and onions and fry in a little oil for 2 minutes. Chop the green pepper and add to the pan with the fennel seeds, salt and pepper and, finally, the grated cheese. Pour a thin layer of oil into a casserole large enough to hold the marrow rings in a single layer and place the stuffing in the centres of the rings. Bake in a moderate oven for 1 hour.

Mushrooms

One has only to wander round the food markets of Europe to realize just how conservative we are about mushrooms. In France, Germany and Italy, in the mushroom season, hundreds of different species of edible fungi are gathered and sold fresh each morning. Here only two main species are regularly on sale: the common field mushroom, or *Agaricus campestris*, and the champignon, the *Psalliota campestris*, both cultivated all the year round. The flavour of these mushrooms is good, but it is a pity that we never see the beautiful yellow chanterelles, the delicate shaggy parasol mushrooms, the Boletus, the blewits or the giant puffballs, all of which are left to grow undisturbed and practically unknown, although they are excellent for eating.

Mushrooms with Garlic and Lemon

Slice the mushrooms and fry in a little butter or margarine, with a scrap of crushed garlic, and finish with a squeeze of lemon juice. All species of mushrooms and fungi can be cooked like this. The garlic and lemon enhance their flavour and it is a good way of sampling the less familiar species. Some of the wild fungi will take slightly longer to cook than the common field mushrooms, which take, at the most, 5 minutes.

Baked Mushrooms and Tomatoes

Serves 2 to 3

¼ lb/125 g large flat mushrooms	sprinkling of oil
1 tbs lemon thyme and basil, chopped finely	½ lb/250 g tomatoes
1 tbs breadcrumbs	1 clove garlic, chopped
	salt and pepper

Halve the tomatoes; remove the mushroom stalks and chop them. Mix the stalks with the herbs, salt, pepper and breadcrumbs. Layer the mushrooms, tomatoes and chopped garlic in a flat ovenproof dish, sprinkle the breadcrumb mixture and oil over the top and bake in the oven at gas mark 4 (350°F, 180°C) for ½ to ¾ hour.

Mushroom and Onion Flan

Serves 4

6 oz/175 g shortcrust pastry (see page 150)	butter or margarine
3 large or 4 small eggs	3 tbs sour milk or yoghurt
¼ lb/125 g mushrooms	salt and pepper
2 large onions	1 tsp mixed herbs (preferably fresh)

Make the pastry and line an 8-inch/20-cm flan tin. Prick the bottom, line the pastry with greaseproof paper and a few dried beans and bake blind with the oven at gas mark 6 (400°F, 200°C) for 15 minutes. Meanwhile, slice the onions and fry in a little butter or margarine until soft. Slice the mushrooms thinly and mix with the onions, salt, pepper, herbs, the beaten eggs and the sour milk or yoghurt. Pour into the half-baked pastry case and return to the oven for 20 minutes until the filling is set and risen.

Mushroom Crumble

Serves 6

FOR THE CRUMBLE:

6 oz/175 g 100 per cent
   wholemeal flour
2 tbs chopped nuts
pinch cayenne pepper
3 oz/75 g margarine
1 tbs sesame seeds
2 oz/50 g grated cheese
large pinch salt
1 egg

FOR THE MUSHROOM
MIXTURE:

1 lb/500 g button
   mushrooms
3 sticks celery
½ pint/300 ml cider or white
   wine
1 oz/25 g margarine
salt and pepper
½ lb/250 g onions
1 heaped tbs flour
¼ pint/150 ml milk
½ tsp nutmeg

Mix the dry ingredients for the crumble and rub in the margarine and the grated cheese. Lastly mix in the egg. For the filling: Slice the onions and the celery and stew gently until softened in the margarine. Stir in the flour and gradually add the milk and the cider or wine, stirring all the time. Simmer for 10 minutes. Wipe the mushrooms, slicing the larger ones, stir them into the sauce, remove it from the heat and season to taste with salt, pepper and nutmeg. Pour the filling into a casserole dish, cover with the crumble and bake with the oven at gas mark 3 (325°F, 170°C) for 45 minutes to 1 hour.

To adapt this recipe for Vegans: replace 2 oz/50 g of the flour for the crumble with soya flour, and omit the egg and the cheese but use 5 oz/150 g margarine; for the filling, omit the milk and use ¾ pint/450 ml cider or white wine.

Mushroom and Almond Pâté

Serves 4 to 6

4 oz/125 g mushrooms
2 onions
1 stick celery
1 tbs oatmeal
salt and pepper
1 oz/25 g margarine or
   butter

2 oz/50 g almonds, roasted
1 small strip lemon peel
2 tbs soft breadcrumbs
   (soaked in water, mashed
   and squeezed dry)
1 egg

Chop the onions and celery very finely and fry gently in the butter or margarine. Grate or chop the almonds and mix with the finely chopped mushrooms and lemon peel, the oatmeal and the breadcrumbs. Add the cooked onions and celery and mash the mixture well with a fork. Season and bind with beaten egg. Bake until set in an ovenproof dish, covered with a layer of greaseproof paper, for 40 minutes at gas mark 3 (325°F, 170°C). Remove from the oven and cool with a weight on top. Serve with toast.

Mushroom Stalks and Peel

There is no need to remove the stalks and peel of young and tender mushrooms, but sometimes large old ones need to be trimmed if they are to be stuffed or used raw in a salad. Chop the trimmings finely and cook them until they are dry in butter, oil or margarine (flavourless). Store them in an airtight jar and use for flavouring.

Mushroom Stalk and Leek Leaf Sauce

¼ lb/125 g mushroom stalks
1 oz/25 g margarine or
   butter
1 pint/600 ml sour milk*

green tops from 1 lb/500 g
   leeks
1 heaped tbs flour
salt and pepper

Chop the mushroom stalks and leek leaves finely. Fry both together in the margarine or butter until softened. Add the flour, stirring well over the heat, and add the milk bit by bit. Stir until the sauce has thickened, season and simmer for 15 minutes. Serve with baked, grilled or steamed fish, pieces of chicken or steamed cauliflower.

Nasturtiums

The use of these attractive plants in the kitchen has largely been forgotten. When nasturtiums were introduced here in the seventeenth century, they were known as 'Indian cress' and the bright orange flowers and the leaves were used as a garnish for salads. All parts of the plant can be eaten and they have a pleasant fresh peppery flavour.

For a recipe for pickled nasturtium seeds, which can be used as a substitute for capers, see page 161. For the following recipe, the leaves should be large (about 4 to 5 inches/10 to 12 cm across) or, alternatively, two smaller leaves can be used together. Take care that they are not infested with blackfly, to which this plant is particularly prone. If they are, spray the plants with a safe insecticide such as soapy water or a nicotine solution.

*Use milk that has gone slightly sour in white sauces instead of fresh milk. It is particularly good with mushrooms, onions or cheese – the flour in the white sauce prevents the milk from curdling as it is cooked. Sour milk can also be used for making scones and bread.

Stuffed Nasturtium leaves

1 dozen large nasturtium
   leaves (the size of a saucer
   if possible) and a few
   extra for lining the dish
2 cups cooked brown rice or
   bulgur wheat
½ lb/250 g cooked green
   beans, chopped

1 raw onion, finely chopped
1 large tsp French mustard
4 cloves garlic
1 red pepper, chopped
1 tsp pickled nasturtium
   seeds
salt and pepper
1 tbs oil

Place the nasturtium leaves in a large bowl, cover them with boiling water and immediately pour the water away – they must not get too soggy at this stage. Mix the rest of the ingredients, except the garlic and oil, for the stuffing, place a dessertspoonful in the centre of each leaf and wrap up into a parcel. Line a flat dish or heavy metal casserole with the extra leaves and lay the stuffed leaves, open sides down, over them. Slice the garlic cloves and distribute them between the stuffed leaves. Pour the oil and a little water (2 tablespoons) over the top, cover the dish and either bake in a slow oven for 1 hour, or simmer very gently on top of the stove. Can be served hot or cold.

Nettles

Common stinging nettles make a good and nutritious vegetable – they are one of the richest sources of iron. They must be picked when they are very young and tender, but wear gloves as a precaution! Nettles can be cooked in exactly the same way as spinach.

Nettled Eggs

PER PERSON:

½ lb/250 g young nettles
salt and pepper

1 egg
butter or margarine

Pick the nettles and strip the leaves from the stalks. Steam the leaves for 5 to 10 minutes until tender. Meanwhile poach the eggs; if you do not have a poacher, bring a pan of water to the boil, carefully break an egg into a soup ladle and slowly lower it into the water. Allow the egg to cook for about 15 seconds before you let it drop from the ladle. This way the egg white won't go all over the saucepan in strips. Poach for 3½ to 4 minutes and remove with a slatted spoon. Drain the nettles, and if you like rub them through a sieve or a *mouli-légumes*, season, dot with butter or margarine and place the egg on top.

Onions

Probably used more often than any other vegetable as an ingredient in soups, casseroles and salads, onions are exceptionally delicious on their own, roasted in their skins.

Cut off the roots and stand the onions in a tray with a little oil at the bottom. They will take about 1½ hours in a moderate oven, depending on their size.

Parsnips

Parsnips, despised by the French as cattle food, were one of the earliest root crops grown in this country. A predecessor of the parsnip was common during the first millennium B.C., and parsnips and turnips were widely eaten as a staple food until they were supplanted by potatoes in the seventeenth century.

Parsnip Casserole

Serves 4

4 parsnips
2 large onions
4 sage leaves or 1 level tsp dried sage
1 oz/25 g margarine or butter

salt and pepper
1 large cooking apple
2 cups oats
1 cup milk and a little extra to moisten the oats
grated cheese

Chop the onions and cook them until soft in the margarine. Add the oats and the sage, cook for 5 minutes and add some milk to moisten the oats. Peel and slice the apple and the parsnips. Grease an ovenproof dish and layer the parsnips and apples with the oats, seasoning each layer and finishing with a layer of oats. Pour the cup of milk over the casserole and sprinkle grated cheese on top. Bake with the oven at gas mark 5 (375°F, 190°C) for ½ to ¾ hour.

Peas

The season for peas is from May to September and they are well worth buying fresh as the pods are so useful for soups (see page 48). Peas are rich in vitamins A, B and C. The vitamin B content is increased when peas are dried, but the vitamin content is altogether reduced in the canning process.

Jugged Peas

Serves 4 to 5

This is an Edwardian method of cooking peas.

2 lb/1 kg peas
1 tsp sugar
a few mint leaves

1 oz/25 g margarine or butter
large pinch salt

Shell the peas and place in a large pickling jar with the margarine or butter, sugar, salt and mint. Cover the jar tightly and stand in a pan half filled with water. Boil for ½ hour, after which the peas, as long as they are young, should be cooked. Once the peas inside the jar are hot, the remainder of the cooking could be done in a hay-box (see page 36).

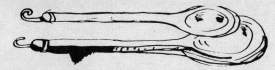

Puréed Peas

This is a good way of using peas which are too old and too tough to serve plain. Shell them and cook them in a little water with salt and a few mint leaves. Pass through a sieve or *mouli-légumes* and heat through with salt, pepper and a knob of butter or margarine mixed in.

Pea Pilau

This recipe was given by Chris Mason.

1 lb/500 g peas (weighed when podded)	2 tsps cumin
1 large onion	2 tsps coriander
2 cloves garlic	¼ lb/125 g mushrooms
1 small green pepper	2 large peeled tomatoes
1 tbs oil	½ lb/250 g rice, cooked
2 hard-boiled eggs, chopped	1 tsp garam masala
½ tsp paprika	½ tsp ginger

Dice the onion, garlic and green pepper and fry gently in the oil until the onion has browned. Add the spices and continue frying for a few minutes. Slice the mushrooms and tomatoes and add to the mixture, stirring in a little water if it is too dry. Cook the peas separately and add to the mixture with the rice and eggs. Heat through thoroughly before serving.

Green Pea Flan

Serves 4

6 oz/175 g wholemeal shortcrust pastry (see page 150)
2 tbs chopped fresh mint
½ lb/250 g curd cheese or ½ lb/250 g sieved cottage cheese mixed with a little milk

1 egg
½ lb/250 g peas, shelled and cooked
salt and pepper

Roll out the pastry and line an 8-inch/20-cm flan tin. Mix the peas with the cheese, mint, seasoning and the beaten egg. Spread the mixture in the flan case and bake with the oven at gas mark 5 (375°F, 190°C) for ½ hour. Serve cold.

Green Peppers

Green peppers are relative newcomers to this country. A few years ago they could only be bought occasionally in specialist food shops in large cities. Now they can be bought almost anywhere, almost all the year round. They grow quite easily if they are started early under glass and can even be grown in flowerpots on a sunny windowsill.

Grilled Green Peppers

Allow 1 pepper per person. Slice the top off each one and rinse out the seeds. Brush them inside and out with oil and grill them, turning them frequently so that they get evenly charred. Rub off the skin and serve.

Stuffed Green Peppers

Serves 4

4 even-sized peppers
½ lb/250 g minced meat or
   cooked aduki beans
1 onion, finely chopped
2 cups cooked brown rice,
   barley, bulgur wheat or
   millet
salt and pepper

FOR THE SAUCE:

1 lb/500 g tomatoes
1 tbs paprika
a little oil
1 large onion, chopped
salt and pepper

Make the stuffing for the peppers: sauté the onion and the minced meat (or aduki beans) for 15 minutes, add the rice or barley, mix well and season with salt and pepper. Pile the stuffing into the peppers, which should have had their tops sliced off and the seeds removed. Replace the caps.

Stew the onion for the sauce in a little oil in a saucepan large enough to hold the peppers standing up. Peel and chop the tomatoes and add them with the paprika and salt and pepper. Stand the peppers in the sauce, put the lid on the pan and simmer slowly for an hour or so, by which time the peppers should have softened and the stuffing should be cooked through.

After ½ hour of cooking, some small scrubbed potatoes can be added to cook in the sauce with the peppers. This dish is rather heavy and filling so, if other courses are to be served at the same meal, they should be light and refreshing – perhaps a cucumber and yoghurt soup to start with and fresh fruit afterwards.

Eggs with Green Pepper and Tomatoes

Serves 4

1 large onion
4–5 tomatoes
salt
oil for frying
1 large green pepper (with
   seeds removed)

cayenne pepper or chilli
   powder
4 eggs

Slice the onion, pepper and tomatoes. Simmer in oil in a shallow saucepan, or frying pan with a lid, for 10 minutes, with a pinch of cayenne or chilli powder and salt. Break the eggs over the top, sprinkle with salt, place the lid on the pan and leave to simmer until the eggs are set. This should take about 15 minutes.

Alternatively, the partly-cooked vegetables can be divided between four individual fireproof dishes, with an egg broken over each one, and baked in a moderate oven until the eggs are set.

The vegetables in this dish can be infinitely varied – sliced courgettes, chopped cucumber and green beans are all very good used together with, or instead of, the above vegetables.

Potatoes

The potato was introduced into Ireland in the last years of the sixteenth century. It proved an ideal crop to grow in Ireland's deep moist soil and windy climate, and by the end of the seventeenth century it had become the staple food for nearly the entire population and their animals as well. The widespread potato blights of the mid 1840s consequently caused immense suffering, famine and poverty throughout Ireland. As a result, the population was more than halved and many of those who remained strong were forced to emigrate to

America. Many of these American-Irish felt very bitterly against the English who were blamed for the misfortunes they had suffered. 'It may truly be said that it was the potato which determined the atmosphere in which the subsequent relations between Americans, Irish and English were to develop in the next hundred years' (Salaman, *The History and Social Influence of the Potato*).

Five million tons of potatoes are eaten in Britain every year. Potatoes contain some vitamin C – 5 to 10 mg per 100 g when boiled. This is much less than that contained in cabbage, cauliflower, Brussels sprouts or citrus fruits, yet, because they tend to be eaten every day, potatoes can be a major source of vitamin C in winter.

Potato Pancakes

Makes 10 to 12 pancakes

1 lb/500 g potatoes	salt and pepper
1 egg	1 tsp caraway seeds
1–2 tbs water	4 tbs oil
1 onion	

Peel the potatoes and grate coarsely. Grate the onion into the same dish and season with salt, pepper and caraway seeds. Beat the egg and mix into the potato mixture with the water. Leave to stand for about ½ hour. Heat the oil in a frying pan until smoking. Put in as many tablespoons of the potato mixture as possible, leaving a little space between them and flattening each one well. Fry for about 5 minutes on each side or until browned. Keep the first batch hot in the oven while the others are frying. Serve with a rather sharp, lemony apple purée.

CUCUMBER

Provençal Potatoes

Serves 3 to 4

1 lb/500 g potatoes	salt and pepper
2 tbs tomato purée	5–6 tomatoes
2 tbs oil	2 cloves garlic
1 cup water	6 black olives

Steam the potatoes in their skins for 10 minutes, and slice them thickly. Chop the tomatoes and simmer in oil with the crushed garlic, tomato purée and water until reduced and thickened a little. Season highly with salt and pepper and mix in a casserole with the potatoes and olives. Bake in a moderate oven for 1 hour.

Half-Baked Potatoes

Serves 4

4 large potatoes	2 tsps cumin or caraway
4 tbs oil	seeds
	1 tsp salt

Scrub the potatoes and cut them in half. Lay them face down in a baking tin or large flat casserole. Pour the oil and sprinkle the cumin seeds and salt over them, and bake for 1 hour at gas mark 6 (400°F, 200°C).

Potato Goulash

Serves 4

1½ lb/750 g waxy potatoes, scrubbed and cubed	1 tbs paprika
½ lb/250 g onions, sliced	¼ pint/150 ml yoghurt
1 tbs oil	salt and pepper
	½ tsp roasted caraway seeds

Fry the potatoes and onions together in the oil until they begin to soften. Season highly with salt and pepper; add the paprika, caraway seeds and yoghurt. Place the lid on the pan and leave to simmer very slowly for about 40 minutes, adding a little water every now and then.

Alternatively the potato mixture can be cooked in water and the yoghurt added at the end of the cooking time, when the potatoes are soft.

Potatoes and Sesame

Serves 4

1½ lb/750 g potatoes	1 egg, beaten
sesame seeds for coating	oil for frying

Scrub the potatoes and cut in ½-inch/1-cm slices. Steam them until only just done. Dip the slices into the beaten egg and then into the sesame seeds, coating them thoroughly. Fry the slices in hot oil until they turn brown. Turn each slice once. Serve with home-made tomato or apple sauce.

Radishes

Radishes were cultivated by the Romans, who ate them with a pepper sauce. They were used in the Middle Ages as a remedy for heaviness in the belly, and in the sixteenth century young radish leaves were a common salad ingredient. The leaves are also good cooked and served as a purée or a base for soup. They should be prepared exactly as for spinach. The radishes themselves, though, become rather bland and characterless when cooked. There are many varieties of radish, from the red globes we all know, to long tapering black, white or purple roots which are better known on the Continent. All types of radish are best served either whole, if they are small, or thinly sliced, with salt, or in salads. Radishes are quite rich in vitamin C.

Rampion

Rampion is a native British plant of the Campanula tribe, with long fleshy white roots. It used to grow wild much more commonly than it does now, and both the roots and the leaves were eaten in the seventeenth century. This recipe is included as a curiosity in case anyone happens to grow rampion – it is certainly never on sale in the shops. It is from a vegetarian cookery book of the 1920s, *May Byron's Vegetable Book* (Hodder & Stoughton).

Wash and scrape 1 dozen roots, throw them into a bowl of cold water with 2 tablespoons vinegar or lemon juice and leave 5 minutes. Have boiling ½ pint/300 ml water, ¼ pint/150 ml milk, ½ oz/10 g butter, 2 slices lemon, ½ teaspoon salt. Plunge the roots into this liquid and boil them until tender. Remove and drain them and thicken the sauce to serve with them.

Salsify

Salsify (or oyster plant) was grown much more in the sixteenth and seventeenth centuries than it is today. The well-known herbalist, Gerard, writing in 1597, said it was cultivated 'in gardens for the beautie of the flowers, almost everywhere'. The roots are usually served hot but are also good cold in a salad. They are very easy to grow and need no attention. They are ready for use from mid-October and can be lifted for storing or kept in the ground.

To cook: Wash the roots and boil until tender in water. Rub off the peel, cut them into 2-inch/5-cm lengths and place in a flat fireproof dish with knobs of butter or margarine, a squeeze of lemon and a tablespoon of chopped parsley. Heat through in the oven for 10 minutes. This makes a good first course.

Salsify Fritters

Allow 1 large or 2 small salsify per person. Cook and peel salsify as above and cut into 2-inch/5-cm lengths. Marinate for ½ hour in lemon juice, parsley, salt and pepper.

FOR FRYING BATTER:

3 oz/75 g flour
4 tbs water
pinch salt

2 tbs oil
1 white of egg, stiffly beaten
oil for frying

Beat the 2 tablespoons oil and the water into the flour; add the salt and lastly the stiffly beaten egg white. Leave to stand for at least ½ hour. Dip salsify pieces into frying batter and fry in hot oil (about ¼-inch/5 mm layer). Drain and place on a hot dish. Sprinkle parsley and salt over before serving.

Salsify Leaves

You can only get hold of these if you grow salsify in your garden, as the leaves rarely, if ever, make an appearance in the shops. The leaves should be eaten when young, and have a delicate flavour rather like a cross between asparagus and spinach. They can be picked until June, after which they become tough and stringy. Steam the leaves from several salsify roots over boiling water (the leaves from 1 root would be sufficient for 2 people) for 7 to 8 minutes. Drain and dot with margarine or butter. Season and serve hot.

Samphire

Samphire is a common sea-weed which grows in the mud along the coasts, particularly those of eastern England, where it is often sold in fish shops in summer. It has fleshy jointed leaves and yellow flowers.

To prepare: Rinse well and cut off the woody stems and roots. Plunge into boiling unsalted water and cook for about 10 minutes. Serve like asparagus – each leaf is dipped into melted butter and the flesh sucked from it. Samphire has a strong salty flavour.

It is sometimes pickled with elder buds, horseradish, peppercorns, vinegar and cider.

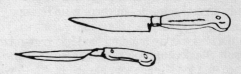

Scorzonera

Scorzonera (viper's grass) is a root vegetable which is similar to salsify, except that the roots are black (it is sometimes known as black salsify). Sow the seeds in April/May and the roots will be ready to eat by October.

Scorzonera was introduced to Britain from Spain in 1576. According to Gerard's herbal, 'Viper's grasse is called of the Spaniards Scorzonera, which soundeth in Latine Viperaria, or Viperina, or Serpentaria, so called because it is accounted to be of force and efficacie against the poisons of vipers and serpents, for Vipera, or a viper is called in Spanish Scurzo.'

The roots, like salsify, have a delicate taste which can best be appreciated by simple treatment and any salsify or asparagus recipe can be used for scorzonera.

Seakale

Seakale beet or Swiss chard sometimes grows wild on the coasts. It is really two vegetables in one: the white fleshy midribs can be cooked and eaten like asparagus, with melted butter, and the green leaves can be cooked and eaten like spinach.

Spinach

'I'm Popeye the Sailorman,
I'm Popeye the Sailorman.
I fights to the finish
Cos I eats me spinach,
I'm Popeye the Sailorman!'

Popeye may have felt stronger and healthier after his daily dose of spinach but there is no reason, nutritionally, why he should have done so. The fame of spinach as a body-building food has grown largely as a result of a decimal point being inserted in the wrong place in a food analysis published in 1870, which claimed that spinach was exceptionally rich in iron. This was quoted repeatedly, until 1937 when spinach was re-analysed and found to contain only one tenth of the amount of iron stated in the 1870 report. What is more, very little of the iron (or the calcium) in spinach is available to the human body, as oxalic acid is also present in amounts large enough to inhibit their absorption. A new variety of spinach called Monnapa, which is low in oxalic acid, has been developed and the seeds are available from Thompson & Morgan Ltd.

All varieties of spinach are good sources of protein and vitamins A and C.

Spinach Lasagne

Serves 3 to 4

1 lb/500 g spinach
¼ lb/250 g lasagne, cooked
salt and pepper
1 onion, sliced
margarine or butter
½ lb/250 g tomatoes, sliced

CHEESE SAUCE:

1 oz/25 g butter or
 margarine
¾ pint/450 ml milk
1 heaped tbs flour
4 oz/125 g grated cheese

Cook the onion in margarine or butter for a few minutes; wash and chop the spinach and mix with the onion. Make a white cheese sauce and layer the lasagne, spinach mixture, cheese sauce, tomato slices and salt and pepper in a casserole, starting with lasagne and finishing with lasagne and cheese sauce on top. Bake in a moderate oven for 35 to 45 minutes.

Spinach with Olives and Capers

Serves 3 to 4

This is best served with a bland accompaniment like rice or potatoes.

1 lb/500 g spinach
1 heaped tbs green olives
1 tbs oil
1 heaped tbs capers or
 pickled nasturtium seeds
salt and pepper
2 cloves garlic

Wash the spinach and steam for 5 minutes. Drain well and chop roughly. Stone and chop the olives. Heat the oil in a large frying pan with a lid, add the garlic, squeezed through a garlic press, the capers and olives. Fry for 2 minutes and then add the chopped spinach, salt and pepper. Mix well for a few minutes and place the lid on the frying pan. Cook for a further 5 to 10 minutes or until the spinach is soft.

Spring Onions

Many people eat only the white part of spring onions. Chop the green leaves finely and use them instead of chives in salads or as a garnish for soups, casseroles or stews. They are good sprinkled over plain boiled potatoes.

Sprue

Sprue is hardly ever seen in the shops nowadays. It has

been entirely replaced by asparagus, of which it is regarded as the poor cousin. It looks very like a green version of grape hyacinth. Sprue is much more tender than asparagus and requires a shorter cooking time (5 to 10 minutes). It should be served in the same way as asparagus and it tastes every bit as good.

Swede, Turnip or Potato Kebabs

Serves 3 to 4

Kebabs will be familiar to travellers in Greece or Turkey. The little aromatic cubes of meat and vegetables, threaded on skewers and cooked over charcoal, are becoming commoner in Britain as Greek and Turkish restaurants proliferate in our cities. The following kebab recipes will be less familiar as they use the same method but different ingredients – common English vegetables like swedes, potatoes and turnips. The marinade is based on the Greek version, but there is much scope for experiment with different herbs and spices. Try, for instance, marinading the partly cooked potatoes in yoghurt and cumin or caraway seeds, or wrapping the turnips in bacon. It is not necessary to have a barbecue or charcoal grill – any gas or electric grill will do.

1 lb/500 g swedes, potatoes or turnips (or a mixture of all three)

FOR THE MARINADE:

2 tbs olive oil

1 tbs finely chopped parsley
1 clove garlic, crushed
2 tsp oregano
1 onion, finely chopped

Cut the vegetables into cubes and steam them for 15 minutes. While they are still hot, mix the marinade ingredients and put the vegetables into it, turning them frequently so that they absorb as much as possible. When they have cooled, thread them onto skewers and grill them for 10 to 15 minutes, turning and brushing them frequently with the remainder of the marinade.

Other vegetables can be threaded onto skewers (e.g.

onions or mushrooms, neither of which need pre-cooking). If meat and vegetables are used together, the meat should be threaded onto skewers and cooked a little first, so that the vegetables do not get mushy and charred.

Stuffed Swedes

Serves 3 to 4

1 lb/500 g swedes (small-sized)
2 cups stock

FOR THE STUFFING:

1 cup pearl barley

1 onion
1 tsp herbs
salt and pepper
½ lb/250 g minced meat (or cooked black-eye beans)
1 clove garlic, crushed

Prepare the stuffing: Cook the pearl barley as for brown rice, in plenty of boiling unsalted water for about 30 to 40 minutes. In the meantime, fry the onion and meat in a little oil, add the garlic and herbs when the meat has browned and simmer the mixture for about 10 minutes. Peel the swedes and slice a cap off the top. Scoop out the centres with a sharp knife and a teaspoon, leaving a shell ½ inch/1 cm thick. Stand the swede shells in water that has come to the boil, for 5 minutes, so that they soften slightly. Drain the barley and add to the meat mixture with the chopped pulp scooped out from the centre of the swedes. Add salt and pepper. Drain the shells, pile the stuffing into them and replace the caps. Stand the swedes in stock in an ovenproof casserole and bake for 1 hour in a moderate oven, basting every now and then.

Sweetcorn

Maize seeds were first brought to Europe from Cuba by Christopher Columbus, who wrote that the vegetable was 'most tasty, boiled, roasted or ground into flour'.

For corn on the cob: Allow one per person and peel

off the leaves and the silky strands underneath (these are *not* good to eat – I have tried them!). Trim the stems, plunge the cobs into boiling water and cook, covered, for 10 to 20 minutes. Drain the cobs and serve with melted seasoned butter.

Sweetcorn Fritters

Makes about 12 fritters

2 corn cobs
salt and pepper
2 tbs oil for frying

FOR THE BATTER:

4 oz/125 g flour
1 egg, beaten
¼ pint/150 ml milk
pinch salt
1 tbs oil

Cook the sweetcorn until tender, drain and cut away the kernels with a knife. For the batter: Sift the flour and salt into a bowl. Make a well in the centre and tip in the egg and the oil. Mix the flour gradually into the centre with a fork. Mix into a smooth paste with the milk and beat well until the mixture is glossy and free of all lumps. Leave to stand for ½ hour and then mix in the sweetcorn kernels. Season with salt and pepper. Heat 2 tablespoons oil in a frying pan until smoking. Drop spoonfuls of the batter into the oil and fry on both sides until brown and crisp. Keep the fritters hot in the oven until they are all ready.

Succotash

Serves 3 to 4

This is an American Indian dish and one of the first dishes adopted by the Pilgrim Fathers on settling in the New World. It is basically a mixture of equal quantities of dried beans and sweetcorn kernels. It is particularly good with black-eye beans.

2 corn cobs
1 tbs finely chopped parsley
¼ lb/125 g black-eye beans

1 oz/25 g butter or
   margarine
salt and pepper

Cook the corn cobs in boiling water until they are tender and strip off the kernels with a knife. Soak the beans in boiling water for 1 hour (or in cold water overnight) and cook them until they are tender. Strain, keeping the water for stock. Melt the butter or margarine in a saucepan and stir in the beans and the corn kernels with the chopped parsley and plenty of salt and pepper. Serve when heated through.

Tomatoes

Tomatoes were introduced to Britain in the fifteenth century, but were grown as a curiosity until the last century, when they were finally accepted as a source of food, and grown in greenhouses. Tomatoes are now grown commercially in vast greenhouses along the Lea Valley in Hertfordshire and sent from there all over England. Unfortunately these are invariably the thick-skinned, watery, prolific varieties, and it is well worth growing some of the thin-skinned, tastier varieties at home, even if the only space is in a window-box or a flowerpot indoors. (See the chapter 'Growing Your Own' at the end of the book.)

Tomato Flan

Serves 4

6 oz/175 g wholemeal
   shortcrust pastry (see
   page 150)

FOR THE FILLING:

4 oz/125 g onion
2 oz/50 g wheatgerm
1 clove garlic, chopped

2 oz/50 g margarine
2 oz/50 g roasted chopped
   nuts
12 oz/350 g tomatoes
½ tsp dried oregano
salt and pepper

Chop the onion and fry in $1\frac{1}{2}$ oz/40 g of the margarine. When soft, add the roasted nuts and wheatgerm. Mix well, season and remove from the heat. Line a flan tin with the pastry. Spread half the wheatgerm mixture in a layer on the bottom. Slice the tomatoes and lay these over the wheatgerm, sprinkling the garlic, oregano, salt and pepper amongst them. Cover with the remainder of the wheatgerm mixture, dot with the rest of the margarine and bake in the oven at gas mark 4 (350°F, 180°C) for 40 minutes.

Tomato Pizza

For 1 large pizza to serve 2 to 3

FOR THE DOUGH:

8 oz/250 g wholemeal flour
$\frac{1}{4}$ oz/5 g fresh yeast (or $\frac{1}{2}$ tsp dried)
$\frac{1}{2}$ tsp salt
$\frac{1}{4}$ pint/150 ml warm water
$\frac{1}{2}$ tsp sugar

Dissolve the yeast in the water with the sugar and mix into the flour and salt. Knead well, adding a little more water if necessary (or flour) to make a smooth, pliable dough. Cover and leave to rise in a warm place until doubled in bulk (about 2 hours).

FOR THE FILLING:

1 lb/500 g tomatoes, peeled and chopped
2 tsps mixed herbs (oregano, basil, marjoram, rosemary)
1 tsp chopped capers or pickled nasturtium seeds
2 onions
2 cloves garlic
6–8 black olives
2 tbs oil
salt and pepper

Optional extras (one of the following): few sliced mushrooms, small slices ham or salami, handful cooked mussels or shredded white fish, few strips salt anchovy, 2 tbs grated cheese, sliced green pepper, 2 eggs (broken over the pizza before the addition of the herbs and seasoning)

Slice the onions and the garlic and stew in 1 tablespoon of the oil. When beginning to soften, add the tomatoes and simmer until most of the liquid has evaporated. Roll out the risen dough to a large thin circle or rectangle and place on an oiled baking sheet. Spread the tomato mixture evenly over the surface and sprinkle with the herbs, capers and olives, salt and pepper and the remaining oil. (Add any of the extras at this stage, except the cheese, which should be sprinkled over the pizza halfway through baking.) Leave the pizza to prove on the stove while the oven heats up to gas mark 7 (425°F, 220°C). Bake for 20 to 30 minutes and serve immediately.

Tomatoes Stuffed with Broad Beans

Serves 4

1 lb/500 g tomatoes, preferably large
1 clove garlic
$\frac{1}{2}$ lb/250 g broad beans
salt and pepper
oil

Cook broad beans and drain; cut the tomatoes in half crossways and scoop out the middles. Chop these and fry in a very little oil with the chopped garlic clove. Pour 1 tablespoon of oil in the bottom of a flat ovenproof dish and place the tomato halves in this. Mix the beans and tomato pulp together and spoon into the shells. Cook in the oven at gas mark 5 (375°F, 190°C) for 20 minutes. Good hot, but better cold.

Stuffed Turnips

Serves 3 to 4

1 lb/500 g small turnips
   (about 5 or 6)

FOR THE STUFFING:

2 thick slices stale brown
   bread
4 rashers streaky bacon or
   ¼ lb/125 g bacon pieces

1 dsp parsley
1 glass cider
1 medium onion
½ dozen black olives
   (optional)
1 tbs oil
salt and pepper

Peel the turnips and steam for about 8 minutes until they are softened, but not mushy. Leave to cool a little and then scoop out the centres. Cut the bread into small cubes and fry until crisp in hot oil. Cut the onion and bacon into small pieces and add to the bread. Chop the pulp from the turnips and, when the onion and bacon are crisp, add to the pan with the parsley, olives (if used) and seasoning. Stuff the turnips with as much as possible of this mixture and lay them in a casserole. Spread any stuffing that remains over the top, pour the cider over them and bake, uncovered, in a moderate oven, for 20 minutes.

Mixed Vegetables

Winter Ratatouille

Serves 6

1 lb/500 g parsnips
½ lb/250 g greens
oil
2 cloves garlic
a sprig rosemary
½ tsp thyme
1 cup water

1 lb/500 g turnips
4 onions
1 tbs tomato purée or
   ½ lb/250 g bottled
   tomatoes
½ tsp marjoram
salt and pepper

Wash, peel and dice all the vegetables. Stew them in oil; add crushed garlic, herbs, tomato purée or bottled tomatoes and 1 cup water. Simmer until all the vegetables are soft, adding a little more water if they begin to dry out. Season well with salt and pepper before serving.

Stir-Fried Mixed Vegetables

Serves 4

a mixture of winter
   vegetables, e.g. 2 carrots,
   2 parsnips, 2–3 sticks
   celery, 1 onion, 1 bundle
   greens
2 cloves garlic

1 strip lemon peel
a 1-inch/2.5-cm piece of
   ginger
2 tbs oil
soya sauce
cornflour (optional)

Clean and slice all the vegetables very thinly. Also slice the garlic, ginger and lemon peel thinly. Put the oil into a pan and heat until it smokes. Add the onion, ginger, garlic and lemon peel and fry very quickly. Almost immediately add all the other vegetables except the greens, stir quickly over the heat for a minute and then add the greens. Stir-fry for ½ minute, dribble some boiling water down the side of the pan and tip the pan so that the steam rises through the vegetables. Add 1 to 2 tablespoons soya sauce, mixed with some cornflour if you want the sauce thick. Mix well into the vegetables and serve immediately. Good with brown rice.

Summer Vegetable Hot Pot

Serves 6

This is based on a war-time recipe issued by the Ministry of Food.

1½ lb/750 g potatoes	½ lb/250 g runner beans
½ lb/250 g young carrots	bunch spring onions
stock or water	salt and pepper
small bunch fresh herbs	1 lb/500 g peas

Wash and slice the potatoes, beans, carrots and spring onions. Put them all together in a casserole with enough stock or water to come half way up the vegetables. Add salt and pepper to taste and push the herbs into the centre of the pot. Cover closely and simmer for ½ hour. Remove the herbs, add the peas and cook for a further 10 minutes. Serve very hot.

Savoury Vegetable Pancakes

Makes about 10 pancakes

FOR THE PANCAKE
BATTER:

4 oz/125 g 100 per cent wholemeal flour	pinch salt
1 egg	
1 tbs oil	½–¾ pint/300–400 ml milk or water

Sift the flour into a mixing bowl. Make a well in the centre and break the egg into it with a little of the milk or water. With a fork, gradually mix the flour at the centre of the well into the egg and milk, until it is a paste. Add the oil and carry on mixing, gradually adding the rest of the milk or water. Beat the mixture more quickly now, always mixing into the centre of the bowl or the paste will become lumpy. When all the liquid has been added, sprinkle in a large pinch of salt and beat the mixture vigorously, preferably with an egg whisk, until it is smooth. Leave for ½ hour to settle.

When the pancakes are ready to be cooked, heat a heavy frying pan for a few minutes, then grease lightly with oil. Ladle in a spoonful of the batter and swirl it round the pan to make an even, thin coat. (The first pancake is always the hardest, so don't worry if it is a strange shape; once the pan has been used a few times and is evenly greased, then the process becomes easier.) When the whole surface of the pancake is dull, then it is ready to turn. Loosen the edges with a knife or spatula and, if you are daring, toss it by tipping the pancake away from you over the edge of the pan and then flipping it quickly upwards and towards you, so that it turns and settles in the middle of the pan. If you are not quite so daring, flip it over with a knife. The other side will cook more quickly than the first, so take care that it doesn't burn. As the pancakes are made, slide them onto a sheet of greaseproof paper and keep them warm in a slow oven until they are all ready.

Pancakes can be made several hours before they are needed; if they are made in advance, wrap them in greaseproof paper or a clean tea-towel to keep them soft, and reheat them slowly in the oven, brushing the top one with oil to keep it moist. The most spectacular way of serving savoury pancakes is to make a number of fillings of different flavours, textures and colours. Have some cooked fillings and others crunchy and raw, and arrange them on the table in small dishes. Everyone can then stuff their own pancakes with whatever fillings they choose.

SUGGESTED FILLINGS FOR PANCAKES:

Chopped cooked spinach, mixed with herbs and garlic and
    cottage or curd cheese (serve hot);
shredded raw leeks or spring onions;
tomatoes, peppers and courgettes, simmered in oil with
    garlic;
grated raw carrots with lemon juice, salt and pepper;
chopped nuts sautéed with onions;
plain grated cheese;
cooked broccoli spears with fresh herbs;

purée of broad beans or peas, mixed with lemon juice, chilli
   powder and chives;
chopped asparagus spears.

Pancake Rolls

Allow 2 to 3 per person

Place 2 tablespoons of a hot filling in the centre of each
pancake (see above) and roll it up into a sausage-shaped
parcel, tucking in the ends. Lay the pancakes side by
side in a flat ovenproof dish, and heat through with the
oven at gas mark 6 (400°F, 200°C) for 20 minutes.
Creamy fillings are best for this method of serving
pancakes, e.g. spinach and curd cheese; plain grated
cheese; vegetables, meat or fish in a béchamel sauce. It
is an ideal way of using up small quantities of left-overs.
Rolled up pancakes could also have some grated cheese
on top, or a béchamel or tomato sauce, sour cream,
wine or cider poured over them, before cooking.

Palatschinken

This is another good way of using up left-overs, and is a
very attractive dish.
   You will need a cake tin, preferably one with a
detachable bottom, the same diameter as the pancakes.
Grease the tin well and lay a pancake (see page 95) at
the bottom. On this spread a layer of one sauce –
perhaps a ratatouille, or a mixture of cooked
mushrooms and onions. Place another pancake over
this and then spread a layer of a different sauce –
maybe a cheese one or a vegetable purée. Carry on
layering the pancakes and the two alternate sauces
until the cake tin is full or until the pancakes and
sauces are used up. Grate some cheese over the top and
bake in a moderate oven for $\frac{1}{2}$ to $\frac{3}{4}$ hour. To serve, turn
out and cut in wedges like a cake.

Food from the Hedgerows

The idea of getting something for nothing always seems
appealing but, as the American ecologist, Barry
Commoner, says in his book *The Closing Circle*, 'There is
no such thing as a free lunch.' Applied to the eating of
wild plants, the cost of uprooting or destroying a plant
may be the complete removal of that plant species from
an area and even its ultimate extinction.
   There are, however, many wild plants which can be
used for culinary purposes, providing certain basic rules
are followed. These can be summarized as:

1. Only take small quantities of leaves, berries or
   flowers from each plant, so that its appearance and
   health are not affected. Cut plants with a knife,
   scissors or secateurs.
2. Don't pick the flowers or seeds of annual plants.
3. Under the Conservation of Wild Creatures and Wild
   Plants Act 1975* it is illegal to uproot a plant
   without reasonable excuse (outside your own
   property) without the owners' permission. It is also
   illegal to pick any of the twenty-one protected plants
   without a licence.

   Some further precautions are advisable when
collecting wild food. It would be wise not to take plants
from the verges of roads which are heavily used,
especially by large lorries, as the plants may be
contaminated by cadmium and lead. It would also be
prudent to refrain from taking plants from land which
has recently been sprayed with weedkillers or
insecticides. In any case, wash thoroughly any foods
gathered from the wild.
   Some plants which are easily identifiable and unlikely
to suffer from over-zealous picking are the dandelion

*Available from H.M.S.O.

Taraxacum officinalis), shepherd's purse (*Capsella bursapastoris*), chickweed (*Stellaria media*), stinging nettle (*Urtica dioica*), hop (*Humulus lupulus*) and plantain (*Plantago major*).

The fruits and flowers of the following can also be taken without permission: blackberry (*Rubus fruticosus*), rosehip (*Rosa canina*), sloe or blackthorn (*Prunus spinosa*), rowan (*Sorbus aucuparia*), elder (*Sambucus nigra*), lime (*Tilia europaea*) and hawthorn (*Crataegus nigra*). The following nuts may also be taken: hazel (*Corylus avellan*), sweet chestnut (*Castanea sativa*), beech (*Fagus sylvatica*) and oak (*Quercus robus*).

Useful field guides for identifying wild plants are *The Concise British Flora in Colour* by W. Keble Martin (Ebury Press/Michael Joseph, 1965) and *The Wild Flowers of Britain and Northern Europe* by Richard Fitter, Alastair Fitter and Marjorie Blamey (Collins, 1974), *Food for Free* by Richard Mabey (Collins, 1972) and *Hedgerow Cookery* by Rosamond Richardson (Penguin, 1980).

Pulses

(legumes (pulses)

let them sit in water OVER NIGHT

o R.

chick peas

8.

HERE IS HOW SOME OF THEM LOOK.

nd Cereals.

POUR BoiLing water over Them

Put a lid on AND LEAVE for one or 2. hrs.

Yum Yum.

BUT, DON'T BE TOO IMPULSIVE.

Then said Daniel to Melzar, whom the prince of the eunuchs had set over Daniel, Hananiah, Mishael and Azariah,

'Prove thy servants, I beseech thee, ten days; and let them give us pulse to eat, and water to drink.

'Then let our countenances be looked upon before thee, and the countenance of the children that eat of the portion of the king's meat: and as thou seest, deal with thy servants.'

So he consented to them in this matter, and proved them ten days.

And at the end of ten days their countenances appeared fairer and fatter in flesh than all the children which did eat the portion of the king's meat.

Thus Melzar took away the portion of their meat, and the wine that they should drink; and gave them pulse.

Daniel 1:11–16

Pulses

Pulses or legumes, as the Bible story indicates, are a very valuable food, rich in protein, iron, thiamine, niacin and calcium. Wild varieties of pulses – chick peas, beans and lentils – are known to have been eaten in the Near East, Central America and parts of Europe since at least 10,000 B.C.

Although the Heinz variety of bean is now the best known, at least in Britain, there are many others, varying considerably in size, colour and flavour.

There are two main genera of bean: the Vigna and the Phaseolus. The Vigna category includes three principal varieties: the cow pea, the green gram (green mung bean) and the black gram (black mung bean). There are 170 variations of these species, mostly native to Africa and India.

Phaseolus is the larger group and includes all the important and common beans of Central and South America. Phaseolus beans grow mainly in semi-tropical arid or humid regions but some varieties, the haricot, French and kidney beans, for instance, have become well established in Europe and were grown originally from seeds brought over by the Spanish and Portuguese in the sixteenth century.

To prepare pulses: pick them over to remove small stones and twigs, put the pulses in a sieve and rinse them under running water. All pulses except orange lentils need to be soaked before cooking (you can manage without soaking brown lentils too, but they will take rather longer to cook than soaked ones). Either leave them to soak overnight in plenty of cold water, or, if you are in a hurry, pour boiling water over them and leave to soak, covered, for an hour.

The cooking time depends on the size and age of the beans. Generally, small beans (brown lentils, green mung, small haricots, small black-eye beans) take from 20 minutes to ½ hour, whereas the larger beans (red beans, black beans, pinto beans, etc.) take about an hour. The biggest, dried broad beans, butter beans and chick peas, take about an hour and a half. Beans are ideal for pressure cooking. At 15 lb pressure, the cooking time will be cut by two thirds. If you follow the instructions supplied with your pressure cooker, allow slightly less time than they suggest, unless you want your beans to be very mushy and falling apart. It is important not to add salt to the beans until the end of the cooking time, otherwise they become very hard.

Dried beans, peas and lentils keep well for up to a year. Once they get too old, they do not cook evenly and may be impossible to cook at all, even after hours of boiling!

Most types of beans and grains, tahini (sesame seed cream) and miso (soya bean paste) can be bought at good whole-food shops, Greek or Oriental grocers.

Aduki Beans

In Japan and China, the aduki bean (*Vigna angularis*) is the second most important crop after the soya bean. It is not produced as widely elsewhere, but it has recently been introduced to Zaire, South America and the United States.

Aduki plants are erect, bushy annuals with clusters of bright yellow flowers. The pods grow up to 4 inches/

10 cm long and contain twelve small oblong seeds: these are usually dark red, but can be straw-coloured, brown or black.

Aduki beans are pleasant and nutty in flavour. They are better for stews than eaten on their own.

Aduki Bean, Orange and Tomato Casserole

Serves 4

1 lb/500 g aduki beans
1 lb/500 g tomatoes
2 onions
1 clove garlic

1 orange (small)
1 tsp marjoram
1 tbs oil
salt and pepper

Soak the aduki beans overnight (or in boiling water for 1 hour); boil for 20 minutes. Alternatively, cook them in a pressure cooker for 5 to 7 minutes. Slice the onions and stew them in oil until softened. Skin and chop the tomatoes and add them with the orange, sliced very thinly, the marjoram, garlic and seasoning. Simmer for 15 minutes or so, until thickened. Drain the beans and add them to the sauce and simmer for a further 20 minutes.

This is also good layered with fried aubergine, marrow or courgette slices, and baked with cheese and breadcrumbs on top for 20 minutes in a moderate oven.

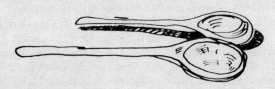

Black Beans

A variety of the *Phaseolus vulgaris*, the black bean is a member of the haricot bean family. The seeds are quite large, shiny and black, looking very much like black kidney beans.

Black Beans with Soya and Ginger

Serves 4

½ lb/250 g black beans
1 onion
oil for frying
1 clove garlic, crushed

½-inch/1-cm piece root ginger, peeled and grated (or a flat tsp of dried ginger)
2 tbs soya sauce

Soak and cook the beans, using any of the methods outlined in the introduction to this chapter. Peel and chop the onion finely and fry gently in the oil. When softened, add the garlic and ginger. Drain the beans and stir them into the mixture with the soya sauce; add a little of their cooking liquid. Simmer gently for 5 minutes.

Serve as a side dish with rice and vegetables.

Broad Beans or Horse Beans

The broad bean (*Vicia faba*) can be left to dry on the plant. The dried seeds are wrinkled and dark brown in colour. Their texture is rather floury and they are best cooked in stews or puréed for soups or pâtés.

English Field Bean Pâté (page 109) or Bean Cake (page 104) can be made with dried broad beans.

Butter Beans or Sieva or Lima Beans

This bean (*Phaseolus limensis*) is very well known in this country and is usually served plain, boiled, as an accompaniment to meat stews. The beans are delicious marinaded, while still hot, in a French dressing and served cold with chopped chives and crushed garlic. There are two main species. Lima beans originated in Peru and are the bigger butter beans which are common here, with large flat white seeds. Sieva beans originated in Mexico and have smaller seeds, variously coloured.

Chick Peas

Widely grown in India, Burma, the Middle East, southern Europe and Ethiopia, the chick pea (*Cicer arietinum*) has recently been introduced to South America and Australia. Chick peas like quite a dry atmosphere and are not suitable for growing in warm, humid climates. The plants are erect and quite small (about 2 feet/60 cm tall); the flowers are white, pink, pale blue or purple, producing small pods containing one or two spherical seeds. The pods, leaves and seeds are used as a vegetable in those countries where chick peas are grown. Some 6 million tonnes of chick peas are grown per annum, mostly for human consumption. The seeds are eaten whole, ground to produce flour, or split to produce dahl.

Chick Peas and Aubergines en Croûte

Serves 10

A very special party dish this. It was served last Christmas by John Pudduck, who kindly donated the recipe. He shaped the pastry into a magnificent 2½-foot/75-cm carp and it looked as splendid as it tasted.

FOR THE DOUGH:

2 lb/1 kg wholemeal flour
½ pint/300 ml warm water
1 oz/25 g fresh yeast (or ½ oz/10 g dried)
2 tbs sugar
2 tsps salt
8 oz/250 g butter or margarine
1 egg for glazing
sesame seeds or poppy seeds (optional)

FOR THE FILLING:

1½ lb/750 g chick peas, soaked (see page 100)
4 aubergines
1 lb/500 g chestnuts
1 large red pepper
3 medium onions, choppe..
3 cloves garlic
2 chillies, chopped
1 egg
1 tsp chopped sage
¼ pint/150 ml water
1 lb/500 g haricot or butt.. beans, soaked
4 tbs fresh, chopped herbs (parsley, sage, oregano, thyme, rosemary, lemo.. balm)
12 oz/350 g basmati rice
3 tbs oil
salt and pepper

Dissolve the yeast and sugar in the warm water. Melt the margarine or butter and rub into the flour and salt. Add the yeast mixture and knead until the dough is smooth. Set the dough aside in a warm place until doubled in bulk.

Slice the aubergines lengthwise, salt them well and leave to drain for at least ½ hour. Rinse off the salt and fry the slices in 2 tablespoons of the oil. Drain and leave to cool. Cook the rice and the haricot or butter beans separately. Fry the onions, chillies and crushed garlic in 1 tablespoon oil until the onions are slightly browned. Mix with the rice and the water and bake in a moderate oven for 20 minutes, adding more water if necessary. Add the haricot or butter beans, the chopped red pepper and the teaspoon of chopped sage. Boil the chick peas and, when soft, add them to the rice and onion mixture. Season to taste with salt and pepper and bind with a beaten egg.

Prick the chestnuts and plunge them in boiling water, or grill them for a few minutes to split the skins. Peel them and steam until soft, then mash into a purée.

Roll out the dough on a floured surface to a thickness

of $\frac{1}{4}$–$\frac{1}{2}$ inch/5–10 mm. Lift onto a large baking sheet and, in the centre, place the aubergine slices, then the chopped herbs, then the rice and chick-pea mixture and finally the chestnut purée. Wrap the pastry around the filling to make a rough oval shape, pointed at each end. Pinch the sides together, sealing with egg or water. Use the pastry trimmings to make fish scales, fins and a tail. Brush the pastry with beaten egg and sprinkle with sesame or poppy seeds. Bake for 1 hour in a fairly hot oven (gas mark 5–6, 375°–400°F, 190°–200°C).

Chick Pea Curry

Serves 4

$\frac{1}{2}$ lb/250 g chick peas, whole or split	1 tbs ground coriander
2 parsnips	2 tsps ground cumin
2 turnips	1 tsp chopped fresh ginger (or $\frac{1}{2}$ tsp dried)
2 onions	1 tsp miso (soya bean paste)
2 carrots	2 tbs oil
3 cloves garlic	

Soak the chick peas (see page 100). Transfer them to a saucepan, cover them completely with water and boil until they are just soft. Chop all the vegetables and fry in oil until slightly browned. Add the spices, fry for a minute, then stir in the miso and the chick peas with all their cooking liquid. Simmer until most of the liquid is absorbed.

Hummus

Serves 6

$\frac{1}{2}$ lb/250 g chick peas	5 tbs olive oil
juice of 2 lemons	salt and pepper
2 cloves garlic	water

Soak the chick peas (see page 100) and cook them until soft. Mash them with a fork or press them through a sieve or a *mouli-légumes*. Mix well with the rest of the

ingredients and add water until the paste is the consistency of thick cream. Check the seasoning and serve as a dip with hot Greek bread. One tablespoon, or more to taste, of tahini (sesame cream) can be added to the basic mixture.

Cow Peas

The cow pea (*Vigna ungulata*) was probably cultivated in Ethiopia or West Africa over 4000 years ago. Seeds were taken to southern Europe c.3000 B.C., to India c.1500 B.C., and to America in the seventeenth century.

The plants are annuals with large snowy white flowers, though only two to four fruits are produced by each plant. Seeds can be white, brown or black. The seeds, pods and leaves are used as a fodder crop, especially in Nigeria, which produces some 75 per cent of the world output, estimated overall at 1 million tonnes. The best known variety sold for human consumption is the black-eye bean.

Black-eye beans have a delicious creamy flavour, a softer texture and thinner skins than many of the other varieties of dried beans. They need no elaborate treatment and are best served quite plain with butter or margarine, chopped fresh herbs and salt and pepper. They go well with sweetcorn (see Succotash, page 92) and are also very good cold in salads.

Potted Beans

This is best made with black-eye or small haricot beans.

$\frac{1}{2}$ lb/250 g beans	2 tbs cider or white wine
$1\frac{1}{2}$ oz/35 g butter or margarine	dash tabasco sauce
1 egg	1 tsp dried sage
$\frac{1}{4}$ lb/125 g mushrooms	1 tsp tomato purée
	salt and pepper

Soak the beans overnight and cook them until soft. Chop the mushrooms finely and fry them in the margarine or butter. When they have cooled, mix them with all the other ingredients, adding the beaten egg last.

Divide the mixture between four greased ramekin dishes, stand them in a tray of warm water and bake – covered with a sheet of greaseproof paper – for 20 minutes with the oven at gas mark 4 (350°F, 180°C). Serve cold.

Haricot Beans

The haricot bean (*Phaseolus vulgaris*) is part of the largest family of beans which includes kidney beans, black beans, pinto beans and French beans. Beans of this genus grow on bushes 8 inches to 2 feet/20 to 60 cm tall, or are climbing plants 6 to 10 feet/2 to 3 metres tall, with white, pink or purple flowers. The pods contain four to six seeds.

Haricot beans make a good base for casseroles or purées. Haricots can be used for either of the soya bean recipes on page 107.

Bean Cake

Serves 6 to 8

½ lb/250 g haricot beans	1 tsp powdered coriander
3 medium onions	½ tsp powdered cumin
3 carrots	1 tsp powdered mustard
½ lb/250 g greens	1 tbs salt
1 tbs chopped parsley	1 tsp pepper
1 tbs peanut butter	2 eggs
2 green chillies, chopped (optional)	

Put the beans in a bowl, pour boiling water over them so that they are covered by about 1 inch/3 cm and leave to soak, covered, for about 1 hour. Drain the beans (keeping the water) and put them through a fine hand mincer. Mince the onions and the carrots separately.

Simmer the minced beans with their soaking water, and 1 mugful extra, for about ¾ hour. Stir occasionally to prevent the beans sticking to the bottom of the pan. Add the minced carrots and onions and cook the mixture a little longer until all the liquid is absorbed and the beans and vegetables are soft. Remove from the heat. Steam the greens until they are soft and chop them finely. Tip the greens, beans, herbs, spices, peanut butter and seasonings into a large bowl and mix thoroughly with a fork. Add the eggs to the mixture, beating them in well.

Grease a 2-lb/1-kg cake tin or ovenproof dish, and fill with the bean mixture. Bake for 1 hour in a moderate oven (gas mark 4, 350°F, 180°C).

Good hot as a main course, but equally good cold, served with bread and salad.

Kidney Beans

A member of the haricot bean family, the kidney bean (*Phaseolus vulgaris*) is rich in colour and in flavour. A beautiful salad can be made with kidney beans, pinto beans (pale pink with red speckles) and black beans, cooked separately and mixed together while still hot, with French dressing.

Red Bean Goulash

Serves 8

½ lb/250 g kidney beans,
   soaked (see page 100)
4 carrots
4 onions
4 potatoes
1 green pepper
1 tsp roasted caraway seeds
1 tbs paprika (mild
   Hungarian)

1 pint/300 ml water
1 tbs tomato purée
¼ pint/150 ml yoghurt
1 tbs oil
optional: ¼ lb/125 g bacon
   pieces, or belly pork,
   sliced very thinly

Scrub the potatoes and carrots and cut into cubes. Peel and slice the onions. Fry the vegetables in the oil (with the pork or bacon), add the water and cover the pan. Simmer for 20 minutes. Stir in the paprika, the caraway seeds and the sliced green pepper and simmer for 5 minutes. Add the beans, the tomato purée and the yoghurt and continue simmering for another 20 minutes. Season and serve with a plain salad.

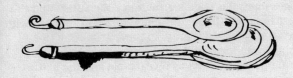

Lentils

One of the oldest legumes, the lentil (*Lens esculenta*) is cultivated in Italy, the Middle East and India. The plants are low – up to 1½ feet/40 cm – and bushy. They mature three to four months after sowing. The flowers are white tinged with purple, the pods flattened and broad, up to ½ inch/12 mm long. The lens-shaped seeds can be light brown, red or greenish-grey, often speckled with black. Total world production is 1 million tonnes per annum.

Baked Lentils

Serves 4

½ lb/250 g brown or green
   lentils
2 onions
¼ lb/125 g mushrooms
1 egg

1 tsp thyme
4 oz/125 g grated cheese
salt and pepper
oil for frying

Cook the lentils (they will need 40 to 50 minutes without soaking, 15 to 20 minutes if pre-soaked). Slice and fry the onions. Drain the lentils and mix them with the onions, the mushrooms, sliced or chopped, the grated cheese and the thyme and seasoning. Bind with egg. Bake for 30 minutes in a moderate oven.

Lentils, Pasta and Sesame

Serves 4 to 5

A well balanced protein dish, with an agreeable contrast in textures.

1 cupful brown lentils
8 oz/250 g spaghetti
1 tbs sesame seeds

a little oil
salt and pepper

Boil the lentils in plenty of water. After 30 minutes, add the spaghetti, broken into short lengths, adding more boiling water if necessary. When both lentils and spaghetti are soft, drain well in a colander, rinse with freshly boiled water and keep warm. Clean the saucepan, heat a little oil and fry the sesame seeds for a minute or two. Add the lentils and the pasta, season and stir well with two forks until well heated through. Serve immediately as an accompaniment to a stew or casserole, or simply on its own with grated cheese on top.

Spiced Red Lentils

Serves 3 to 4

This recipe was given by John Pudduck. It is quick and easy to make.

½ lb/250 g red lentils	½ tsp turmeric
1 medium onion	¼ tsp cayenne pepper
1 level tsp cumin seed, crushed	½ tsp salt
1 tbs oil	¾ pint/450 ml warm water

Chop the onion and fry in oil until soft. Add the lentils, spices and salt and continue frying for a minute or two. Allow to cool slightly and pour in the warm water. Simmer without stirring until the lentils are soft (about 15 to 20 minutes). Just before serving, whisk with a fork.

onions

Green Mung Beans or Green Gram

(*Vigna radiata*), a native of India, is also grown in China, Iran, Japan and parts of Africa, the West Indies and the United States. The plants are annuals, producing prolific crops of small yellowish or purple flowers and then long pods containing ten to fifteen green seeds each. Mung beans are grown as forage and manure crops as well as for food. They can be cooked, but are more usually sprouted. The simplest way to do this is to soak them in cold water for a few hours, drain them and tip them into a jar. Cover the jar with a layer of muslin, secured with a rubber band, and turn it on its side. Every day, rinse the beans with tepid water and pour out the excess through the muslin. The bean sprouts will be ready to eat in four to five days when they are about 1 inch/3 cm long.

Pulse Chutney

This is an African recipe – use fewer chillies if you don't want it so hot.

2 oz/50 g mung beans	4 green chillies
1½-inch/3½-cm piece of root ginger	salt
	lemon juice

Soak the green mung beans for 3 to 4 hours. Allow to sprout. Mince the green chillies and the fresh root ginger, and add salt. Flavour with lemon juice.

Black Gram or Urd

Another variety of mung bean, the black gram or urd (*Vigna mungo*) is widely grown in Asia, Africa and the West Indies. In India, it is often grown in rotation with rice. The black seeds grow in narrow pods up to 2½ inches/6 cm long on a spreading, heavy plant. The young pods are eaten as a vegetable and the mature seeds are used whole, split or powdered to make dahl or flour.

Iddli

Another African recipe.

4 oz/125 g rice	salt
2 oz/50 g black mung beans	water

Soak the rice and the black mung beans separately for about 2 to 3 hours. Pound each to a smooth paste. Mix and add salt. Ferment in a warm place for 15 to 20 ours. Add water to make a thick batter consistency. Place the mixture in small cups and steam until cooked.

Soya Beans

The soya bean (*Glycine max*) is widely grown in Japan, China and eastern Asia, Australia, Africa, India, South America and the United States.

The plants thrive in temperatures between 10°C and 38°C (50°F and 100°F) with short day lengths. They require fertile, acidic soil and can withstand long droughts. Their climatic requirements are similar to those of maize and in the United States they are often grown with maize.

In the Far East, soya beans are used mainly for the manufacture of various fermented products: bean curd, soya sauce and miso. But the bulk of the world crop (in excess of 80 million tonnes) is processed by the food industry into animal feed cake and other soya by-products: flour, oil and texturized vegetable protein (T.V.P.). The protein content of soya beans is higher than that of other beans and as such it is thought that they will be increasingly useful in the future when there are likely to be protein shortages. Already, Corn-Soy-Milk, a drink made from maize flour, soya flour and non-fat milk solids, is being used as a food for children in developing countries.

But it must be borne in mind that the soya by-products are available largely because the soya beans are grown principally as an animal feed. Thus the food industry derives a maximum profit from the beans – by supplying the factory farming industry with high-protein feedstuffs, and by converting the waste products by energy-intensive processes into meat substitutes (T.V.P.) which can then, with the addition of flavourings, be sold as expensive, ready-to-serve meals.

In some ways this is admirable, as the optimum use is made of a single product, but also, from the industry's point of view, soya beans provide an excellent vehicle for value-adding, and it is this aspect that needs watching. Soya beans could easily be used to fill the protein gap, but their usefulness will be diminished if they are converted mainly into animal feed and into products which are imitations of, and as expensive as, meat.

Soya Nut Rissoles

Serves 4

½ lb/250 g soya beans	1 egg
1 large carrot, grated	salt and pepper
1 medium onion	2 tbs oil
2 oz/50 g chopped nuts	flour for coating

Soak and cook the soya beans until they are soft. Press them through a sieve or a *mouli-légumes*, or mince them finely. Slice the onion and fry in a little of the oil for 2 minutes. Mix the onion with the carrot, beans, nuts and seasoning, and bind with egg. Shape the mixture into rissoles and roll them in flour. Fry in the remaining oil until crisp. Serve with a tomato sauce.

Baked Soya Beans

Serves 3 to 4

A fresh version of the beans that Heinz baked. This dish can also be made with butter beans or haricot beans.

½ lb/250 g soya beans	1 clove garlic, crushed
1 lb/500 g fresh peeled tomatoes (or bottled tomatoes)	1 tsp marjoram, oregano or basil
	salt and pepper
1 large onion	1 tbs oil

Soak and cook the soya beans until soft. Slice the onion and fry in the oil. Chop the tomatoes finely and add them with all the remaining ingredients. Bake for 1 hour with the oven at gas mark 3 (325°F, 170°C).

Split Peas

A split pea is a pea (*Pisum sativum*) stripped of its membranous covering, dried and halved. Seventy-four thousand acres of peas are grown commercially for drying, in this country. Home-grown peas can be left to dry in their pods on the plant at the end of the season. One of the best-known English dishes for dried vegetables is the subject of the famous nursery rhyme, 'Pease Pudding'. It is also one of the oldest dishes and is a speciality of many regions. The following recipe makes a type of pease pudding, but it is spiced and served cold.

Spicy Split Pea Pâté

Serves 6

½ lb/250 g split peas
1 small onion, chopped
    finely
1 clove garlic, crushed
1 fresh green chilli, finely
    chopped (or 1 tsp chilli
    powder)

3 tbs olive oil
juice 1 lemon
1 heaped tsp salt
½ tsp black pepper

Soak the split peas and simmer them until soft (about 1 hour in a saucepan or 20 minutes in a pressure cooker). Mash them with a fork, or rub them through a sieve or a *mouli-légumes*. Beat in the oil and lemon juice and, if the purée is still too stiff, add more of either to taste. Mix in the remaining ingredients and taste for seasoning. Chopped fresh tomatoes can be added as well, in season. Pile into a dish and serve as a pâté or a dip. Very good as an accompaniment to vegetable or meat kebabs.

Tic Beans

These are small round beans with brown skins, which are grown in England. In seed catalogues, they are called tic beans, daffa beans or brown Dutch beans. They are used mainly for animal feed and they can be bought cheaply from pet shops and seed merchants. In wholefood shops they are sometimes sold as 'English field beans'. They are very similar to *foul* beans, which are a staple food in many parts of the Middle East and North Africa.

English Bean Roast

Serves 4

½ lb/250 g tic beans
2 oz/50 g hazelnuts
1 medium onion
oil

½ tsp ground cumin
2 eggs, beaten
salt and pepper

Soak and cook the beans and mince them finely, or press them through a *mouli-légumes*. Slice the onion and fry in a little oil until slightly browned. Chop the hazelnuts and add them to the bean purée with the rest of the ingredients. Bake in a greased ovenproof dish in a moderate oven for 1 hour.

Shirley's Foul Medames

Serves 4

½ lb/250 g tic beans (or foul
    beans)
1 bunch watercress
2–3 tomatoes
2 hard-boiled eggs

1 heaped tsp cumin
4 tsps tahini (sesame paste)
2 tbs oil
juice 1 lemon
salt and pepper

Soak and cook the beans in plenty of water until they are soft. Chop the watercress and the tomatoes and slice the hard-boiled eggs and put them into separate bowls. Mix the cumin, tahini, oil and lemon juice (the quantities can be varied according to taste) in another bowl. Drain the beans, and reserve their cooking liquid. Each person takes a helping of beans and mixes them with some of each of the other ingredients, moistening with the bean water and seasoning with salt and pepper. *Foul medames* should be eaten with hot, Greek bread to mop up the juices.

In the Sudan, *foul medames* is eaten every day, at each meal, and no one ever tires of it.

English Field Bean Pâté

Serves 4 to 6

½ lb/250 g English beans
approx. ¼ pint/150 ml olive
    oil
salt and pepper

1 large clove garlic
1 tsp strong flavoured herb,
    e.g. thyme, sage or
    rosemary

Soak the beans in water overnight. Boil them in plenty of unsalted water for about 1 hour, until they are soft. (They can be cooked in a pressure cooker very successfully for 20 minutes at 15 lb pressure.) Mash them with a fork, pound them in a pestle and mortar, or press them through a sieve or *mouli-légumes*. Add the olive oil, the finely chopped herbs and garlic and the seasoning. If the purée is too stiff, add some lemon juice, water or more oil. Chill and serve with toast.

Cereals

Nutritionally, pulses and cereals complement each other admirably, as they compensate for one another's amino acid deficiencies. Cereals are not normally thought of as foods which are rich in protein, but an average helping can supply from 7 to 15 per cent of a daily requirement. Altogether some 90,000 acres of farmland in Britain are devoted to cereals, most of which are used as animal feeds. Ironically, it is only rice, the one cereal which cannot be grown here, which is universally popular. Some of the other cereals make very good alternatives, and, as indigenous foods, they really should be exploited a lot more for human consumption.

Wheat

Wheat is very rarely eaten as a grain in this country, and is usually found in the form of bread, flour or breakfast cereal. Wheat grains can be bought in various forms for use in vegetable dishes: whole wheat berries; wheat flakes – which are similar to oat flakes, but need slightly longer cooking; cracked wheat and bulgur wheat – cracked, steamed and toasted wheat grains. All these should be available from good wholefood shops.

Wholewheat Risotto

Serves 4 to 6

The whole wheat grains, or berries, need a lot of cooking for them to be digestible. They are delicious, but chewy, so serve them in small quantities.

½ lb/250 g wholewheat,
    boiled for 1–1½ hours in
    plenty of water
½–1 oz/10–25 g dried
    mushrooms (the quantity
    depending on their
    strength)

½ lb/250 g cottage cheese,
    sieved
½ pint/300 ml milk
salt and pepper

Mix all the ingredients together, thoroughly, and bake for at least 1 hour with the oven at gas mark 3 (325°F, 170°C).

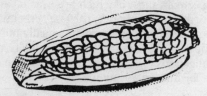

Frumenty

This very simple dish is as old as the invention of cooking pots. In the Middle Ages, frumenty was probably eaten more widely as a staple food than bread, and was used as a savoury or a sweet dish, depending on what was added to it. It is still quite common in many parts of England, served for breakfast with milk or eggs, honey and spices, or as a sweet with fruit and cream. It was originally cooked next to the fire. It is ideal for cooking in a thermos flask or a haybox.

Wash the wheat and place it in an earthenware crock or casserole with three times its volume of boiling water. Put the dish in a hot oven and, after a few minutes, turn off the heat and leave undisturbed for 24 hours. The husks should have burst by that time, and the wheat set to a thick, creamy-white jelly.

Cracked Wheat

Cracked wheat can be cooked in the same ways as whole wheat berries. Cracked wheat is sometimes used as a topping for bread, and in the Middle East it is often used as a coating for rissoles.

Wheat Flakes

Wheat flakes can be used to make porridge, but will need longer cooking than oats. They are good as a topping for vegetable dishes and as a base for stuffing.

Bulgur Wheat

As bulgur wheat is partly cooked already, it takes much less time to prepare than whole or cracked wheat. It should first be sautéed in oil, then boiled in one and a half times its volume of water, for about 20 minutes. Good as a grain on its own, as an alternative to rice, and very useful as a base for stuffings (see Stuffed Aubergines, page 68) as it is somewhat lighter and less stodgy than rice.

Buckwheat

Not actually wheat at all, buckwheat groats are the seeds of a cereal plant related to dock and rhubarb, which are sold ready hulled and cracked.

To prepare: Mix 1 cupful buckwheat groats thoroughly with 1 beaten egg and leave for an hour to dry. Tip the groats into a dry pan and stir them over a high heat until the grains are separate. Pour in 2 cupfuls boiling water, cover the pan, turn heat down very low and leave to steam for 30 minutes. Remove the lid and fluff the grains with a knob of butter or margarine and salt. Serve it as you would rice. One cupful serves two people.

Millet

Millet is widely eaten in China, the Middle East and parts of Asia and Africa. It is grown in England and can be bought whole or as flakes. It has a pleasant nutty flavour. The flakes can be cooked in the same ways as flaked oats and are good as a base for stuffings and casseroles. Whole millet can be cooked in the same way as buckwheat. Millet gives a delicious flavour to pastries (page 151).

Rice

Towards the end of the nineteenth century, polished rice became very popular in the Dutch East Indies. The poor people, for whom rice was the main item of diet, quickly began to contract beriberi, a disease which leads to wastage of muscle tissue, damage to heart and lungs

and, eventually, death. The Dutch became so concerned about the number of deaths from the disease, that they sent out a team of doctors to investigate. They found that the removal of the outer husk of the rice during polishing led to a dietary deficiency which caused the disease. The vital nutritional factor was later identified as vitamin B_1, which is absent in white or polished rice.

For most purposes in this book, we have used round-grain brown rice, which should be quite easily available from wholefood shops and good grocers. It has a strong flavour which tends to dominate very delicate foods, so where the type of rice has not been specified, make your own choice. For stuffings and risottos, a soft round-grain rice from Spain or Italy is best, but it does tend to taste and act like blotting paper, so you may prefer to use millet or bulgur wheat instead.

To cook plain brown rice: Rinse the rice first, then cook it in plenty of boiling unsalted water for about 40 minutes. Drain, return to a low heat to dry and add salt and a knob of butter or margarine, or a few drops of oil. Fluff up with a fork and serve.

Savoury Rice

Serves 3 to 4

1 mugful brown rice	1 tsp yeast extract
2 mugfuls boiling water	1 tbs soya sauce
1 tbs oil	

Rinse the rice. Heat the oil in a saucepan until it is smoking and fry the rice, stirring until all the grains are well coated with oil. Mix the boiling water with the soya sauce and yeast extract and pour into the rice. Cover the pan and simmer for 30 to 40 minutes until all the liquid is absorbed and the rice is soft. The rice grains will be shiny and brown with a rich savoury flavour.

Rice Croquettes

Serves 4 to 6

The quantities here are for uncooked rice. This recipe is also ideal for using left-over rice or risotto, in which case, use 1 egg per $2\frac{1}{2}$ cupfuls of rice. The spices can, of course, be varied.

2 cups uncooked round-grain brown rice	deep fat for frying
	salt and pepper
2 onions	2 eggs
oil	1 tbs flour (may not be necessary)
3 tsps Indian curry powder	

Cook the rice until it is soft and almost mushy, in plenty of boiling water. Drain well. Chop the onions and fry them in a little oil until softened, adding the curry powder at the last minute. Mix the onions with the rice and season rather highly with salt and pepper. Beat the eggs and mix in with the rice. Leave to stand for $\frac{1}{2}$

hour. The mixture should be firm enough to roll into balls, but if it is too runny, add a little flour, and roll into balls the size of a walnut. Fry in deep fat until golden. Serve hot or cold.

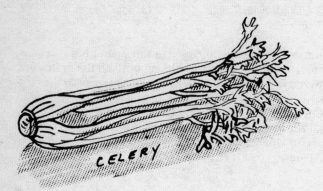

Barley

Barley is available in several forms. Whole barley is similar to wholewheat and can be cooked in the same ways. Pot or Scotch barley is the whole seed with only the husk removed, and pearl barley is the de-husked seed, steamed, rounded and polished. Pot barley can be cooked in exactly the same way as unpolished rice, and makes a very good alternative. It also has the advantage of containing more vitamins and protein and of being grown extensively in this country – over 50,000 acres are devoted to barley.

Pearl barley is more easily obtainable than pot barley, but, as the outer layers of the grain are removed, it is not as nutritious – it is to pot barley what white rice is to brown rice, though the levels of nutrients are slightly higher than those of white rice.

Barley swells up considerably during cooking, so it needs to be boiled in plenty of unsalted water for about 40 minutes. Drain, season and dot with margarine or butter.

Barley Pilaff

Serves 4

½ lb/250 g pot barley	1 tbs raisins
1 onion	1 tbs oil
1 tbs chopped nuts	parsley

Cook the barley in plenty of boiling water as above. Slice and fry the onion until soft, then add the nuts and raisins. Drain the barley and add to the onion mixture. Heat through and stir with a fork until the flavours have blended a little. Sprinkle the top with parsley and serve as an accompaniment to kebabs or plain vegetable dishes.

Oats

Oatmeal porridge is well known as the Scots' national dish. In Scotland it is often made with sour milk or buttermilk. Oatmeal makes a good coating for fried fish or rissoles and can also be used as a base for stuffings. Oats are quite a good source of protein; a 1-oz/25-g helping can provide 7 to 8 per cent of the daily requirement.

Oat Dumplings

3 oz/75 g rolled oats	1 small egg
1 small onion	salt and pepper
¼ tsp sage or thyme	

Mix the oats, finely chopped onion, herbs and seasoning and mix in enough egg to make a stiff dough. Roll into balls. The dumplings can be cooked in clear soup or stews or they can be used as forcemeat balls in meat or vegetable pies.

Oatmeal Stuffing

4 oz/125 g oatmeal
1 oz/25 g walnuts
1 onion
strip lemon peel, chopped
salt and pepper

1 dsp currants
1 small green pepper,
   chopped
1 egg, to bind

Mix all the ingredients and season quite highly with salt and pepper. This makes a good stuffing for baked onions, fish, bacon rolls or chicken.

vegetables

STILL LIFE with MEAT VEGETABLES and.
water
chicken
SPINACH
POTATOES
LEEKS
SALAMI
SWEET CORN

Meat: A Little Goes a Long Way

One of the central themes of this book is that we should eat less meat (see the Introduction and Chapter 1, 'All Flesh is Grass'), so, by conventional cookery-book standards, this chapter is rather short.

Meat does not have to be eaten in large quantities to be enjoyed. Of course that depends entirely on the way in which the meat is served. A dinner guest would be justifiably disappointed if he or she were served with a miserable 2-oz steak, but if the 2-oz steak was incorporated into a rich stew containing lashings of fragrant vegetables and herbs, that would be quite a different matter. Most of the recipes in this chapter are for combinations of meat, including offal and game, with vegetables, pulses or pasta, where the meat is used as a flavouring rather than as the main constituent of the dish.

Stews, casseroles and stuffed and braised meats can be quite delicious. The methods are adaptable to many cuts that have not been used, and with all these recipes none of the precious juices are lost and a little meat goes a long way.

'A large quantity of vegetables should be constantly mixed with animal food, to take off its putrescency and to prevent it from corrupting while it continues in the stomach. In short, we should eat in great moderation and make vegetables the principle part of our food' (W. Smith, *A Sure Guide to Sickness and Health*, 1776).

Although the language used by modern nutritionists is rather more technical, it is interesting that, in the light of research into the correlation between the incidence of digestive diseases and the consumption of animal fats, many have reached the same conclusions as W. Smith!

Free-range meat, other than chicken and game and Argentine beef, is the hardest of foods to buy, but there are a few suppliers. Wholefood, Paddington Street, London is a butcher's shop selling exclusively free-range meat. The Organic Food Service publishes a list of farms selling free-range produce. It should be possible, by making inquiries in your locality, to find other sources of supply. The more people that do so, the better.

Shirley Bennett's Stew

Serves 6 to 8

1 lb/500 g stewing beef	a 1-inch/2.5-cm piece fresh
1 lb/500 g parsnips	ginger, chopped
1 lb/500 g leeks	1 tsp cumin
4 carrots	1 tbs mixed herbs
4 onions	2 tsps yeast extract
2 green peppers	1 dsp miso (soya bean paste)
6-8 potatoes	pepper and salt
1 chilli	1-2 tbs oil
6 cloves garlic, chopped	

Cut the meat into small pieces and fry in oil until browned. Transfer it to a large casserole. Prepare all the vegetables except the potatoes, cutting them into large slices, and fry them in oil together with the ginger and the garlic. Transfer them to the casserole and add the herbs, the cumin, the chopped chilli and the yeast extract. Cover with boiling water and cook, covered, at the lowest possible oven temperature for 8 hours. Alternatively, cook in the oven at gas mark 3 (325°F, 170°C) for about 4 hours. This recipe would also be ideal for pressure, haybox or thermos cooking. Cook the potatoes separately and add them to the stew, with the miso and any extra seasoning, $\frac{1}{2}$ hour before serving.

Summer Cottage Pie

Serves 6

1½ lb/750 g potatoes	2 cloves garlic, chopped
½ lb/250 g minced lamb or beef	4 oz/125 g grated cheese
	salt and pepper
1½ lb/750 g tomatoes	rosemary
¾ lb/350 g onions, sliced	nutmeg

Scrub the potatoes and slice them very thinly (a *mandoline* is the ideal tool for this as, the thinner the slices, the lighter the dish). Fry the minced meat with the onions and garlic and, when the meat is browned, add the tomatoes, peeled and chopped. Add 1 teaspoon rosemary, the salt and pepper and simmer for 20 minutes. Layer the potatoes, meat mixture and grated cheese in a casserole, starting and finishing with the potatoes. Season each layer of potatoes with salt, pepper and nutmeg. Leave a little grated cheese for the top. Bake, covered, with the oven at gas mark 3 (325°F, 170°C) for 1½ to 2 hours.

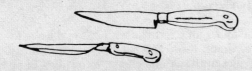

Lamb or Mutton with Chick Peas and Tomatoes

Serves 6

1 lb/500 g stewing lamb or mutton
¾ lb/350 g chick peas
1½ lb/750 g tomatoes
3 onions, sliced

2 cloves garlic
1 tsp cumin
½ tsp allspice
salt and pepper
1 tbs oil

Soak the chick peas overnight in cold water, or for 1 hour in boiling water. Cook them for 30 minutes (or in a pressure cooker for 10 minutes at 15 lb pressure). Fry the pieces of lamb in the oil until well browned, then remove them from the pan and fry the onions. Peel and chop the tomatoes and add them to the onions, with the chopped or crushed garlic, the spices and seasoning, the chick peas and the chick pea water. Simmer for 10 minutes and add the lamb. Cook very slowly indeed, either on top of the stove or in the oven, for 3 hours. Serve with green vegetables or a salad.

Meat and Vegetable Loaf in Pastry

Serves 6

8 oz/250 g puff pastry
1 lb/500 g minced meat
1 lb/500 g spinach or young greens
½ lb/250 g mushrooms
½ lb/250 g onions
1 tsp pickled nasturtium seeds or capers

2 cloves garlic, crushed
½ tsp cumin
small sprig tarragon, chopped
1 tbs chopped parsley
2 eggs
salt and pepper
a glass of cider

Chop the onions very finely. Slice the mushrooms; cook, drain and chop the greens. Mix the vegetables, herbs, pickled nasturtium seeds, spice and garlic thoroughly into the meat, season and bind with the beaten eggs (leaving aside a little for glazing the pastry). Form into an oval loaf shape and bake for ¾ hour in a moderate oven on a flat tray. Remove and leave to cool, keeping the pan juices to make gravy. Roll out the pastry into a large oblong. Carefully lift the meat loaf out of the tin and lay in the centre of the pastry. Wet the edges of the pastry and wrap securely around the meat, trimming away the excess. Turn the loaf over and return it to the tin. Brush with egg and decorate with pastry leaves, make a few incisions in the top and bake in the oven at gas mark 6 (400°F, 200°C) for about 40 minutes, or until the pastry is crisp and golden. Make a gravy from the pan juices, a few extra capers or nasturtium seeds and a glass of cider.

Pork, Leek and Apple Pie

Serves 4 to 5

¾ lb/350 g pork (spare rib
    chops, but buy 1 lb/500 g
    to allow for the weight of
    the bones)
2 large cooking apples
½ tsp sage
1½ lb/750 g leeks
salt and pepper
½ lb/250 g half-wholemeal
    flaky pastry (see page
    150)
egg or milk for glazing

FOR FORCEMEAT BALLS:

1 cup soft breadcrumbs,
    soaked in water or milk
    and mashed with a fork
1 onion, finely chopped
3–4 mushrooms or
    mushroom stalks, chopped
    (optional)
1 strip lemon peel, chopped
pinch thyme
1 egg, to bind
flour, if necessary, to thicken

Core the apples and cut them into slices. Wash the leeks well and slice into rounds. Bone the meat and cut into cubes.

To make the forcemeat balls: mix the breadcrumbs with all the other ingredients, bind with egg and add some flour until the mixture is firm enough to roll into balls.

Line a 10- by 8-inch/30- by 20-cm dish or tin with half the pastry, rolled out quite thinly. Layer the pork, leeks and apples evenly and season with salt, pepper and sage. Lay the forcemeat balls evenly on top and cover with the remaining pastry. Make a hole in the top to allow the steam to escape or use a pie funnel in the centre. Brush with egg or milk and bake in the oven at gas mark 6 (400°F, 200°C) for ½ hour, then place a sheet of damp greaseproof paper over the top and bake for another hour at gas mark 4 (350°F, 180°C).

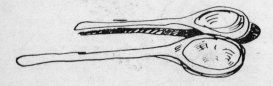

Chicken, Prune and Aubergine Pie

Serves 4 to 6

8 oz/250 g pastry
    (shortcrust or half-
    wholemeal flaky pastry)
egg or milk for glaze

FOR THE FILLING:

12 oz/350 g chicken meat,
    cut into small pieces
12 prunes, soaked in tea,
    stoned and chopped

1 large aubergine
8 oz/250 g onions
2 cloves garlic
1 tsp tomato purée
1 tbs soya sauce
1 tbs oil
black pepper

Halve the aubergine, sprinkle with salt and leave to drain for ½ hour. Rinse and pat dry. Grill the aubergine on both sides until soft and chop it into cubes. Chop the onions and fry in the oil with the chicken pieces for a few minutes. Add the remaining filling ingredients and stir over a low heat for about 5 minutes. Roll out two thirds of the pastry and line a 10-inch/25-cm pie dish. Pour in the filling and cover with the remaining pastry, making a hole in the centre to allow the steam to escape during baking. Bake in the oven at gas mark 5 (375°F, 190°C) for 40 to 45 minutes. The pastry can be glazed before it is baked with beaten egg or milk mixed with a little salt.

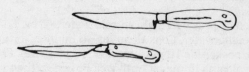

Schinkenfleckeln

Serves 4

This is an Austrian dish, literally 'Ham Noodles'. In Austria, it is made with sour cream. This version is less rich.

½ lb/250 g (dry weight)
pasta squares, cooked
(either make your own or
use lasagne and cut it into
squares when cooked)
½ lb/250 g cottage cheese,
sieved

¾ pint/450 ml milk
½ lb/250 g cooked bacon or
ham, cut into squares
salt and pepper
1 oz/25 g margarine
2 eggs
pinch nutmeg

Cream the margarine and mix into a smooth paste with
the sieved cottage cheese. Separate the eggs and add the
yolks to the cheese and margarine. Stir in the milk and
the bacon or ham and the pasta and season with salt,
plenty of pepper and the nutmeg. Whip the egg whites
until stiff and fold into the mixture. Pour into a greased
flat ovenproof dish or baking tin and bake in the oven
at gas mark 4 (350°F, 180°C) for ½ to 1 hour, until well
risen and brown and crisp on top.

If you are buying bacon for a dish such as a pâté or a
flan which does not require whole rashers, it is much
cheaper to buy bacon scraps or offcuts. These are not
always displayed in butchers and grocers but they are
usually available for half the price, or less, of the
complete rashers. Bacon pieces are often very fatty. If
you are using only the lean pieces, don't throw the fat
away but render it down in the oven (while cooking
another dish) and use it for cooking. Bacon fat is ideal
for frying the bread for Hungarian Bread Soup (see page
43).

Liver with Yoghurt and Mushrooms

Serves 3 to 4

½ lb/250 g liver (lamb's or
pig's), cut into small
pieces
1 tbs flour
½ tsp cinnamon

½ lb/250 g mushrooms
½ pint/300 ml yoghurt
salt and pepper
margarine or butter for
frying

Dredge the liver slices in a mixture of flour, cinnamon,
salt and pepper and fry in margarine or butter for 5
minutes. Slice the mushrooms and fry with the liver for
a minute or two; then add the yoghurt, stirring well.
Leave to simmer for 5 minutes, adjust the seasoning
and serve, maybe with a rice pilaff and a selection of
two or three vegetables.

Potatoes Baked with Kidneys

Serves 4

4 large potatoes
butter or margarine

4 sheep's or pig's kidneys
salt and pepper

Scrub the potatoes well and cut each one in half. Scoop
out a cavity in the centre of each half potato. Clean the
kidneys and leave them whole. Place one in each pair of
potato halves, with a knob of butter or margarine and
salt and pepper. Tie the two halves of each potato
together securely with string and bake until the
potatoes are soft. The flesh of the potatoes will absorb
the juice from the kidneys. Use the left-over potato flesh
for soup.

Stuffed Hearts

Serves 4 generously

The quantities of stuffing and the cooking time for this
dish will vary according to the kind of hearts used. Ox
hearts are the largest and will need about 2½ to 3 hours
to cook; pigs' hearts will need about 1½ hours and
sheeps' hearts about an hour. Before making the
stuffing, clean the hearts, removing all the tubes and
blood (not a very pleasant task!) and adjust the amount
of stuffing according to the size of the cavity.

STUFFING: (quantities for 1 ox heart, 3 pigs' hearts or
4–5 sheeps' hearts)

2 tbs breadcrumbs, soaked
  in milk and mashed with
  a fork
1 onion, finely chopped
½ tsp each sage and thyme
½ tsp chopped lemon or
  orange peel

3 rashers bacon, chopped
  into small pieces
1 small egg to bind
salt and pepper

Mix together all the stuffing ingredients except the egg –
the onion and bacon can be fried a little first, but if they
are finely enough chopped it will not really be
necessary. Finally, add enough of the egg to bind the
mixture. If the mixture is too slack add a little flour. It
should be the consistency of pastry, otherwise it will fall
out of place and mix with the sauce. Stuff the cavities of
the hearts and wrap each one in a rasher of bacon
secured with a toothpick. Brown the hearts in hot
dripping or oil and place in a casserole.

SAUCE:

2 onions
oil
1 or 2 carrots
2 small turnips

3–4 sticks celery
1 tsp thyme
1 bay leaf
1 tbs flour
1 pint/600 ml water

Chop the onions roughly and fry lightly in oil. Halve the
carrots and celery and chop the turnips into large pieces
and add to onions. Add the thyme, bay leaf and flour.
Gradually add the water and bring to the boil. Pour
over the hearts in the casserole, adding more water if
they are not covered with liquid. Bake in a moderate
oven until the hearts are soft. Cut them in slices for
serving.

Beuschel

Serves 6

This is a Viennese dish for lights (lungs). Lights here are
usually fed to pets, but they are eaten a lot in Austria
and can be quite tasty if well cooked.

1 lb/500 g ox lights
1 ox heart weighing about
  1 lb/500 g
1 bay leaf
½ tsp thyme
1 onion
4 carrots
2 cloves
6 peppercorns

FOR THE SAUCE:

2 oz/50 g butter or
  margarine

½ tsp finely chopped lemon
  peel
2 tbs flour
2 tbs finely chopped onion
4 anchovy fillets (or 2 tbs
  anchovy essence)
12 capers (or pickled
  nasturtium seeds)
1 small clove garlic
1 tsp finely chopped parsley
1 tsp made mustard
juice ½ lemon
salt and pepper

Wash and trim the lights and the heart. Put them in a
large saucepan with the bay leaf and thyme, the whole
unpeeled onion, the carrots (scrubbed), the cloves and
peppercorns. Cover with water and simmer for 1½ hours
or until quite tender.

For the sauce: Melt the butter or margarine. Add the
flour and cook until brown, stirring frequently. Add the
onion, lemon peel, anchovies, capers and garlic, all
finely chopped. Strain the stock from the lights and the
heart and stir into the sauce mixture. Bring to the boil
and simmer for 10 minutes. Cut the lights and heart
into matchstick-sized strips, trimming away all the
membranes. Mix into the sauce with the lemon juice,
mustard and chopped parsley. Heat through slowly,
season with salt and pepper and serve with boiled
potatoes or dumplings.

Brawn

Quantities for a 2-pint/1-litre basin

1 pig's head
4 onions
2 celeriac roots (or cut the
*   lower 4 inches/10 cm*
*   from a whole head of*
*   celery)*
12 sticks celery

12 peppercorns
4 pig's trotters
8 carrots
4 bay leaves
½ lb/250 g ham
salt and pepper

Cover the pig's head, trotters, onions, celeriac, carrots, bay leaves and peppercorns with water and simmer for 3 hours, adding the celery sticks after 2 hours. Strain off the liquid, leave to cool and skim off the fat. Cut all the meat from the head and trotters into small pieces. Cut the ham into strips and cut the carrot and celery into small pieces. Boil up the strained stock, season and pour over the meat and vegetables in two 1-pint/500-ml basins. Keep the remaining stock for soup. Leave the brawn to set, stirring occasionally to distribute the meat evenly. Turn out and garnish with chopped onions and gherkins. Serve with a vinaigrette dressing.

Game

Venison

Deer – the largest of our wild animals – are the most productive. About 200,000 red deer range freely over 3 million acres of the Scottish Highlands, and approximately 30,000 are killed each year. The farming of red deer is in its infancy in Scotland but output could be increased considerably. Domesticated deer reach commercial body weight within fifteen months, compared to five years in the wild. Other deer (roe, fallow, etc.) are also killed for food but most venison comes from red deer, and, at the moment, most of it is exported to Europe. Owing to the rising price of venison, poaching has increased on a vast scale and new legislation is currently being formulated to control the sale of venison.

Venison Casserole

Serves 6

1 lb/500 g stewing venison
4 carrots
4 onions
2 turnips
¼ lb/125 g bacon or ham,
*   diced*
a little fat
1 tsp capers or pickled
*   nasturtium seeds*

½ tsp thyme
pinch nutmeg
1 tbs flour
1 pint/600 ml water or
*   game stock*
2 tbs sour cream or thick
*   yoghurt*
salt and pepper

Clean the vegetables and cut them into large pieces. Fry the vegetables and bacon or ham in a little fat, stir in the flour and cook until brown. Add the venison, cut into small pieces, season with salt, pepper and thyme, add the capers or nasturtium seeds, cover with the water or stock and simmer slowly for about 2 hours or until the venison is tender. Ten minutes before serving, add a pinch of nutmeg and the sour cream or yoghurt.

Rabbit

Rabbits can provide a useful addition to the diet. They are gradually developing a degree of immunity to myxomatosis (although the disease hasn't completely died out) and are beginning to reach pest proportions again. Until a few decades ago, rabbit fur was very much in demand for making felt hats and some farmers found it more profitable to breed them in vast warrens than to grow crops. A solution to the rabbit problem, now, might be to farm them for their meat.

Rabbit and Tomato Casserole

Serves 6 to 8

2 lb/1 kg small rabbit joints	½ tsp sage
2 lb/1 kg tomatoes	2 tbs flour
4 carrots	1 pint/600 ml stock or
2 large onions	water
¼ lb/125 g bacon	salt and pepper
1 clove garlic	oil or margarine for frying
½ tsp thyme	

Mix together the flour, herbs and some salt and pepper. Coat the rabbit joints with this, brown them in oil or margarine and place in a large casserole. Fry the bacon, carrots and onions (all sliced) for a few minutes. Add the crushed garlic and peeled, halved tomatoes, simmer for a minute or two and then tip all the vegetables into the casserole with the rabbit. Pour over them the boiling water or stock and mix well. Add more salt and pepper and bake in a moderate oven for about 1½ hours.

Sliced mushrooms (¼ lb/125 g) could be added 20 minutes before serving.

Hare

There are two species of hare in Britain – the brown hare of the lowlands and the smaller mountain or blue hare of the Scottish Highlands. The latter species is usually too stringy to eat. Hares may be shot all year round but may not be sold during the close season for game (1 March to 31 July). The flesh of hare is darker than that of rabbit. Hares should be hung (head downwards) for six to twelve days if freshly killed.

Hare in Guinness

Serves 6

1½ lb/750 g hare joints (leg)	oil
1 lb/500 g carrots	3 cloves
½ lb/250 g onions	1 tsp mustard
2 parsnips	¾ pint/450 ml Guinness
2 tbs flour	¼ pint/150 ml water
1 tsp thyme	1 tbs redcurrant jam or jelly
salt and pepper	(blackcurrant or plum will do)

Cut the hare joints into small pieces. Coat them in flour and brown in hot oil. Remove them from the pan and add the onions, peeled and roughly chopped, and the carrots and parsnips, scrubbed and cut into large pieces. Fry for a few minutes, adding any remaining flour and the thyme, cloves, salt, pepper, Guinness and water. Bring to the boil and pour over the hare joints in a casserole. Simmer in the oven for 2½ hours at gas mark 3 (325°F, 170°C). Twenty minutes before it is to be served, stir in the mustard and the jam, adjust the seasoning and return the dish to the oven to finish cooking.

Pigeon

Wood pigeons are not usually classed as game birds and are considered to be pests by most farmers. About 2½ million are shot each year for food.

Stuffed Braised Pigeons

Serves 4

2 wood pigeons	4 rashers streaky bacon
2 turnips	
2 carrots	FOR STUFFING:
1 bay leaf	
fat or oil for frying	3 tbs soft breadcrumbs
1 tbs flour	1 onion
1½ pints/850 ml water or	2 sticks celery
stock	1 tsp parsley
1 wineglassful orange juice	grated rind 1 orange
salt and pepper	egg to bind
	salt and pepper

To make the stuffing: Chop the celery, onion and parsley very finely. Season with salt and pepper and mix with the breadcrumbs and grated orange rind. Bind with egg and stuff the pigeons with this mixture. Wrap them in the bacon rashers and secure with toothpicks. Fry the vegetables (coarsely chopped) and the bay leaf in a little fat or oil. Add the flour and cook until brown. Add the pigeons, brown them on all sides, pour in the stock and leave them to simmer, covered, for about 1 hour or until tender. At the last minute, add the orange juice and adjust the seasoning.

*

British birds are well protected under the Protection of Birds Acts 1954–67 and it is illegal to kill them or to take their eggs. There are exceptions for pests, wildfowl and game birds for which open seasons are set. Grouse, pheasant and partridge shooting is big business, yet the amount of food produced from these birds is negligible. Of the 7 million pheasants which are shot each year in Britain, Dr Kenneth Mellanby reckons that each person would only receive 2 oz/50 g a year if the total was divided equally amongst the population. Apart from the poor return of food from these birds, their rearing often involves the ruthless destruction of all the animals which might prey on them: stoats, weasels, hedgehogs, foxes, otters, rooks, magpies, crows and even, in some instances, protected species such as birds of prey. Vast numbers of pheasants and partridges are artificially reared and then released into the wild. Many of the birds are so tame that the beaters have difficulty in getting them to fly over the sportsmen's guns. The high energy input in the production of ammunition makes the shooting of small game animals and birds hardly worth the effort.

Salads are perfect and easily prepared summer food. Not the depressing canteen variety, with endless variations on the theme of soggy lettuce, cucumber and tomato; but large bowls of absolutely fresh crisp vegetables and fruits, garlic and herbs, tossed at the last minute with a good oily dressing.

Winter vegetables are quite different in character from summer ones and they can be made into good salads, providing a crisp texture and a fresh taste as a welcome change from the traditional hot stews and starchy puddings.

It is often said that it is important to eat some raw foods in any season. This is very true, but it must be qualified. Starchy foods need to be cooked if they are not to be totally indigestible. Surprisingly, carotene, or vitamin A, is more easily absorbed from cooked vegetables than from raw. A raw carrot may be good for your teeth, but only one sixth of its vitamin A is digestible, whereas one third is digestible when it is cooked. On the other hand, vitamin C is easily destroyed by cooking. This vitamin is particularly scarce in winter food, and the cheapest source, apart from citrus fruits, is from raw winter vegetables. Brussels sprouts, for instance, contain 100 mg of vitamin C per 100 g of sprouts, which is reduced on cooking to 35 mg.

Dressings

French Dressing

A real French dressing is nothing more and nothing less than a mixture of good olive oil, wine vinegar, salt and pepper. The proportions are normally three parts oil to one part vinegar, though they can be adjusted to suit individual needs and tastes. Cucumbers and potatoes, for instance, both go best with a dressing that is slightly on the vinegary side, whereas lettuce is better with an oily dressing.

Some people like to add a little sugar to their French dressing; herbs or herb-flavoured vinegars, mustard and garlic are also often used to vary the basic recipe.

Honey and Lemon Dressing

$\frac{1}{4}$ pint/150 ml thin honey $\frac{1}{4}$ pint/150 ml lemon juice
1 tsp chopped mint, chives
　or parsley

Beat the honey and lemon juice together. Chop the herbs finely and add them. Leave to stand for an hour or two before using, to allow the flavour of the herbs to penetrate. Good with cabbage and carrot salads, and mixed salads, especially those with fruit amongst the ingredients.

Mayonnaise

2 egg yolks, at room $\frac{1}{2}$ pint/300 ml olive oil, also
　temperature   at room temperature
$\frac{1}{2}$ tsp salt   mustard (optional)
juice $\frac{1}{2}$ large lemon

Beat the egg yolks in a bowl with a wooden spoon. When they are creamy, begin to add the oil, drop by drop, stirring all the time. Make sure that each drop of oil is amalgamated before adding more – in the later stages, the oil can be added in slightly larger quantities. The mayonnaise will get thicker and thicker and harder to stir as it progresses. When all the oil is used up, thin the mayonnaise with the lemon juice, adding more if necessary. Season with salt and perhaps a little mustard.

Mayonnaise can be a little temperamental: if the oil is added too quickly, if the eggs and oil are at different temperatures, or if there is a little egg white adhering to the yolks. If it looks as though it is beginning to curdle, it can be saved with the addition of a little drop of boiling water. If it is too late and it has curdled, start again with another egg yolk in a fresh bowl, adding the curdled mixture drop by drop, as you did with the oil.

Various flavourings can be added to mayonnaise, such as: chopped gherkins, capers, hard-boiled eggs and parsley to make *sauce tartare* for serving with fish or vegetables; chopped herbs, spinach and anchovy fillets to make *sauce verte* for fish, vegetables or eggs; tomato purée to make the standard sauce for prawn cocktail; garlic for aïoli; and so on.

Salads

Aïoli with Vegetables

This can be a beautiful dish and it makes a perfect summer lunch served with thick slices of brown bread.

FOR THE AÏOLI:

2 cloves garlic, crushed
½ pint/300 ml olive oil
juice ½ lemon or 2 tsps
vinegar

2 egg yolks
salt and pepper

Pound the garlic with the egg yolks until they form a smooth purée. Then proceed as for mayonnaise, adding the oil drop by drop, beating all the time with a wooden spoon. When all the oil has been used up, thin to the consistency of thick cream with lemon juice or vinegar.

Prepare a selection of vegetables, some crisp and raw, some cooked: sprigs of cauliflower, young carrots, spring onions, cooked new potatoes, celery sticks, cucumber cut into strips, cooked or raw beetroot are all suitable. Arrange the vegetables in mounds around the edge of a large oval meat plate and place the bowl of aïoli in the centre. Each person takes a selection of vegetables and dips them into the aïoli. Only one or two vegetables need be used, but a large variety of different tastes, textures and colours makes the dish more attractive to look at, and to eat.

Beetroot Leaf Salad

Serves 2 to 3

Wash the leaves from the tops of young red or golden beets. Steam them for a few minutes, or boil in a very little water. When they are soft, drain and chop them and, while they are still hot, mix them with a little French dressing.

Beetroot leaves taste like a cross between beets and greens. They can be added to a mixed salad, or to a salad made with the beets themselves. They also make a good soup.

It was only after the sixteenth century that the roots of beets began to be eaten. Beets were cultivated by the Greeks and Romans for their leaves alone.

Beetroot Salad 1

Serves 2

1 large or 2 small raw
  beetroots, peeled
1 good-sized cooking apple,
  cored
¼ cup soaked raisins or
  sultanas

salt
1 tbs oil
juice of ½ lemon

Mince or grate the beets and the apple. Mix together with the other ingredients, adding salt to taste.

Beetroot Salad 2

Serves 4 to 6

1 lb/500 g beetroots
½ cup French dressing

1 lb/500 g onions

Boil or bake the beetroots in their skins. Rub off the peel and, while they are still hot, slice them thinly and mix them with the onions, also thinly sliced. Mix well with the French dressing and leave to cool, turning occasionally.

Raw Brussels Sprouts with Hazelnut Dressing

Serves 3

1 lb/500 g sprouts	1 tbs hazelnuts, roasted
2 tbs plain yoghurt	2 tbs oil
salt and pepper	lemon juice (optional)

Wash the sprouts thoroughly, dry and slice them very thinly. Grate or chop the hazelnuts and mix with the yoghurt, oil, salt and pepper. Pour this dressing over the sliced sprouts, adding more seasoning and a little lemon juice if you want the dressing sharper. Chill before serving.

Celeriac Salad

Serves 4

Wash and peel 1 or 2 celeriac roots. Cut in matchstick-sized pieces (the crinkly blade of the *mandoline* is ideal for this) and mix immediately (to prevent browning) with a simple French dressing and 1 teaspoon mustard.

The French often cook the celeriac lightly before mixing it, while still hot, with a little dressing and adding mayonnaise when the celeriac has cooled.

Coleslaw

Serves 4

1 lb/500 g Dutch white cabbage	1 cooking apple (or a large sweet apple)
1 small onion	salt and pepper
2 carrots	
French dressing or mayonnaise	

Coleslaw was originally a Dutch dish – *kool*: cabbage, *sla*: salad – the name was corrupted when the dish was introduced by settlers to America.

Remove the thickest stalks from the cabbage (save these for stock, or they can be stir-fried like the cauliflower stalks on page 75) and slice the rest very thinly. Shred, slice or grate the carrots, the onion and the apple, mix with the cabbage and dress the salad straight away, before the apples turn brown. (Sprinkle lemon juice over the salad first if you are using mayonnaise.)

This salad can be served as it is, or it makes a good base for all sorts of variations and additions such as: chopped orange and orange peel, beanshoots, watercress, finely chopped raw spinach, nuts, raisins or sultanas, garlic, capers, gherkins, chopped parsley.

Hungarian Cucumber Salad

Serves 3 to 4

1 large cucumber	2 onions
1 tbs salt	2 tsps oil
1 tsp vinegar	pepper
¼ pint/150 ml thick yoghurt	1 tsp paprika

Slice the cucumber and onions very thinly. Sprinkle with salt and leave to marinate for several hours, by which time the juices and salt will have formed a brine. Drain the cucumber and onions in a colander, rinse out all the salt and squeeze dry (the only way is by hand). Return to the dish and mix well with the oil, vinegar, pepper and yoghurt. Sprinkle the top with paprika and chill before serving.

Always test a little piece from the end of a cucumber before slicing it, to make sure it is not bitter. If it is, cut it lengthwise down the centre and rub the two halves together. The bitter juices will rise to the surface and can be rinsed off.

Cucumber and Bean Salad

Serves 3

1 cucumber
French dressing

½ lb/250 g tender young
    green beans

String the beans if necessary. Slice and cook them. Slice the cucumber (peeled or unpeeled) thinly or cut into small cubes and mix with the hot beans and a rather vinegary French dressing. Chill before serving.

Leek Salad

Serves 3

Wash 1 lb/500 g leeks well and steam them whole for 10 to 15 minutes, or until tender but not completely limp. Cut into slices while still hot and mix with French dressing. Leek salad is also good with raw leeks but the flavour is rather more pungent. The leeks, green leaves and all, should be washed very thoroughly and cut into very thin slices before being mixed with a dressing.

Lentil Salad

Serves 3 to 4

½ lb/250 g small green or
    brown lentils
parsley

1 onion
French dressing

Wash the lentils. Tip them into a bowl, cover them with boiling water, put a plate on top and leave them for 1 hour. Slice or chop the onion finely. Drain the lentils and add the onion to them. Toss in French dressing and sprinkle chopped parsley on top. As the lentils are uncooked they will still be crunchy yet soft enough to eat, but the method will not work if they are too old.

Mediterranean Salad

Serves 3 to 4

6 tomatoes
1 small onion
sprig basil
1 green pepper
½ cucumber

FOR THE DRESSING:

3 tbs oil
1 clove garlic
juice ½ lemon
salt and pepper

Make the dressing ½ hour before you need it to allow the flavour of the garlic to penetrate, or use garlic oil (see page 78).

Slice the tomatoes and lay them in the middle of a flat dish. Slice the pepper, onion and cucumber very thinly and arrange around the edge of the tomatoes. Sprinkle with chopped fresh basil and serve the dressing separately, first removing the garlic.

Melon and Grape Salad

Scoop out the flesh and the seeds from a small canteloupe melon. Chop the flesh and return to the melon shell with an equal quantity of white grapes. Mix with a simple French dressing and chill. Allow one of these little melons per person. Don't throw away the melon rind. See page 161 for a recipe for melon rind pickle.

Both melons and grapes can be grown quite successfully in this country, particularly in a dry hot summer such as we had in 1976. Melons were grown in the gardens of rich houses in the sixteenth century, and in the Middle Ages a large amount of white wine was brewed from monastery vines. These vines disappeared with the dissolution of the monasteries. 'Many monasteries in the kingdome hauing Vineyards, had as much wine made therefrom, as sufficed there couents yeare by yeare: but long since they haue been destroyed, and the knowledge how to order a Vineyard is also utterly perished with them' (John Parkinson. 1629).

There are now a few vineyards in the south and east of England producing English wine very successfully.

Mushrooms in Red Wine

Serves 4

1 lb/500 g mushrooms
4 shallots, finely chopped
2 cloves garlic, finely chopped or crushed
2 tsps coriander seeds, crushed
2 wineglasses red wine
4 tsps fresh thyme or parsley, chopped

3 tbs olive oil
1 tbs wine vinegar
4 tomatoes, skinned, de-seeded and chopped
1 tsp ground cumin
salt and black pepper

Wash and trim the mushrooms – use them whole if they are small button mushrooms, halve them if medium-sized and quarter them if large. Heat the olive oil in a heavy frying pan and fry the shallots, mushrooms, garlic and coriander briskly for about 3 minutes, stirring all the time. Remove the mixture from the pan and pour in the wine. Boil until reduced by half. Add the wine to the mushrooms, together with the tomatoes, vinegar, cumin and herbs. Season well, cover and leave to cool. Serve cold with hot Greek bread, rye bread or crusty wholemeal bread.

Mushroom and Watercress Salad

Serves 3 to 4

¼ lb/125 g mushrooms
2 tbs oil
salt and pepper

1 bunch watercress
juice of ½ lemon

Slice the mushrooms; wash and chop the watercress roughly. Mix with the oil, lemon juice and seasoning. This can also be made with equal quantities of mushrooms, watercress and beanshoots.

Finely sliced nasturtium leaves make a good and unusual addition to summer salads. They taste slightly peppery and are particularly good with mushrooms and with lettuce.

Orange Salad

Serves 4

Peel 4 oranges, cut them across in thin slices and mix with 2 onions cut into thin rings. Sprinkle with salt and pepper and olive oil.

Potato and Bean Salad

Serves 4

1 lb/500 g new potatoes
¼ lb/125 g black olives
salt and pepper

1 lb/500 g tender green beans
½ cup French dressing

Scrub and boil the potatoes in their skins. Peel them while still hot and slice them into the French dressing. Cook the beans, slice them while still hot and mix with the French dressing. Add the olives and some extra salt and pepper and serve cold.

Hot Potato Salad

Serves 3

Boil or steam 1 lb/500 g potatoes in their skins. While they are still hot, slice them into a bowl and mix in ¼ cup highly seasoned French dressing, most of which will be absorbed immediately. Serve at once.

Variations: Add a finely chopped raw onion to the salad; roast a teaspoonful of caraway or cumin seeds under the grill and add to the hot sliced potatoes; sprinkle a teaspoonful of paprika over the salad.

Rice and Red Kidney Bean Salad

Serves 4

½ lb/250 g rice, cooked
French dressing

½ lb/250 g red kidney beans, cooked
chopped parsley or chives

Toss the rice, beans and dressing together (preferably when hot so that the taste of the dressing is absorbed more thoroughly). Sprinkle chopped parsley or chives on top. Leave to cool before serving.

Grated Swede Salad

Serves 3 to 4

1 large swede
1 medium onion
1 tbs chopped parsley
lemon juice and honey
    dressing (page 126)

1 large cooking apple or 2
    eating apples
1 tbs raisins, soaked
salt and pepper

Wash, peel and grate the swede; core and grate the apple, chop the onion and parsley. Mix everything together with the drained raisins and add the lemon and honey dressing, salt and pepper.

The nicest way to round off a good meal is with a large basket of fresh fruits. Especially in summer, the season for soft fruit is so short that it seems a pity to do anything but enjoy them just as they come off the bush.

Here are a few puddings for those occasions when a special effort is called for, but if your taste is for elaborate confections drenched in cream and sugar, then you must look elsewhere. The puddings in this chapter are generally quite simple: based on fruit and eggs, nuts and milk, with just enough sugar to give a hint of sweetness. No one using these recipes need worry too much about their waistline, or their teeth!

Sugarless Apple Purée

Serves 4

1 cup water
handful of raisins
pinch salt
2 cloves
¼ tsp cinnamon

1½ lb/750 g apples (cookers
  or eaters), peeled, cored
  and sliced
2–3 drops vanilla essence
¼ tsp allspice

Bring the water to the boil and add all the ingredients. Simmer until almost all the water is gone, making sure it doesn't burn. Cool before serving.

Chaffcombe Apple Pudding 1

Serves 4

3 cooking apples, grated
juice and grated rind of 1
  orange

1 oz/25 g margarine or
  butter
2 tbs sugar
6 tbs oat flakes

Mix the grated apples, orange juice, orange rind and half the sugar in an ovenproof dish. Melt the margarine or butter over a low heat and stir in the rest of the sugar until it melts. Add the oats and stir until they are coated with the sugar and margarine. Spread them over the apple mixture and leave to stand for 1 hour before baking for 20 to 30 minutes with the oven at gas mark 5 (375°F, 190°C).

Chaffcombe Apple Pudding 2

Serves 4

1 lb/500 g apples, grated
  (cookers or eaters)
3 digestive biscuits (see page
  151)

2 tbs oatflakes
grated rind and juice of 1
  lemon

Crush the digestive biscuits, mix all the ingredients together and chill. Roasted chopped nuts can be sprinkled on top if liked.

Apple Strudel

Serves 6 to 8

You will need a large table and a clean, boiled cloth on which to spread the dough.

FOR THE PASTRY:

5 oz/150 g strong plain
  white flour
pinch salt
1 small egg
2 tbs oil or 1 oz/25 g lard
2 tbs warm water

FOR THE FILLING:

4 oz/125 g breadcrumbs,
  toasted, or

4 oz/125 g digestive biscuit
  crumbs
3 oz/75 g sugar
juice 1 lemon
1 tsp cinnamon
2 oz/50 g chopped walnuts
6 tbs oil or 3 oz/75 g lard
2½ lb/1¼ kg Bramley or
  other cooking apples
2 oz/50 g sultanas

Make the pastry: Sift the flour and salt onto a board or into a bowl. Rub in the oil or lard; mix in the warm water and egg and knead until absolutely smooth and free of bubbles (about 5 minutes). Cover the dough with flour and wrap in a warm cloth and leave to rest for ½ hour while you prepare the filling.

For the filling: Peel, core and slice the apples very thinly. Place them in a bowl with the nuts, sultanas, sugar and lemon juice. Stir well and leave aside until needed. Prepare the breadcrumbs or the digestive biscuits. Set the oven to gas mark 4 (350°F, 180°C).

Cover a large table with a clean cloth sprinkled with flour. Place the ball of dough in the centre and roll it out in all directions, as far as it will go, with a floured rolling pin. Now, with your hands underneath the dough, start from the centre to ease it very gently outwards, taking care not to pierce it with your fingernails. Carry on easing and pulling until the surface of the table is mostly covered with a thin film of dough – so thin that you can read a newspaper through it. This is not as hard as it sounds, as the pastry is very pliable and easy to work. Should you happen to pierce it, just pinch the edges back together again and take care not to put too much pressure on this area again. Cut off the thick edges of the dough with scissors and then brush the whole surface with the melted lard or oil. Spread the dough with the breadcrumbs, leaving a 2-inch/5-cm margin on three sides. Cover the breadcrumbs with the sliced apples, nuts and sultanas, and sprinkle with cinnamon. It is now ready to roll up. Starting at the end with no margin of dough, take up the cloth with both hands and pull upwards, so that the dough starts to roll over by itself, and continue until it is all rolled up. Pinch in the ends to seal the filling. Ease the roll of dough onto a baking sheet. This is a little tricky and the easiest way is to put the cloth over the edge of the tray and roll the strudel onto it in the same way that you rolled it up. Make sure that the open edge is underneath so that the strudel doesn't split on baking. Brush the surface with a little more oil or lard and bake for ¾ hour. Should the finished strudel be longer than the baking tin, form it very gently into a crescent shape before easing it onto the tin. Either use two spatulas to ease the dough onto the tray or roll out the cloth from under the strudel, moving the tray under the strudel as you do so.

Apple and Rice Snow

Serves 4

2 tbs round grain rice (white or brown)	3 tbs sugar
1 lb/500 g cooking apples	1 pint/600 ml milk
strip lemon peel	1 egg
1 oz/25 g margarine or butter	

Melt the margarine or butter, add the milk and then the rice and 2 tablespoons of the sugar. Cook very gently indeed until the rice is tender and the mixture is thick and creamy. It will take a good hour or more, depending on the rice. Stir once or twice while cooking. Stew the apples with 1 tablespoon of sugar (or more to taste) and the lemon peel. Separate the egg and, when the rice is cooked, beat in the yolk. Add the apples (first removing the lemon peel) and leave to cool. Whip the egg white until stiff and fold in gently. Serve well chilled, piled into a glass bowl or individual dishes.

This is also good made with stewed blackberries, apricots, plums, black or red currants.

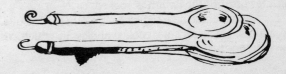

Apricot Pizza

Serves 4 to 6

A sweet pizza sounds an odd idea but is in fact very good. The juices from the fruit seep into the pastry and make an aromatic and succulent pudding.

FOR 1 LARGE PIZZA:

3 oz/75 g wholemeal flour
2 oz/50 g oil or margarine
1 tsp sugar
pinch salt
3 oz/75 g strong plain white
    flour
1 tsp crumbled fresh yeast
    or ¼ tsp dried yeast
about 4 fl oz/150 ml water

FOR THE FILLING:

1 lb/500 g ripe apricots
2 tbs sugar
few cracked kernels
4–5 drops vanilla essence

The method for the dough is the same as for wholemeal bread dough on page 147, except that this mixture contains more oil and is rather richer.

Stew the apricots whole with a tiny bit of water to prevent them from sticking to the pan. They should be soft but not mushy. Leave them to cool a little, halve them and remove the stones. Crack a few stones, remove the kernels and chop them: they are rather like bitter almonds and a few go a long way. When the dough has risen to twice its bulk, knock it down and knead for a few minutes; roll it out to a large circle or oblong as thinly as possible, and place on a greased baking tray. Spread the apricots over it; sprinkle them with the sugar, vanilla essence and chopped kernels. Leave to prove and then bake in a hot oven for 30 minutes or until the dough is cooked.

This pizza can be adapted for many other soft fruits, e.g. plums, blackcurrants, cooked apples, in which case use almonds instead of apricot kernels.

Damson Purée

Serves 3 to 4

1 lb/500 g damsons
sugar to taste – approx. 2-
    3 oz/50-75 g should be
    ample

pinch bicarbonate of soda

Damsons are the tastiest of the English plums. They are tiny and blue-black and very sour, so they need to be cooked with sugar. A war-time tip comes in useful here – add a pinch of bicarbonate of soda to damson purée and the amount of sugar can be reduced. Damsons only make a short appearance in the shops around September; they are unpopular as they are somewhat fiddly to stone. The following purée is worth all the effort of sieving the fruit and is a beautiful deep red colour and rich in flavour.

Simmer the damsons with a little water until they are quite soft. Rub them through a sieve or mouli-légumes, extracting as much as possible of the flesh from the stones. Heat the purée gently, add the bicarbonate of soda and the sugar and stir until the sugar has melted. Pour the sweetened purée into a bowl and leave to cool.

Elderflower Fritters

Makes about 15 fritters

¾ lb/350 g plain unbleached
    flour
½ oz/10 g fresh yeast
½ pint/300 ml elderflowers,
    stripped from stalks
¾ pint/450 ml lukewarm
    water
1 tsp sugar

pinch salt
granulated sugar

SYRUP:

½ lb/250 g clear honey
juice ½ lemon
¾ pint/450 ml water

Sift the flour and salt into a bowl. Dissolve the yeast with the sugar in a little of the water and leave until frothy. Mix the yeast into the flour and gradually add the rest of the water, beating all the time to make a thick, smooth batter. Leave to rise in a warm place for 1 hour, then beat vigorously again, until the dough is elastic. Leave to rise for another hour, then beat in the elderflower petals and leave the dough to rest once more.

Make a syrup with the honey, water and lemon juice and allow it to get quite cold – in a refrigerator if possible. Deep fry small teaspoonfuls of the batter mixture, a few at a time, in a bland vegetable oil. As they cook, they will turn deep golden, expand and rise to the surface. Drain the fritters and keep them hot and crisp in the oven. Just before serving, pile them onto a plate, pour the cold honey syrup over them and sprinkle them with a little granulated sugar.

Orange and Hazelnut Tart

Serves 4 to 6

8 oz/250 g soya pastry or ordinary shortcrust pastry (see page 150)	2 eggs, separated
	2 large oranges
4 oz/125 g hazelnuts	½ lemon
	3 oz/75 g brown sugar

Pare the rind from 1 of the oranges and boil in a little water for 10 to 15 minutes, until soft. Roast the hazelnuts under the grill and grate finely. Squeeze the juice from the oranges and the half lemon. Add the sugar, egg yolks and grated hazelnuts. Mash the orange rind with a fork until it is almost a purée and mix well into the orange juice and hazelnut mixture. Line a flan tin with the pastry and bake blind for 15 minutes. Whip the egg whites until stiff, fold into the orange mixture, pour into the half-baked pastry case and return to the oven for a further 20 minutes or until well risen. Serve cold.

Orange or Lemon Peel

The following are two wartime tips: when oranges and lemons were so scarce, people were loath to waste even the peel.

Remove the pith from orange or lemon peel. Cut the peel into small shavings and dry on a tray in a low oven until all the moisture has gone. When cooled, put into jars and use instead of candied peel for flavouring cakes and puddings or savoury stews and stuffings. Delicious also for flavouring tea.

Orange Firelighters

Dry orange peel, complete with pith, in a low oven, to drive off all the moisture. Use the dried peel for lighting fires. It sounds a strange thing to do with orange peel, but it works. The peel is very oily and stays alight for a long time. Grapefruit and lemon peel also work.

Pear Crumble

Serves 4 to 5

FOR THE CRUMBLE:	FOR THE FILLING:
6 oz/175 g wholemeal flour	1½ lb/750 g pears (comice are best)
4 oz/125 g margarine or butter	1 tbs honey
pinch salt	
2 oz/50 g grated hazelnuts	
1 tbs brown sugar	

Sift the flour and salt into a bowl and rub in the margarine. Mix in the sugar and nuts. Slice the pears into a deep ovenproof dish and stir in the honey. Spread the crumble over the top and bake for 1 hour in a moderate oven.

Curd Cheese and Pear Flan

8 oz/250 g quantity of shortcrust pastry, with 1 tbs sugar and grated rind of 1 lemon added to the basic mixture

FOR THE FILLING:	
8 oz/250 g cottage cheese, sieved	1 lb/500 g sweet pears (Comice or Williams), peeled and quartered
1 egg	4 oz/125 g plain yoghurt
	½ tsp vanilla essence

Roll out the pastry and line a flan tin or dish 8 inches/20 cm across and 1½ inches/4 cm deep. Beat the cottage cheese with the yoghurt, vanilla essence and egg and pour into the flan case. Arrange the pear slices in a circle on the cheese mixture, pressing them in slightly. Bake with the oven at gas mark 3 (325°F, 170°C) for 1 hour, then turn off the oven, leaving the flan in until it is cooled.

N.B. If you have some pastry scraps left over, roll them out again, cut them in strips and use them to make a lattice pattern over the flan before it is baked.

Apple quarters or apricot halves could be used in place of the pears.

Rhubarb

Rhubarb became popular in the late eighteenth century. It was such a novelty, that the Royal Society offered a prize for its cultivation.

Cold Rhubarb Charlotte

Serves 4 to 6

Place 1½ lb/750 g stewed, sweetened rhubarb with strips of orange peel in layers in a deep bowl with slices of stale bread. Put a plate and weight on top and leave overnight. Turn out and sprinkle strips of orange peel on top.

Rhubarb is high in oxalic acid and a little more than 4 lb/2 kilos may provide a fatal dose, so don't eat too much at once!

Rhubarb, Lemon and Date Compote

Serves 4

1 lb/500 g rhubarb
½ lb/250 g stoned dates

juice ½ lemon and grated rind
1 cup water

Trim the rhubarb and cut into 1-inch/3-cm lengths. Simmer until soft with the dates, lemon juice and rind and 1 cup water. Chill well before serving.

A little grated fresh ginger root (or powdered dry ginger) could be added to the compote while it is simmering, as well as, or instead of, the lemon.

Magic Fruit Syllabub

Serves 4

This recipe was given by Marianne Sekules. It is a war-time recipe, invented when cream was impossible to get. It is light, delicious and very cheap to make.

1 tea cup pure fruit juice, such as orange or lemon
1 tea cup soft brown sugar
1 egg white

Whisk all three ingredients together in a bowl until light, stiff and frothy. Don't lose heart – it takes a long time to whip but it works in the end.

Brown Bread Summer Pudding

Serves 4 to 6

6 slices brown bread
½ lb/250 g redcurrants
½ lb/250 g raspberries
a little sugar

Cut the crusts off the slices of bread. (The number of slices rather depends on the size of the loaf, but there should be enough to line a round pudding basin.) Cut the slices into triangles and moisten slightly to make the bread hold together better. Line the basin with some of the slices almost to the rim, overlapping them slightly. Stew a mixture of raspberries and redcurrants with a little sugar. Pour off most of the juice into a jug and put aside. Pour the fruit into the basin and cover with more slices of bread, making sure that there are no cracks. Cover with a plate of exactly the same diameter as the circle of bread or, alternatively, several layers of greaseproof paper with a 1-lb/500-g weight placed on

op. Leave overnight. The next day, turn the pudding
out onto a plate, pour the remaining juice over the top,
as the juice in the fruit will only partly have penetrated
the bread, and serve.

Raspberry Snow

Serves 4 to 6

1 lb/500 g raspberries　　*2 egg whites*

Pass the raspberries through a sieve (a nylon one, to
stop them discolouring). Whip the egg whites until stiff
and whisk into the raspberry purée. It shouldn't need
any sugar if the raspberries are ripe and sweet.

Schaumomelette or Foam Omelette

Serves 3

This recipe was given by Marianne Sekules.

2 eggs
3 tsps sugar
pinch salt
2 tbs blackcurrants,
*　raspberries or*
*　redcurrants, sweetened if*
*　necessary (jam can be*
*　used instead)*

1 heaped tsp flour
½ cup milk
grated rind 1 lemon
butter for frying

Separate the eggs. Add the flour, 1 teaspoonful of the
sugar, salt, lemon rind and milk to the egg yolks and
mix well. Whip the egg whites very stiffly with the rest
of the sugar. Fry the egg yolk mixture slowly in a small
frying pan in a little butter. When the bottom is just set
and the top still moist, spread the egg whites over the
top. Leave for 1 minute and then fold the two opposite
sides upwards and towards the middle, to make a boat
shape. Put the whole pan in a medium oven for 5
minutes, to set the whites. Spoon the fruit along the
centre of the whites and cut in slices to serve.

(The *Schaumomelette* can be made larger, in which
case a bigger frying pan is needed. It will only work if
the pan does not stick.)

Strawberry Sorbet

Serves 4 to 6

1 lb/500 g strawberries　　*2 tbs sugar*
1 tbs water

Mash the strawberries thoroughly with a fork so that
they are reduced to a pulp. Pass through a nylon sieve
(a metal sieve tends to discolour the fruit). Make a syrup
with the sugar and water and mix this well into the
strawberry purée. Put into ice trays in the freezing
compartment of the fridge until frozen solid. Remove
and tip the block into a large bowl. Leave for about 20
minutes to thaw out a little, break it up into little pieces
and beat it with an egg whisk until it is foamy and
light. This should be done just before it is to be served,
although, once whipped, it could be returned to the
freezing compartment until 5 minutes before serving.

Whipped Strawberries and Curd Cheese

Serves 4 to 6

½ lb/250 g strawberries　　*a little sugar or honey*
½ lb/250 g curd cheese or
*　sieved cottage cheese*

Mash the strawberries well with a fork and sweeten to
taste with honey or sugar. Mix with the curd cheese
and whip with an egg whisk until light and fluffy.

Dried Fruit Compote

Serves 4 to 5

1 oz/25 g prunes	*2 oz/50 g dried apples*
2 oz/50 g dried pears	*2 oz/50 g dried raisins*
2 oz/50 g dried apricots	*3 tsps rosewater*

Cover the fruit with water and leave to soak for 1 hour.
Put the fruit into a saucepan with ¼ pint/150 ml of the
water used to soak the fruit and simmer for ½ hour until
soft. Leave the fruit to cool, add the rosewater and chill.
Delicious served with yoghurt.

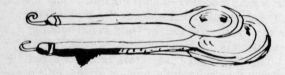

Yoghurt

1 pint/600 ml milk   *1 tbs plain yoghurt*

Heat the milk to boiling temperature, turn the heat
down very low and leave it barely simmering for a
minute or two. Leave to cool for 5 to 6 minutes to
hand-hot temperature (about 113°F or 45°C). Skim off
all the skin which will have formed on the surface and
beat the skimmed milk, a spoonful at a time, into the
yoghurt (preferably in a heavy earthenware casserole
with a lid as this will retain the heat well). Cover the
dish, wrap it in a thick blanket or eiderdown and leave
quite untouched in a warm place for about 12 hours.

Alternative Methods:

Pour the mixed yoghurt into a warmed thermos flask
and leave for 8 to 12 hours.

Use skimmed milk or Long Life milk instead of fresh,
and simply heat it to about 113°F (45°C) before mixing
with the yoghurt.

For thick high protein yoghurt: add 1 oz/25 g
skimmed milk powder to the yoghurt before mixing in
the milk.

For low fat yoghurt: Make up 1 pint/600 ml skimmed
milk from powder. Heat to about 113°F (45°C) and mix,
spoonful by spoonful, into 1 tablespoonful of beaten
yoghurt in a bowl. Pour into a thermos, or wrap bowl
in a blanket, and leave in a warm place for 8 to 12
hours.

Sometimes home-made yoghurt separates and
becomes grainy if the milk was mixed in at too high a
temperature. Should this happen, it is not wasted. It can
be drained overnight through a colander lined with
muslin to make a delicious soft sweet curd cheese. This
cheese can, of course, be made just as well with yoghurt
that has not failed. It is one of the cheapest ways of
making curd cheese.

Raisin and Nut Yoghurt

Serves 3 to 4

This is delicious for breakfast or as a pudding.

ALLOW PER PERSON:

2 oz/50 g raisins	*1 oz/25 g nuts (hazelnuts*
¼ pint/150 ml yoghurt	*are best)*

Soak the raisins in plenty of water for a few hours until
they are plump. Chop the nuts and roast them until
well browned. Drain the raisins and mix together with
the nuts and yoghurt. Chill before serving.

Christmas Pudding

Makes about 6 pints/3 litres

This recipe was given by John Pudduck.

lb/250 g wholemeal flour
lb/250 g brown
  breadcrumbs
lb/250 g Barbados sugar
lb/500 g prunes, stoned
  and chopped
lb/250 g currants
lb/250 g raisins
2 oz/50 g cut mixed peel
4 oz/125 g shredded
  almonds
juice and grated rind of 2
  lemons
3 eggs
approx. ½ pint/300 ml
  brown ale or Guinness
2 tsps ground cinnamon

2 tsps salt
1 lb/500 g margarine
½ lb/250 g dried apricots,
  chopped
½ lb/250 g dates, stoned and
  chopped
½ lb/250 g sultanas
¾ lb/350 g cooking apples,
  peeled, cored and grated
juice and grated rind of 2
  oranges
½ lb/250 g black treacle
¼ pint/150 ml brandy
2 tsps mixed spice
2 tsps ground ginger
¼ grated nutmeg

Sift flour, salt and spices into a large bowl and add breadcrumbs and sugar. Mix together the dried fruit, apples, mixed peel, almonds and grated orange and lemon rinds and add to the flour. Melt the margarine and add to mixture. Beat orange and lemon juice with the treacle and eggs and add to the mixture with brandy and brown ale or Guinness to make a dropping consistency, adding more ale if necessary. Place mixture in pudding basins and cover with greaseproof paper and foil tied on with string. Steam for 4 hours (or about 2½ hours in a pressure cooker). Steam for a further 3 hours (1 hour in a pressure cooker) before using.

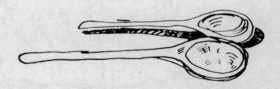

Bread and

12.

Baking

RISE

RISE

of the wholemeal loaf.

Bread

The Fall and Rise of the Wholemeal Loaf

Bread has been an important food ever since man first learnt how to grind cereals into flour. The earliest loaves were simple unleavened cakes of flour and water, dried in the sun. Bread of this kind has been found in Stone Age settlements. Leavened bread is mentioned in the earliest chapters of the Bible and seems to have been invented, most probably by accident, by the Egyptians. The Romans brought bread-making to a fine art. Their flour, made from barley, rye, millet or wheat, was ground between circular millstones. The resulting flour was leavened with brewer's barm, kneaded mechanically and baked in clay ovens.

In old-fashioned stone mills, the grain is still ground between two grooved circular millstones. The lower stone is stationary and the top stone revolves as the grain is fed through its axle. The heat generated during milling distributes the nutrients and flavouring constituents evenly throughout the meal, and the resulting flour is 100 per cent wholemeal, consisting, in the case of wheat, of coarse and fine bran, endosperm and wheatgerm.

For centuries this type of flour has formed the basis of the bread of both the rich and the poor. The bread of the poor was coarse, heavy and brown. It was the staff of life, being, in times of extreme hardship, almost the only food they knew. The rich have always preferred a lighter, more refined bread, more suitable as an accompaniment to rich meats and sauces. For their bread, the meal was sieved through a silk bolting cloth to remove the coarsest particles of bran. White bread thus became a status symbol – the whiter the bread, the richer the household. It was not long before this was exploited by the bakers. Slaked lime, alum and chalk were in common use until well into the eighteenth century to improve the whiteness of inferior flour.

In the 1870s the invention of a new roller milling process for flour put pure white bread within reach of everybody, rich and poor alike. Roller mills work by cracking the wheat grains between sets of increasingly fine grooved rollers, during which process the constituents which give the flour a coarse texture and a dark colour, the bran and the germ, are blown off giving a fine flour of 70 per cent extraction. Unfortunately, the bran and the germ, although they form a small proportion of the wheat grain, contain most of the nutritional value. The endosperm, of which roller-milled white flour is made, is composed largely of cellulose and starch, with a small amount of protein. As a result, the poor had their white bread at last, but it was nutritionally inferior; they suffered, while the animals who were fed the bran and the germ were thriving! The seriousness of this problem became evident when, at the end of the century, 40 per cent of the recruits for the Boer War had to be rejected on the grounds of stunted growth, poor sight and hearing, heart disease and rotten teeth.

The result was that, during the two succeeding world wars, the British government adopted a nutritional policy, rationing food to ensure an equitable distribution both of quantities and nutrients. During the Second World War, when supplies of imported wheat were interrupted, Britain had to become self-sufficient in flour and all bread flour was milled from English wheat. The extraction rate of National Flour, as it was called, was raised from 70 per cent to 85 per cent, with the double purpose of increasing the nutritional content and making the wheat go further. With the end of rationing, millers reverted, by popular demand, to producing white flour, but the government retained some control over its nutritional content. The 1953 and 1956 Flour Composition Orders stipulated that all flour of 70 per cent extraction had to contain nutrients equivalent to those in National Flour and be fortified with synthetic thiamine, nicotinic acid, calcium and iron. The 1956

Flour Composition Order still stands, and all white flour must contain these four nutrients.

Today's white loaf is a very different commodity from that sold just after the war. The bread market is now dominated by the factory-made wrapped sliced loaf, accounting for 60 per cent of sales and the product of many years of research by technologists in the bread industry. It is designed not only to have a perfect light white crumb and good keeping qualities in order to withstand long periods in storage, but also to be the right shape and size for sandwiches and electric toasters and stacking on supermarket shelves. Flour milled from English wheat alone does not give a springy enough loaf, so 40 per cent of the wheat has to be hard wheat imported from the U.S.A. or Canada. Each batch of wheat naturally varies in quality, but the use of chemical additives and the technique of mixing and baking the dough ensure that the resulting loaves are of absolutely standard quality.

About sixty additives, apart from the compulsory nutrients, are currently permitted in white bread and flour. These are used as bleaching and improving agents, raising agents, enzyme active preparations, yeast stimulating preparations, preservatives, emulsifiers, stabilizers, antioxidants (to prevent fats from going rancid), colouring agents, acids and excipients or diluents. Some of the additives, such as Lecithin (an antioxidant obtained from the soya bean), caramel (the only permitted colouring for use in brown bread) and chalk (a diluent for some of the other additives) are natural substances. Most of the others are chemicals which on rigorous testing have proved to be harmless. However, several of the additives which are currently permitted have been insufficiently tested, and in some cases there is reason to believe that they are unsafe. The most controversial of these, and the one with the nastiest name, is an antioxidant – Butylated Hydroxitoluene, known commonly as BHT. BHT was banned in Sweden and Australia in 1962, following feeding tests on rats which showed considerable toxic effects. In 1963 the Food Additives and Contaminants Committee recommended that its use be discontinued in Britain unless it had overriding advantages over other antioxidants which were known to be safe. It hasn't, but it is still in use today, pending further tests of toxicity.

Arguments about the nutritional value of white bread versus brown have been raging at least since the Second World War. Experts still disagree about the optimum extraction rate of flour: whether it should be 70 per cent with nutritional additives, or 85 per cent or 100 per cent with no additives at all, and whether it matters anyway, as people are eating less bread.

It is now believed, on very good authority, that chemical additives do not adequately replace the nutrients which are removed from 100 per cent flour to make 70 per cent flour. Vitamin B_6, for instance, which plays a role in the nervous system and for which wholemeal bread is the best source, is completely removed and not replaced. Research in the U.S.A. has shown that the removal of chromium, zinc and magnesium has led to widespread deficiencies of these minerals. Moreover, the synthetic thiamine, which is added to flour by law, is heat sensitive and mostly destroyed during baking. Half the vitamin E which is present in the whole wheat is also removed during milling and the portion which remains is completely destroyed when the flour is bleached.

Bread is a good source of protein, calcium and iron and, for these nutrients, wholemeal and white bread are equally valuable. Wholemeal bread contains a lot of fibre and phytic acid, which inhibit the digestion of all three constituents, so that although it contains more than does white bread, the amount actually absorbed by the body is about the same. This fact convinced many nutritionists in the past that there was little to choose between white and wholemeal bread and that the amount of fibre in wholemeal bread could actually prove harmful to those people with delicate constitutions. Recent research has, however, brought to light a fact which was ignored for many years. Certain diseases, such as cancer of the large intestine, diseases of the bowel, deep vein thrombosis and diverticulitis of the colon, are rampant and a major cause of death in communities which eat fibreless white bread and refined foods. In communities which live on a diet of fibrous whole-grain cereals and fresh vegetables, these diseases are absent. Whether or not the circulatory diseases, known as the 'diseases of affluence', are caused entirely by lack of fibre in the diet, fibrous foods such as bran are undoubtedly effective in their treatment and should be a part of everybody's daily diet. The lack of fibre and texture in white bread may also be responsible for the high incidence of dental caries in young people. White bread tends to stick in the mouth and, when it is eaten with jam, it acts like cement in sticking the jam to the teeth – an ideal recipe for dental decay. Wholemeal bread is a simple and effective source of roughage. It is also much tastier than commercially produced white bread. Surely nobody who has tasted a thick slice of crusty wholemeal bread straight from the oven would ever again be satisfied with the meagre sliced white flannel sold all over the country.

Where wholemeal bread is sold, more and more people are buying it and master bakers cannot cope with the demand for 'real' bread from their shops. Where the choice is between spongy white or spongy white dyed brown, the consumption of bread is declining, the more so as bread increases in price. The bread industry has only itself to blame for this trend, by creating a fashion for the sandwich loaf. If the industry joined the master bakers in making a greater variety of breads containing fibre, it would not only be better nutritionally, but we could once again be self-sufficient in flour.

Know Your Loaf

White bread is made with 70 per cent extraction flour with the bran and germ removed. White bread invariably contains a great many additives apart from the compulsory nutrients. Rice flour, soya flour, egg and milk products are permitted ingredients in certain types of loaves.

Wheatmeal or brown bread, not to be confused with wholemeal, which can be a very different product, can be made from flour of 80 per cent to 90 per cent extraction or from 70 per cent flour with added fibre and colouring (caramel). It must contain at least 0.6 per cent fibre and can contain some soya flour. The same additives are permitted as for white bread.

Hovis is a wheatgerm bread. Wheatgerm breads can be brown or white loaves with added wheatgerm and colouring. The same additives are permitted as for white bread.

Granary bread is a wheatmeal loaf with malted wheat and rye grains added. The same additives are permitted as for white bread.

Wholemeal bread is bread made from the entire wheat grain. The use of additives is restricted but colouring, yeast stimulating preparations, emulsifiers, stabilizers and preservatives are permitted and are often used by chain bakeries. In 1976 the Vegetarian Society launched a 'Campaign for Real Bread' to encourage the sale of real wholemeal loaves without additives as sold by most private bakers and health shops.

Flour

Wholemeal flour has by law to be milled from the entire wheat grain. No other additives are permitted or necessary. There are various wheat flours of extraction rates ranging from 70 per cent to 100 per cent which are suitable for baking lighter brown breads, cakes and pastries. Some brands of these contain no additives. It is also possible to buy unbleached white flour from health shops and some grocers. There are many different types of flour apart from wheat, such as barley, rye, maize, rice, potato and soya. These make satisfactory bread when used together with wheat flour but they do not contain enough gluten to rise well on their own.

Baking Bread

The easiest way to ensure that you get 'real' bread is to make your own, using additive-free flours. Bread recipes often sound mystifying and complicated whereas the technique is actually extremely easy, provided a few simple rules are observed.

Yeast
Yeast can be used fresh or dried. Fresh yeast can be bought by the ounce from some bakers and wholefood shops. It will keep well in an airtight container in the refrigerator for up to two weeks, or for several months in a deep freezer. Fresh yeast tastes a little sweeter and milder than dried. Dried yeast is widely available in grocers' shops and keeps indefinitely. Both types of yeast are started in the same way – by sprinkling them into a glass or cup of slightly sweetened warm water and leaving them for a few minutes to dissolve and froth. Yeast is killed by high heat (necessary in baking, of course, but not before), by prolonged contact with metal or by excessive amounts of salt.

Kneading the dough
Bread has to be kneaded until the texture of the dough is smooth and elastic. This not only mixes all the ingredients thoroughly but it also releases the gluten so that the dough can have a good strong rise. Don't be timid when kneading the dough; it can be handled quite roughly, in which case two minutes' kneading each time will be quite sufficient. If the dough is very slightly wet and elastic (not actually slippery though) it will be easier to knead and will also rise more quickly than a stiff dough.

Leaving the dough to rise
After the first kneading, the dough should be left in a floured or greased bowl and covered with a damp tea-towel or polythene bag. It can rise overnight in a cold larder or refrigerator, for two hours or so at room temperature or for one hour or so in a warm place. When the dough has doubled in bulk, knock it down and knead once more – again two minutes will be ample – and leave to rise ('prove') a second time in tins or on a baking sheet in a cool or warm place.

The timing of bread-making can be adapted to suit your own schedule and, provided you give the dough a little help, it will do all the hard work for you.

Basic 100 Per Cent Wholemeal Bread

Makes 1 large loaf

1½ lb/750 g 100 per cent wholemeal flour
½ oz/10–15 g fresh yeast or 1 tsp dried yeast
¾ pint/450 ml warm water
1 dsp brown sugar
1 tsp salt
2 tbs oil or 1½ oz/35 g margarine

Pour ¼ pint/150 ml of the warm water into a small bowl. Stir in the sugar and sprinkle the yeast into it. Leave for 10 minutes or so for the yeast to dissolve and froth (use the same method for fresh or dry yeast). In a large bowl, mix the flour and salt and rub in the fat, making sure that it is evenly distributed throughout the flour. Pour the yeasty liquid into the flour and add most of the rest of the water. Whether or not you need the whole ¾ pint/450 ml will depend on the coarseness of the flour, as even 100 per cent flours will vary. Knead the dough until it is smooth (2 minutes is ample) and leave in the bowl, covered with a damp cloth, to rise. Left in a cool place, the dough will take about 2 hours to rise. In a warm place, it will take about an hour. The time can be cut further by placing the bowl in a polythene bag.

When the dough is double its original size, knock it down and knead until light (again, about 2 minutes is long enough). Press the dough into a greased and floured 2-lb/1-kg tin, or roll it into a ball or sausage shape and place on a baking sheet. Cover again and leave to double in size. Again, this can be done in a cool place (even overnight in the refrigerator). In a warm place it will take from 15 to 20 minutes. Bake for about 40 minutes with the oven at gas mark 8 (450°F, 230°C). Check by removing the loaf from the tin and tapping the bottom. If it sounds hollow, it is done.

Cracked wheat grains, sesame seeds, poppy seeds or any other grains or spices can be pressed into the dough before it proves. The loaves can be glazed before they are baked with a little beaten egg or salted milk, or after they are baked with a light brushing of honey or sugar syrup.

Quick Wholemeal Bread or Graham Bread

An American, The Rev. Sylvester Graham, was one of the first advocates of vegetarianism in the late nineteenth century. He believed, as many doctors do now, that bran should be an important part of the diet. 100 per cent wholemeal flour is still called Graham flour in the United States. This bread tends to be heavier than ordinary wholemeal bread.

FOR 3 LOAVES:

3½ lb/1.5 kg 100 per cent wholemeal flour (or, for a granary loaf, 3 lb/1.25 kg wholemeal flour and ½ lb/225 g cracked wheat and malt, the last two mixed and soaked in cold water for an hour, then drained)

1 oz/25 g fresh yeast or 2 tsps dried yeast
1 oz/25 g brown sugar
1 dsp salt
2¼ pints/1.25 litres warm water

Grease and flour three 1-lb/500-g loaf tins. Mix the flour and salt in a bowl (with the soaked grains if used). Leave in a warm place while waiting for the yeast and sugar to froth with ¼ pint/150 ml of the water. Pour the yeasty liquid and the water into the flour and stir with a wooden spoon. The dough should be so wet that it is almost slippery. Spoon the dough into the tins and leave in a very warm place to rise. This bread is best made when you are cooking other things so that it can be left to rise above the hot stove. Otherwise, put the tins on a wire rack above a radiator or near a fire. When the dough has risen about a third, it is ready to bake. If it rises much higher it will be too open and crumbly in texture. Bake for ¾ to 1 hour with the oven at gas mark 5 (375°F, 190°C). The loaves should sound hollow when they are cooked.

Three Grain Bread

This bread contains soya flour which is about 50 per cent protein. Soya flour is considered to improve the shelf life and volume of bread. It increases the protein content and improves the essential amino acid balance, as soya is high in lysine, and cereals are not. This bread is quite light in colour and has a nutty flavour.

FOR 1 LOAF:

12 oz/350 g 100 per cent wholemeal flour
4 oz/125 g medium oatmeal
2 tbs sunflower oil
1 dsp sugar
1 tsp salt

4 oz/125 g unbleached bread flour
4 oz/125 g soya flour
½ oz/10–15 g fresh yeast or 1 tsp dry yeast
just under ¾ pint/450 ml water

Mix the flours and oatmeal in a large bowl with the salt. Rub in the sunflower oil, making sure that it is evenly distributed. Crumble the yeast into a bowl with the sugar. Pour over ¼ pint/150 ml of the warm water and leave to froth. Pour the yeast into the flour, add the rest of the warm water and knead the dough until smooth.

Leave the dough until doubled in bulk (about 2 hours at room temperature). Knock down and knead again until light. Press into a 2-lb/1-kg tin and leave to prove for 20 minutes in a warm place or 1 hour in a cool place. Bake for 40 minutes with the oven at gas mark 8 (450°F, 230°C) or until it sounds hollow when tapped.

Limpa

This is a Swedish recipe for a rich and spicy dark rye bread.

FOR 2 LARGE LOAVES:

12 oz/350 g rye flour
¼ pint/150 ml milk (or water)
1¾ lb/800 g wholemeal flour
2 tbs molasses
1½ tsps fennel seeds, warmed under the grill and ground
1 tbs oil
¾ pint/450 ml brown ale
1 oz/25 g fresh yeast dissolved in 4 fl oz/100 ml water with 1 tsp molasses
1 dsp grated or chopped orange peel
1 tsp salt

Warm the ale and beat to a thick paste with the rye flour. Leave to stand, covered, for 12 hours.

Crumble the wheat flour, salt, orange peel, fennel seeds and oil with the rye mixture until all the ingredients are thoroughly amalgamated. Pour in the dissolved yeast and the milk, warmed with the molasses. Mix well and knead for 2 minutes. Leave the dough to rise until doubled. Knock down and knead again, divide the dough into two, shape into oblongs, make a few shallow cross cuts in each loaf and leave to rise once more on floured baking sheets. Bake with the oven at gas mark 6 (400°F, 200°C) for 45 minutes. Brush with water once during baking and again on taking the loaves out of the oven. This bread is delicious, particularly while it is still warm, and it will keep well for about a week.

Home-made Baking Powder

2 oz/50 g cream of tartar
3 oz/75 g ground rice
1 oz/25 g bicarbonate of soda

Mix all the ingredients together well and put through a sieve several times.

Plain Scones

8 oz/250 g wholemeal flour or 4 oz/125 g wholemeal and 4 oz/125 g unbleached flour
pinch salt
1 oz/25 g margarine or butter
2 tsps baking powder
1 tsp sugar (optional)
¼ pint/150 ml milk

Rub the fat into the flour, salt and baking powder. Mix in the sugar and the milk (water can be used instead), knead lightly and quickly, roll out to a ¼-inch/4-mm thickness and cut into rounds. Bake for about 15 minutes with the oven at gas mark 7 (425°F, 220°C).

Any mixture containing baking powder should be baked immediately it is moistened. The liquid sets off a chemical reaction, causing the baking powder to aerate the mixture. The reaction stops if the dough is left uncooked for too long.

Bran Scones

4 oz/125 g wholemeal flour
1 tbs brown sugar
1 egg
water if necessary
2 tbs bran
1 tsp baking powder
2 oz/50 g margarine

Rub the margarine into the flour; add the remaining dry ingredients and lastly the egg. Make into a stiff dough, adding water if necessary. Roll out and cut into rounds. Bake in the centre of an oven at gas mark 6 (400°F, 200°C) for 15 minutes.

Herb Scones

To make half rosemary scones and half sage scones:

7 oz/200 g wholemeal self-
*   raising flour*
good pinch salt
1 tsp dried sage or 1 dsp
*   fresh*

3 fl oz/75 ml water
1½ oz/35 g margarine
1 tsp dried rosemary or
*   1 dsp fresh*

Divide the flour into two separate bowls and add the rosemary to one and the sage to the other. Divide the margarine and add one half to each bowl with a little salt. Rub in the margarine and mix in the water. Knead the dough a little, then cut into rounds. Bake in a hot oven for 10 minutes.

Pastry

Pastry made with 100 per cent wholemeal flour tends to be crumbly and, unless you have a particularly light hand, rather tough. Eighty-one per cent extraction flour is more suitable, or half 100 per cent and half unbleached white flour.

Rubbed-in pastry will keep well in an airtight container in the refrigerator for up to two months, and the water can be added as the pastry is needed.

Basic Wholemeal Shortcrust Pastry

Enough for the underneath and top of an 8-inch/20-cm pie.

8 oz/250 g 81 per cent flour
*   or 4 oz/125 g 100 per*
*   cent flour and 4 oz/125 g*
*   unbleached bread flour*

4 oz/125 g soft margarine
3–4 tbs water
pinch salt

Rub the margarine quickly and lightly into the flour

and salt. Mix in the water, using a knife, and knead the pastry a little until smooth. Add a little more flour if the dough is too sticky. Leave in a cool place for ½ hour before using.

Soya Shortcrust Pastry

This is very light and nutty – good for sweet flans. Enough for the underneath pastry for a 10-inch/25-cm flan tin.

2 oz/50 g 100 per cent
*   wholemeal flour*
2 oz/50 g soya flour
3 oz/75 g soft margarine

2 oz/50 g unbleached flour
pinch salt
1–2 tbs water

Mix the flours and salt and rub in the margarine. Moisten with water and knead lightly to mix. Leave for ½ hour in a cool place before rolling out.

Half-Wholemeal Flaky Pastry

This is a very light pastry – good for savoury or sweet flans.

4 oz/125 g 100 per cent
*   wholemeal flour*
6 oz/180 g soft margarine
pinch salt

4 oz/125 g unbleached bread
*   flour*
3–4 tbs water

Mix the flour, salt, margarine and water with a knife. It doesn't matter if there are still small lumps of margarine in the mixture. Flour a pastry board and roll out the pastry to a rectangle. Fold into a rectangle a third of its size by turning two edges into the centre. Give the pastry a quarter turn, roll out and fold again, and repeat once more. Refrigerate for ½ hour before using. If the dough is still streaky, roll out and turn again.

Millet and Wheatgerm Pastry

Another nutty pastry, light and crunchy in texture. Unlike the shortcrusts and flaky pastries, it is only really suitable for a flan and not for a top pastry.

5 oz/150 g 100 per cent
   wholemeal flour
2 oz/50 g wheatgerm
4 oz/125 g soft margarine

pinch salt
1 oz/25 g whole millet or
   millet flakes
4 tbs water

Rub the margarine into the flour, millet, wheatgerm and salt. Mix with the water. Leave the pastry to rest in a cool place before using.

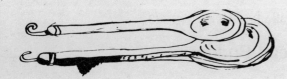

Fatless Pastry

This recipe was published by the Ministry of Food during the Second World War when fats were rationed. Now that we are told to cut down on saturated fats, it comes into its own once more.

8 oz/225 g 81 per cent flour
  or 6 oz/175 g 100 per
  cent wholemeal and
  2 oz/50 g unbleached
  bread flour

1 level tsp baking powder
pinch salt
just under ¼ pint/150 ml
  cold milk

Mix the flour, baking powder and salt. Stir in the milk. Roll out and bake (as soon as it is mixed) for 30 minutes with the oven at gas mark 6 (400°F, 200°C). Serve hot.

   N.B. If this pastry is cooked for too long, it becomes leathery.

Biscuits and Cakes

Digestive Biscuits

4 oz/125 g medium oatmeal
4 oz/125 g wholemeal flour
pinch salt
1 small egg

1½ oz/35 g sugar
3 oz/75 g margarine
small pinch bicarbonate of
  soda

Rub the margarine into the flour and oatmeal. Add the sugar, salt and soda, and bind with as much egg as is necessary. Sprinkle a little oatmeal onto a board and roll out the pastry. Sprinkle more oatmeal on top and roll into the pastry. Cut into shapes and bake with the oven at gas mark 6 (400°F, 200°C) for 10 to 15 minutes.

Carrot Cake

8 oz/250 g wholemeal flour
1 heaped tsp cinnamon
4 oz/125 g sugar
4 oz/125 g chopped walnuts
3–4 tbs water

2 tsps baking powder
3tbs oil
2 eggs, beaten
1 lb/500 g grated carrots

Mix the flour, baking powder and cinnamon; add the oil, sugar and beaten eggs, and beat well. Stir in the nuts and grated carrots and thin to dropping consistency with 3 to 4 tablespoonfuls water. Beat well. Grease and flour an 8-inch/20-cm cake tin, pour in the cake mixture and bake with the oven at gas mark 4 (350°F, 180°C) for about 1¼ hours.

Apple Slice

3 oz/75 g margarine or
  butter
5 oz/150 g flour
2 medium cooking apples

¼ tsp baking powder
3 oz/75 g brown sugar
½ lemon
2 eggs

Cream together the margarine or butter and sugar. Squeeze the juice of the half lemon and grate the rind. Grate the apples, leaving the peel on. Beat the eggs lightly. Mix all the ingredients together well and place in a greased 9-inch/23-cm flan tin. Bake in an oven at gas mark 5 (375°F, 190°C) for 40 minutes.

Apricot and Walnut Loaf

12 oz/350 g bread dough
2 oz/50 g chopped walnuts
1 oz/25 g sugar or honey

4 oz/125 g dried apricots, soaked for 1 hour and chopped
1 oz/25 g margarine or 2 tbs oil

Knead the bread dough and work in all the other ingredients. Leave to rise until doubled in bulk; then put the mixture into a greased and floured tin and prove until well risen. Bake with the oven at gas mark 5 (375°F, 190°C) for 35 to 40 minutes.

This method can be used for many other sweet breads – other dried fruits, such as raisins, dates, figs, can be used instead of apricots; treacle or sugar can be used instead of honey; sweet herbs and spices can be added – the variations are endless.

Apricot Shorties

This recipe was given by Judy Walker.

8 oz/250 g dried apricots
½ level tsp ground cinnamon
¾ pint/450 ml water
6 oz/175 g plain wholemeal flour

1 tbs honey
1 tbs lemon juice
6 oz/175 g butter or margarine
6 oz/175 g oatmeal

Soak the apricots overnight or for a couple of hours in water. Preheat the oven to gas mark 5 (375°F, 190°C). Put the apricots and their juice, honey, cinnamon and lemon juice in a pan. Cook over a low heat until the apricots are soft and the mixture has thickened. Add more water if necessary during cooking. Leave to cool. Melt the butter or margarine over low heat in a large pan. Stir in the flour and oatmeal. Grease a 9-inch/23-cm cake tin. Press half the crumb mixture into the tin, spread cooked apricot mixture on top and cover with remaining crumb mixture. Press down lightly. Cook for 30 minutes; cut into slices while still hot but leave in tin until completely cold. They are best eaten within a few days of being made. (The same recipe can be used with dried dates instead of apricots.)

Left-over Bread

See also Bread Soup, page 43.

Bread Pudding

Serves 6

8 oz/250 g stale bread
4 oz/125 g currants, raisins or sultanas
2 oz/50 g brown sugar or honey
1 tsp mixed spice

1 egg
4-5 dried apricots or dates, chopped
1 tsp candied peel or peel of 1 fresh lemon
2 oz/50 g walnuts

Soak the bread in cold water for an hour or so and then strain and squeeze dry. Mash with a fork until smooth and add the fruits, peel, sugar or honey, nuts and spice. Add the beaten egg last. The consistency should be like creamed cake mixture and drop off the spoon. If it isn't, add some milk, water, beer or cider. Pour into a greased cake tin 8 inches/20 cm in diameter and bake gently for an hour or until firm. Turn out and sprinkle with sugar. Chopped fresh fruit can be used as well as, or instead of, the apricots or dates; the nuts can be omitted, and nutmeg or cinnamon used instead of the mixed spice. Bread pudding keeps well in an airtight container and is in fact better after a few days, as the fruits swell, making the pudding more moist.

Torrijas

This is a Spanish recipe for using up stale bread.

6 pieces stale bread
½ pint/300 ml milk
sugar and cinnamon

1 egg
butter or margarine for
    frying

Beat the egg with the milk in a shallow dish. Lay as many bread slices in this as possible and leave to soak for about 5 minutes on each side, or until they are well impregnated. Heat the butter or margarine in a frying pan and fry the bread on both sides until brown and crisp. Keep one batch warm in the oven or under the grill while the rest is cooking. Serve on hot plates with sugar and cinnamon, or a sugar syrup flavoured with cinnamon and lemon peel.

Breadcrumbs

Dry some left-over toast in a low oven (while other things are cooking). Put through a fine mincer or grater and store in an airtight container.

Rusks

Cut a loaf of stale bread into thick slices. Bake in the oven at gas mark 6 (400°F, 200°C) for 20 minutes.

To Freshen Stale Bread

Dip in water or milk and bake for 15 minutes in a very hot oven.

Croûtons

Dice a few slices of stale bread and fry in oil until crisp, either on their own or with garlic and herbs. Sprinkle onto soups and casseroles just before serving. They keep well in an airtight container and can be reheated when required.

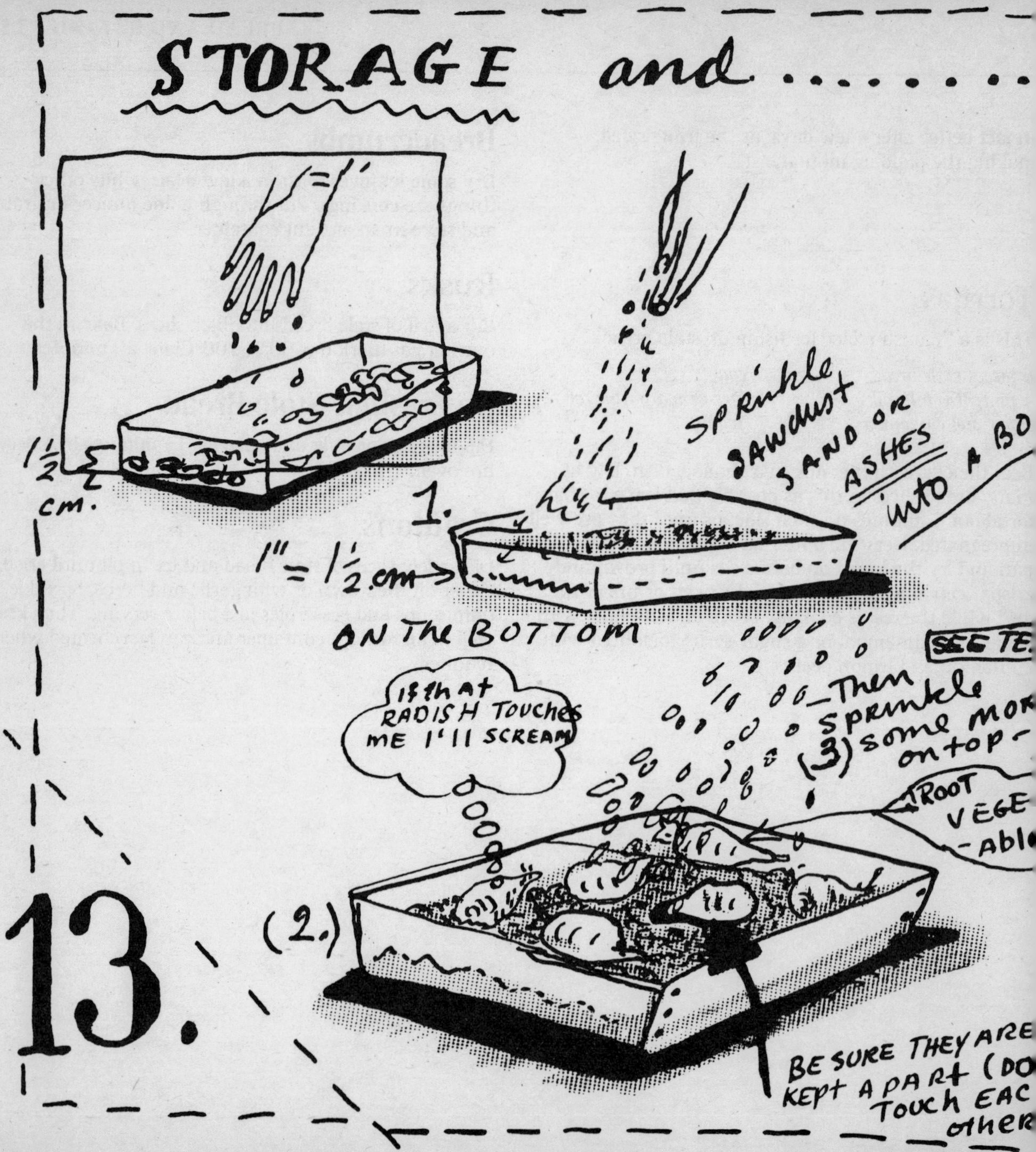
STORAGE and ....
1½ cm.
1.
SPRINKLE SAWDUST SAND OR ASHES INTO A BO
1" = 1½ cm
ON THE BOTTOM
SEE TE
IF THAT RADISH TOUCHES ME I'LL SCREAM
Then SPRINKLE (3) SOME MOR ON TOP -
ROOT VEGE -ABL
13.
(2.)
BE SURE THEY ARE KEPT APART (DO TOUCH EAC OTHER

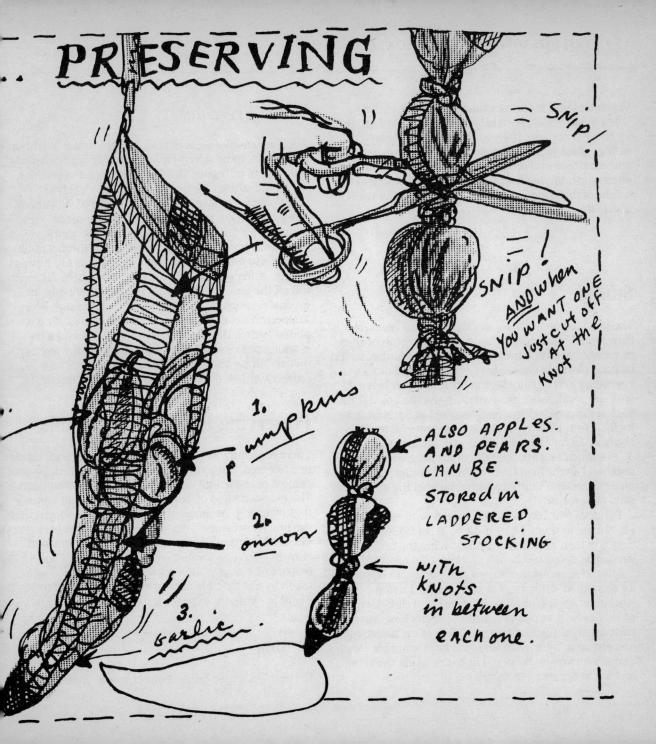

Vegetables and fruits are undoubtedly at their best when fresh (preferably straight out of the garden), but for those times, especially in the winter and early spring, when produce is expensive and the choice limited, stored and preserved foods are invaluable. It is often worth buying fruit and vegetables cheaply at the height of the season, and storing or preserving them for leaner times.

Storage

The ideal temperature for storing fruit and vegetables is between 33° and 40°F (1° and 5°C). A frostproof shed or garage, or a cool and airy room, loft or larder, would be good places to choose for storage. Most root vegetables can be stored for months in boxes layered with dry sand, ashes or sawdust. Raise the box a little so that air can circulate freely around it. Sprinkle a 1-inch/3-cm thick layer of the storing material in the bottom and lay the vegetables on it, ensuring that they do not touch one another. Cover the vegetables with another 1-inch/3-cm layer of the dry matter, and carry on as necessary, finishing with a layer of the ashes, sand or sawdust.

Potatoes will keep well in a sack as long as plenty of air can get at them. Light must be excluded, otherwise they will turn green, thereby producing the toxic substance, solanine.

Marrows, pumpkins, onions and garlic can be hung for storage in string bags or well-laddered nylon stockings. Apples may also be stored in well-laddered nylons as long as a knot is tied in the stocking between each apple, to prevent any possibility of rot spreading. Just cut off a 'knot' each time you need an apple. Apples and pears can also be stored in boxes, using the same method as for root vegetables.

Home Freezing

A freezer enables gluts of food, bought at the height of the season, to be stored for long periods with relatively little loss of nutrients. But frozen fruit and vegetables are no substitutes for fresh ones, as invariably the texture and the flavour are slightly altered. In general, freezers are most useful for storing home-made convenience foods: purées, sorbets, soups, stews, casseroles, bread, cakes, etc. made from surplus produce for use when time and/or fresh ingredients are in short supply. A freezer should be kept at least three quarters full all the time as it is hardly worth investing in an expensive machine for cooling air! A large supply of Tupperware containers, margarine and yoghurt pots, plastic bags, string or covered wire, labels and a few marking pens are essential equipment for the freezer owner. All food should be chilled thoroughly in a refrigerator before being transferred to the freezer.

Preserving Fruit and Vegetables

There are many ways in which fruit and vegetables can be preserved. They can be dried, salted, pickled, bottled, canned or made into chutneys, jams, jellies and sauces. The oldest method of food preservation is undoubtedly that of drying. Archaeological studies have shown that the practice of sun-drying fish and meat goes back 4000 years. The drying of grapes for sultanas, raisins and currants also has ancient origins. Dried soups have been prepared for over 200 years and a cake of dried soup taken by Cook on his voyage around the world in 1772 is still in existence to prove it.

Drying

Herbs, peas, broad beans, runner beans, haricot beans,

mushrooms, plums, apples, pears and apricots, dandelion (for grinding as a coffee substitute) and horseradish roots can all be dried. (Most apples store well in their natural state so only windfalls or varieties which don't keep well need be dried.)

Prepare the food that is to be dried: string runner beans, tie in a muslin bag and dip in boiling water for about 3 minutes, then drain; pod broad and haricot beans and peas (peas may be left in their pods on the bush and gathered after the sun has dried them); core pears and apples and cut into desired shapes (quarters, rings, etc.), then dip immediately into salted water, to prevent browning, and drain.

Spread whatever is to be dried on wire trays or gauze or muslin stretched tightly over a frame, so that plenty of air can circulate. Drying can be done in the oven, using 'left-over' heat (as mentioned in Chapter 4, 'Energy and Equipment'), or on racks on top of the stove when the oven is on. Herbs should be hung in bunches in a dry, dark place, or spread on trays in a cool oven (excessive heat or direct sunlight will quickly destroy their fragrant oils).

All dried foods should be kept in airtight jars and stored in a dark cupboard or larder. Make sure food is really dry before putting it in jars – peas, beans, herbs and roots should be brittle, and mushrooms and fruit like chamois leather.

Fruit should be soaked for 12 hours before being cooked and peas and beans treated as for pulses (see page 100). Mushrooms only need to soak for half an hour.

Salting

Beans are the best vegetables for salting, but cabbage is also suitable. In Germany and Eastern Europe, cabbage is fermented during the salting process to make sauerkraut.

To salt runner beans: String, wash, dry and weigh the beans. Each 1 lb/500 g beans will require 3 lb/1½ kg salt. Layer the salt and the beans, starting and finishing with salt, in a wide necked glass jar or crock, pressing them down firmly. Cover the jar. After 2 to 3 days, when the level has dropped, fill the jar with more layers of salt and beans, finishing again with salt. Then cork or cover the jar tightly and leave in a cool place. Sauerkraut is made in the same way, but the crock is left in a warm place and the surface skimmed every few days and more salt added. It is ready in 2 to 3 weeks.

The beans or cabbage should be washed thoroughly before use and cooked in water without salt. Sauerkraut can be cooked in a mixture of vinegar and water with a few caraway seeds and a little sugar.

Bottling

Most fruits are suitable for bottling. You will need special bottling jars either with screw tops or clips. Ordinary jam jars are not strong enough. First, prepare the fruit by washing, peeling, coring and cutting as necessary. Soft fruit should be rinsed in a sieve with cold water for a minute, then left to drain.

All equipment used for bottling must be scrupulously clean. First, ensure that all bacteria and mould are killed. This can be done in a sterilizer or pressure cooker, but the simplest way is in the oven. Set the oven at gas mark ½ (250°F, 130°C). Fill the bottling jars evenly with the prepared fruit and stand the jars on a wooden board or asbestos mat, ensuring they do not touch each other or the oven walls. Cover the jars with clean lids. The oven time varies according to what is being bottled, but allow about 50 minutes for soft fruits, 1 hour for hard fruits and 1½ hours for tomatoes.

Towards the end of the cooking time, boil the glass lids and rubber rings for 15 minutes (boil metal top rings for 1 minute only or the lacquer will come off). Have ready a wooden chopping board, a wooden spoon and boiling water as the bottling must be done as quickly as possible to prevent bacteria getting in.

Remove the jars from the oven, add a teaspoonful of sugar (salt for tomatoes) to each one and top up with boiling water. Tap the jars to release air bubbles. Put the rings and lids on quickly. After 48 hours test the vacuum by unscrewing the outer ring and lifting the jars by their sealing lids. If they stay on the bottling has been satisfactorily completed. Store the jars in a dark place as light will rob the fruit of its vitamin C content. Jars may be used year after year, but replace the rubber rings each time.

Fresh vegetables can also be bottled but as they are low in acidity the oven method will not sterilize them effectively. A pressure cooker will, at a constant temperature of 250°F (130°C) for 40 minutes at 15 lb pressure. Before bottling, the prepared vegetables (peas, beans, broad beans are best) must first be sterilized in boiling water for 5 minutes. Insufficiently sterilized vegetables are dangerous and it is advisable before contemplating bottling them to consult a detailed manual on the subject such as *Home Preservation of Fruit and Vegetables*, published by H.M.S.O.

Jams and Jellies

Jam-making works on the principle that the water in the fruit is suspended in sugar, which acts as a preservative in stopping the action of bacteria and yeasts. The set of jams and jellies is achieved by balancing the proportions of pectin, acid and sugar. Pectin and acid are found in varying degrees in all fruits. The acid regulates the amount of pectin that is released and the pectin is the substance which regulates the success of the set. Fruits with a high pectin content include: apples, redcurrants and blackcurrants, gooseberries, oranges and lemons. Those with a low pectin content include: blackberries, cherries,

strawberries and rhubarb. These should have pectin added in the form of lemon juice, citric acid, apples (or the cores and pips tied in a muslin bag) or commercially produced pectin (Certo). Most jam recipes use sugar and fruit in equal proportions. The jam will still set if less sugar is used – one of the recipes in this chapter uses twice as much fruit as sugar – but the keeping qualities will not be quite as good, though the flavour will be better. Surprisingly, those fruits which are high in vitamin C retain a considerable amount after boiling. Even one helping of blackcurrant jam can supply 5 per cent of the daily vitamin C allowance.

General Procedure for Jam-Making

The pans for jam-making should be scrupulously clean and preferably made of stainless steel, good quality aluminium or hard enamel.

The fruit should be quite dry and fresh. Simmer the fruit in the pan, with a little water, until it is soft. Stir in the sugar over a low heat until it is dissolved (for most recipes the proportion should be at least 40 per cent sugar to 60 per cent fruit). When the sugar has completely dissolved, the heat can be increased and the jam boiled (without stirring) until setting point is reached – usually after 20 to 30 minutes.

To test whether the jam is set, use one of the following methods:

1. Use a jam thermometer: when the temperature has reached 220°F (105°C) the jam is ready.
2. Put a teaspoonful of the jam onto a cold plate and leave it to cool. (Take the pan off the heat while doing this test in case the jam passes the setting point.) Push it with your finger – if it goes crinkly, the jam is ready; if it is still runny, cook the jam a little longer.
3. Dip a wooden spoon into the jam and hold it

horizontally to let it cool. Turn the spoon vertically and if the juice falls off in a single thick droplet the jam will set. If it runs off the spoon in several drops the jam needs more cooking.

Have the jars ready, dry and warmed and fill them to he brim with jam, covering them immediately. Metal ops will do for jam, but for long-term storage they hould be lined with greaseproof paper or waxed paper ircles; alternatively, use waxed paper circles and ellophane covers. Store the jam in a cool, dry, dark lace.

Chunky Blackberry Jam

nough to fill two 1-lb/450-g jam jars

| lb/1 kg blackberries | juice of 2 lemons |
| 2 oz/350 g sugar | |

lace blackberries in a preserving pan and soften over a ow heat with a little water and the lemon juice. Add he sugar and stir until dissolved. Boil until setting point s reached (about 20 minutes), pour into warmed, clean ars and cover.

Low Sugar Jam

The following is a war-time recipe for jam, when sugar vas in short supply. The use of salt helps preservation nd brings out the flavour of the fruit.

| lb/2 kg fruit | 2 lb/1 kg sugar |
| -2 tsps salt | |

Marinate the fruit with the sugar and salt for 24 hours, nd then treat in the ordinary way.

Once the jars are opened, they should be kept in the efrigerator, or the jam should be eaten up quickly.

General Procedure for Jelly-Making

Jelly-making works on the same principle as that for jam, but it is only the fruit juice which is boiled with the sugar.

Use dry, fresh fruit. Place it in a large pan, together with a few whole spices (or as specified in the recipe). Pour in water until it can just be seen through the top layer of fruit and simmer until the fruit is soft. The mixture must now be strained through a jelly bag or a double layer of butter muslin which should be sterilized in boiling water and used while it is still wet (a dry bag will absorb too much of the precious juice). Leave the bag to strain for several hours, until it has stopped dripping. Strictly speaking, the bag should not be squeezed as this will produce a cloudy jelly, but if you want more jelly and don't mind if the appearance is not perfect, squeeze the bag gently once or twice – not too much or the juice will be bitter. Measure the juice and, for every 3 teacupfuls, use 2 teacupfuls of sugar; then proceed as for jam. Use the juice within 24 hours of straining.

Apple Jelly

Cut any bad sections out of the apples and quarter them. Allow 1 pint/600 ml of water and a quarter of a lemon to each 1 lb/500 g of apples. Bring apples, lemon and water to the boil (with a few sprigs of apple mint, if available), and simmer until apples are tender. Strain the whole mixture through a jelly bag or several thicknesses of muslin, allowing it to drip for a few hours. Measure juice into a preserving pan and, for each 1 pint/600 ml of juice, add 14 oz/400 g of sugar. Heat the juice, stirring until all the sugar is dissolved. Bring to the boil and cook at a medium simmer until the jelly has reached setting point. (Use the same tests as for jam.) Pour immediately into warmed, dry jars and seal.

Elderberry and Hawthorn Jelly

Use equal quantities of elderberries and hawthorn hips (2 lb/1 kg of each will produce about 1 pint/600 ml juice). Pick over the fruit and strip the elderberries from their stalks, though it doesn't matter if a few stalks get in. Simmer the fruit with a cinnamon stick and one or two cloves until it is quite soft. Strain through a jelly bag. Measure the juice and, to each cupful, use the juice of ½ lemon and 1 cupful sugar. Dissolve the sugar in the juice over a low heat, increase the heat and boil until the jelly will set. Pour into warmed, dry jars and seal immediately.

Fruit Butter

Fruit jellies use only a little of the juice from the fruit, especially if the bag is not squeezed, and the remaining pulp is still full of flavour. The pulp can be used to make a fruit butter. Proceed as in the following recipe – the principle is the same for any fruit.

Apple Butter

Pass the pulp left over from making jelly through a sieve. Measure the purée in cups and, to each cupful, allow ¾ cupful of sugar. Mix the pulp and sugar together in a saucepan and add a stick of cinnamon, a few cloves and a strip of lemon peel. Stir over a low heat to melt the sugar and cook slowly for 3 to 4 hours, stirring frequently to prevent it sticking to the pan. When the purée is thick and translucent it is ready. (Test it by dropping a spoonful onto a plate. If it doesn't ooze water, then it is done.) You will find that, as the butter thickens and the temperature rises, it will tend to spatter drops all over the kitchen. Either stand clear and clean up the mess afterwards or cook the purée in the oven at a low temperature.

The remaining pulp from the apple butter can be used to make juice. Half-fill a saucepan with the pulp and fill to the top with water. Simmer for 20 minutes or so, strain and sweeten if necessary. Not many nutrients are left by this stage but the juice tastes good! Uncooked apple peel and cores can be used to make juices in the same way.

Chutneys

Usually apples or marrows are used as bases for chutneys but green or red tomatoes, gooseberries, apricots, pears and plums are also excellent. The ingredients are cooked with vinegar, salt, sugar and spices, which act as preservatives. Chutneys improve in flavour if they are kept for a few months before being used.

No special equipment is needed but, if you are using jam jars with metal lids, line them with greaseproof paper or the vinegar may cause the metal to rust and ruin the chutney.

Hot Apple and Marrow Chutney

Makes about 10 lb/5 kg

4 lb/2 kg apples (preferably Bramleys) peeled, cored and chopped	*5 chillies*
	2½ lb/1 kg sugar
2 lb/1 kg marrow, peeled, deseeded and chopped	*½ lb/250 g raisins or sultanas*
1 lb/500 g onions, chopped	*3 oz/75 g salt*
½ lb/250 g currants	*3 tbs or 1½ oz/35 g mustard powder*
1½ oz/35 g ground ginger	*few blades mace*
½ oz/10 g turmeric	*2½ pints/1.5 litres vinegar*

Place all the ingredients in a preserving pan and leave overnight. The next morning, heat through slowly, bring to the boil and simmer for 2 hours until a rich brown colour. Pour into hot jars and seal.

Special Gothic Apricot Chutney

1 lb/500 g dried apricots,
  soaked for 1 hour or more
  in water
1 pint/600 ml clear malt
  vinegar
1 tsp coriander seeds
1 chilli

2 sticks cinnamon
½ lb/250 g soft brown sugar
6 peppercorns
½ tsp mustard seeds
4 allspice berries
1-inch/3-cm piece of ginger
  root, cut in small pieces

Bring the vinegar to the boil with the spices and sugar. Boil for 15 to 20 minutes until reduced and thickened, then add the apricots. Cook for 10 minutes if you want the apricots to be firm or, if you prefer a thicker consistency, boil for 20 minutes or longer. Seal while hot and keep for at least 3 weeks before using.

Pickles

The general principle of pickling is to soak food (vegetables, fruit, nuts or eggs) in brine and then to pack it into jars with spiced vinegar. The brine can be wet (2 oz/50 g kitchen salt to 1 pint/600 ml water) or dry, in which case the food to be pickled is placed between layers of salt. This stage lasts for 1 to 2 days, after which time wet-brined produce should have the excess salt shaken off. To prepare the vinegar, boil it for 15 minutes with whatever whole spices are required, and strain. Pack the brined foods into jars (ordinary jam jars will do as long as metal caps are lined with vinegar-proof paper). Cover with the vinegar and seal.

Pickled Cauliflower

1 head cauliflower
1 pint/600 ml vinegar
1 pint/600 ml wet brine

1 level tbs mixed pickling
  spices

Break the cauliflower into flowerets and soak in the brine for 24 hours. Make sure that the brine covers the cauliflower completely and, if necessary, put a plate on top to press it down. Boil the vinegar, with the pickling spices, for 15 minutes. The following day, drain and rinse the cauliflower and pack into jars. Cover with the cold vinegar and seal immediately.

Pickled Melon Rind

Makes 2 lb/1 kg pickle

1 lb/500 g melon rind (2
  average-sized honeydew
  melons)
4 oz/125 g salt, dissolved in
  2 pints/1 litre water

¾ pint/450 ml distilled malt
  vinegar
¼ pint/150 ml water
6 cloves
1 stick cinnamon
¾ lb/350 g sugar

Cut the melon rind into strips, cover with salt water and leave to stand for 24 hours. Drain off the water, rinse the rind, cover with fresh water and boil until tender. Pour off the water and rinse the melon rind again. Mix the vinegar, water, sugar and spices. Heat gently to dissolve the sugar, then add the melon rind. Simmer, uncovered, until the syrup is thick and clear. Remove the spices and pack the pickle into sterilized jars. Seal with a vinegar-proof cover.

Pickled Nasturtium Seeds

These taste very much like capers and in some ways are preferable as they have a fresher, more peppery taste and remain crisp after pickling.

The ripe seeds are pea-sized and bright green, with a ribbed surface, and they hang in clusters of two or three on the plant. Regular picking of the seeds encourages the growth of more flowers and hence more seeds. If you are lucky, you may get three or even four crops in a season, especially if the plants are grown in a sunny position.

To pickle the seeds: Separate the clusters, removing the stalks. Wash the seeds and leave them to soak for 12 hours in strongly salted water. Drain and wash the seeds and pack them into small screw top jars. Boil clear malt vinegar (enough to cover the seeds), with pickling spice (about 1 dessertspoonful to 1 pint/600 ml vinegar), for 10 minutes. Strain the vinegar and pour hot over the seeds. Cover the jars immediately. They will be ready in about 2 to 3 weeks. Use them in any recipe where capers are called for.

Nasturtium leaves can be pickled in the same way for use in salads or stuffings. If the leaves are large they can be used instead of fresh ones in the recipe for stuffed nasturtium leaves on page 83; they will not need the preliminary soak in hot water.

Nasturtium flowers can be used fresh in salads and are sometimes used to flavour vinegar. Follow the method for flavoured vinegars, using 4 tablespoons flowers to 1 pint/600 ml vinegar.

Altogether, nasturtiums are very useful culinary plants.

Vinegar

It is possible to make home-made vinegar from wine or cider which has gone off, but it must be confessed that it is not as good as that manufactured commercially. If you find yourself confronted by a quantity of wine or cider which is not good enough to drink, pour it into glass jars and cover them with a double layer of muslin secured by a rubber band. Place the jars in a cool, dark place and forget about them for a year. Then, strain the vinegar and add 1 teaspoonful of brown sugar per pint/600 ml, to take the edge off the sharpness. Pour into screw top bottles.

Tarragon Vinegar

Infuse 4 tablespoons crushed fresh tarragon in 2 pints/ 1 litre wine or cider vinegar, in corked bottles, for 6 weeks, shaking the bottles occasionally. Strain into fresh bottles and put a sprig of fresh tarragon in each one. Delicious for salad dressings.

Garlic Vinegar

Use the same method, with 8 cloves garlic to each 1 quart/1 litre vinegar. Strain and bottle and keep for salad dressings. You may want to dilute it with plain vinegar if you find the flavour too strong.

Spiced Vinegar

Simmer 2 pints/1 litre malt vinegar with 3 tablespoons pickling spice for 15 minutes. Cool, strain and bottle. Use for pickles and chutneys.

Sauces and Condiments

By the late 1700s sauces were being bottled commercially. These, together with sauces created from fresh ingredients, gradually replaced the complicated spicing of many dishes. Today, a wide range of commercially bottled sauces is available but many can easily be home made, and will taste better for it.

Sterilized bottles should be used for sauces, but make sure that they will withstand heat. Place them in a panful of cold water and bring to the boil. Boil them for 5 minutes and pour in the sauces as soon as possible. Always use new corks to seal the bottles, boiling them in the sterilizing pan before inserting them. Dip the tops of the corked bottles into melted paraffin wax to ensure an airtight seal.

Mushroom Ketchup

Makes about 3 pints

3 lb/1½ kg fresh mushrooms
¾ lb/350 g salt

To each quart/litre of the resulting liquor (see below) add:

1 tbs or ½ oz ground ginger
½ tsp powdered mace

1 heaped tsp or ¼ oz allspice
¼ tsp cayenne papper

The mushrooms must be dry. Layer the mushrooms with the salt in a large glass jar. Leave for 3 days, stirring three times daily. Pour the mushrooms and salt into a saucepan and stew very slowly until the juice runs freely. Strain the liquor into a large jar that will withstand heat, add the spices and place the jar in a panful of boiling water. Simmer for 3 hours. Strain several times through muslin, pour into bottles, cork and seal with wax.

Herb Sauce

Makes about 1 pint/600 ml

This is handy for flavouring sauces and stews. It is adapted from a recipe of Mrs Beeton's.

1 stick horseradish
few sprigs winter savory,
   basil, marjoram, thyme
   and tarragon
½ pint/300 ml vinegar

1 pint/600 ml water
2 shallots, finely chopped
6 cloves
thinly peeled rind and the
   juice of 1 lemon

Wash and scrape the horseradish and wash the herbs. Place all the ingredients in a large pan and simmer gently for about 20 minutes. Strain and bottle when cold. Add a fresh bunch of herbs to each bottle. This sauce can be made with dried herbs.

Tomato Sauce

4 lb/2 kg tomatoes
½ oz/15 g salt
½ pint/300 ml vinegar,
   spiced if preferred

2 shallots
pinch cayenne pepper
4 oz/125 g sugar
½ tsp paprika

Chop the tomatoes and slice the shallots and place in a pan. Stir over a very low heat at first, then increase to a simmer and cook the mixture until it thickens. Rub mixture through a sieve, return to the pan and add the remaining ingredients. Continue boiling and stirring until the mixture reaches a creamy consistency (this is important). Pour the sauce into hot sterilized bottles and cork at once. Store in a cool, dry place.

Tomato Purée

For this recipe you will need proper bottling jars (see page 157 for instructions).

For every 2 lb/1 kg tomatoes, allow 1 teaspoonful salt. Cut up the tomatoes and put in a pan with the salt. Bring slowly to the boil, adding a very small amount of water. Cook gently, stirring frequently, until the mixture is a thick pulp. Strain the pulp through a sieve and pour into warmed, dry bottling jars. Cover the jars and immerse them in a pan of water, bring to a temperature of 190°F (85°C) (or a fast simmer), and maintain for 15 minutes. When cool, test seal as for bottling. Store in a cool, dry place.

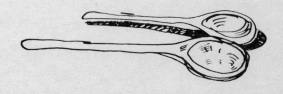

Pesto

Pesto is a famous Genoese sauce for pasta, made with fresh basil, pine nuts, oil and Parmesan cheese. This recipe is based on that sauce but uses ingredients which are more readily available in Britain. It should make enough for four as a sauce with pasta.

1½-2 oz/40-50 g fresh
   parsley, basil or
   marjoram
sprinkling of salt
1 clove garlic

2 oz/50 g walnuts
1 oz/25 g finely grated dry
   cheese
1-2 tbs olive oil

Pound everything except the oil in a pestle and mortar until puréed. Gradually add the oil, drop by drop, stirring all the time, until a creamy texture is reached. The sauce will keep for quite a while in storage jars if a film of oil is left on top. Delicious with pasta; also good for flavouring soups, stews, sauces and vegetables.

Crunchy Mustard

4 oz/125 g white mustard
   seeds
1 tsp ground black pepper
1 sprig tarragon
2-3 blades mace
½ tsp fennel seeds
sweet cider
4 oz/125 g black mustard
   seeds

1 crumbled chilli
1 tsp coriander seeds
1 crushed clove garlic
   (optional)
1 tsp salt
cider or wine vinegar

Put all the ingredients in a bowl and cover with a mixture of sweet cider and cider or wine vinegar. Steep for 24 hours and pound in a pestle and mortar until the mixture reaches the desired consistency. Put into a screw top or corked jar. The mustard may need topping up occasionally with cider or vinegar as it tends to dry out.

Alternatively the seeds can be ground dry in a coffee grinder and then moistened with vinegar and cider.

Brewing :!!

1.

← Bits of Apple + others

FOLLOWING RECIPE - BOIL UP *BRUISED APPLES*, *ELDER FLOWERS*, *OAK LEAVES*, OR *STINGING NETTLES*.

N.B. THESE ARE INDIVIDUAL RECIPES. NOT ALL LUMPED TOGETHER.

2

STERIL-IZED

POUR INTO GALLON FERMENTATION JAR

MORE...

3.

INSERT (BUBBL AIRLOCK THIS PREVENTS VI BACTERIA GETTING INTO WINE.

THE BUB IS A GUIDE TO THE SPEE OF FERMEN

3.

LEAVE FOR A FEW WEE

14

GASES ESCAPE.

4.

WHEN THE WATER LEVEL IS STATIC.

THEN....

5.

WINE SHOULD BE SIPHONED OFF.

LEAVING BEHIND ALL SEDIMENT

PUT INTO GALLON JARS AND LEFT TO MATURE FOR A FEW MONTHS.

6. UNSCREW CAPS FROM TIME TO TIME TO ALLOW GAS GASES TO ESCAPE.

SOME ADDITIONAL FERMENTATION MAY OCCUR.

LATER ON..........

7.

8. LATER ON.....

GLUG GLUG

Wine*

Alcohol is produced when yeast feeds on sugar. Alcoholic drinks are all made on the principle of producing a pleasant environment for the yeast to live and feed in, and this requires not only sugar, but warmth, oxygen and a nitrogenous substance, in an acidic medium. A good recipe will contain a balance of these elements and should naturally ferment to a finish. That is to say, a point should be reached at which the yeast has used up the sugar supply or, alternatively, has produced such a concentration of alcohol that it can no longer survive in the environment it has created for itself. Sweet wines contain unconverted sugar; dry wines have had nearly all the sugar transformed into alcohol.

Various types of yeast are available, ranging from ordinary baker's yeast to special wine yeasts such as champagne or burgundy yeasts. These latter special yeasts (obtainable from home-brewing shops or Boots the chemist) produce a better end result, but the whole wine-making process takes longer if they are used because they work more slowly than baker's yeast. Dried yeast in pellet or tablet form should be activated before being introduced into the basic solution. This is done by putting 2 teaspoons of the yeast into ¼ pint/150 ml warm water (about 75°F, 24°C, or as specified on the packet) mixed with 2 teaspoons of sugar. A baker's yeast will be activated in about 15 minutes but the more refined yeasts will take anything up to 12 hours. Both when starting the yeast and fermenting the wine, it is important to realize that the warmer the environment, the faster the necessary chemical reactions will occur. It is thus preferable to keep these solutions in an airing cupboard or a warm room.

The recipes in this section include enough sugar to make a dry wine. If the fermentation ceases while the liquid is still quite sweet it is most probably because of a lack of warmth, a lack of nitrogenous substance or a lack of acidity. The nitrogen can be supplied by yeast nutrient, which can be bought from a home-brewers' supplier, and the acidity can be supplied most easily by adding lemon juice.

Unless you have almost unparalleled quantities of self-discipline and very few friends, you will find it advisable to think in terms of 5-gallon batches, or 5-gallon sherry containers from wine shops or food stores. By the time you have tested your wine once or twice, sought one or two second opinions and sampled the odd bottle, you will find you have very little change from a gallon – so think big!

Metal spoons or containers should never be used for wine-making, as the metal is likely not only to kill the yeast but also to give the wine an unpleasant taste.

The following recipes assume that the brewers will use jars which have been sterilized with boiling water or Campden tablets, which are available from any shop selling home-brewing equipment. A 'bubbler' airlock should be inserted in the fermentation jars to prevent vinegar bacteria getting into the wine. The bubbler is also a useful guide to the speed of fermentation. When the water level in the airlock becomes static, the wine should be siphoned off and all the sediment of dead yeast and precipitation left behind. The wine should be kept in large containers at this stage – 5-gallon jars are ideal – and left to mature for a few months. Some additional fermentation may occur during this period and it is worth checking the storage jars from time to time and unscrewing the caps to release any gas pressure which has built up.

When tiny gas bubbles are no longer rising in the liquid, fermentation can be said to be finished, but no brewer is ever certain that it will not quite spontaneously begin again. However a 3- to 6-month storage, as well as allowing the wine to mature, will

*The introduction and recipes for the wine section were compiled by Sandy Heslop.

llow some time for this unexpected fermentation to manifest itself. If nothing has happened at the end of his period, the wine may be siphoned off into bottles. Any sediment which settles during storage should be eft behind when the wine is racked off into bottles. Once the wine is bottled, it should be left unopened for at least 3 months.

Wine can be made from almost anything. Very good wines can be made from produce which is free and otherwise unused, e.g. bruised windfall apples or elderflowers, oak leaves and stinging nettles. Some greengrocers are prepared to give away bruised fruit and vegetables at the end of the week – ideal for wine-making.

Elderflower Wine

Makes 1 gallon/4 litres

2 pints/1 litre elderflowers, picked when flowers are dry and full
2 pints/1 litre boiling water
2½ lb/1 kg sugar

juice of 1 lemon
wine yeast (as per instructions on packet), or 2 tsps dried baker's yeast

Pour the water over the elderflowers as if to make elderflower tea. Stir lightly and, after half an hour or so, strain off the liquid onto the sugar. Make this up to 1 gallon/4 litres with cold water and add the juice of the lemon. Start some yeast (see page 168) and, when it is thoroughly active, add it to the liquid. Generally speaking, the more aristocratic the yeast, the more refined the wine. Hence champagne yeast will produce a genuine connoisseur's tipple, whilst ordinary brewer's yeast will produce the equivalent of elderflower beer – potent and pleasant none-the-less.

The wine mixture with its yeast should now be poured into a fermentation jar and an airlock inserted to prevent bacteria from infecting the wine. The length of this fermentation will depend primarily on the warmth of the environment, the type of yeast and the amount of sugar in the solution. An ordinary baker's yeast works quickly and, in a warm room, should ferment out in 2 to 4 weeks. A refined wine yeast may take 6 months or more. Wait until obvious signs of fermentation cease, that is, until bubbles stop rising in the liquid. Siphon the wine off into another clean jar and put an airlock or stopper on it. Leave it to mature in a cool place for at least 3 months, at which time it can be bottled and corked for storage. To produce a champagne-type wine, dissolve a level teaspoonful of sugar in each bottle of wine and tie in the cork. This will allow some additional fermentation to occur in the bottle. Once bottled, leave the wine for at least 2 months before drinking.

Windfall Apple Wine

Makes 1 gallon/4 litres

6 lb/2.75 kg windfall apples
3 pints/2.75 litres cold water
2½ lb/1 kg sugar
wine yeast (as per instructions on packet), or 2 tsps dried baker's yeast

1 tsp pectinase (available from home-brew shops or Boots)
⅓ cup chopped sultanas (optional)

For this recipe the apples need to be crushed when raw. Cider or fruit presses can be bought for this at considerable expense or hired at a nominal charge from some brewing shops. An easy do-it-yourself alternative is to obtain a log about 4 feet/120 cm long, 6 inches/15 cm in diameter and fairly straight. Neatly saw across one end to flatten it, and bounce it up and down on the apples in a plastic bucket or bin. If the base of the container does not rest directly on the ground, it will need reinforcing with a piece of wood shaped to fill the gap. The deeper the bucket or bin, the less spillage will occur and the larger will be the number of apples that can be crushed at one go. Crush the apples, skin, core and all, and add to the cold water. Stir daily for 3 to 4 weeks and then strain off the liquid (through muslin). Add the sugar and stir until dissolved; then add the started wine yeast (see page 168), and then the pectinase to help clear and settle the clouding. Add the chopped sultanas if you want the wine to have body.

To transform into a rich, red wine also add the strained juice from 2 lb/1 kg of blackberries at this point, infused and crushed in 1 pint/600 ml of boiling water.

Transfer the liquid into a fermentation jar and top up with water, if necessary, to make a gallon. Insert an airlock and leave the wine to ferment to a finish. Then siphon it into a clean jar, making sure that the sediment is left behind. Put an airlock or some other stopper in the wine jar and store it in a cool place to mature. After about 3 months, bottle and cork it and leave for at least another 2 months before drinking.

Hawthornberry Wine

Makes 1 gallon/4 litres

This is an old Cornish recipe, from Susan Wood.

1 gallon/4 litres hawthorn berries	6 pints/3 litres water
wine yeast (as per instructions on packet), or 2 tsps dried baker's yeast	2 lemons
	3 lb/1 kg white sugar

Crush the berries in a bowl, add the juice and peel from the lemons (remove all the white pith) and pour on the cold water. Leave for 5 days, stirring daily, then strain and dissolve the sugar in the juice. Put into jars or bottles and add the activated yeast (see page 168). Keep in a warm room on a tray to catch the froth. When frothing stops, wipe the jars clean and insert airlocks.

After fermentation ceases, treat as follows, depending on the type of wine required:

Dry still wine: Put jar in a cool place for 14 days and then siphon into a clean jar. Make sure second jar (storage jar) is completely full and cork. Wax the top of the cork and store in a cool cellar for 6 months. Rack o and bottle and cork firmly. Store bottles on their sides for 6 months before use.

Dry sparkling wine: Leave in a very cold place for 14 days and then siphon off. For each gallon of wine, boil up ¼ lb/125 g sugar and ½ pint/300 ml water, skimming if necessary. When cold, add to wine, mix, bottle and cork. Tie or wire the corks and store the bottles for 6 months on their sides.

Blackberry Wine

Makes 1 gallon/4 litres

4 lb/1.65 kg blackberries	wine yeast (as per instructions on packet),
½ gallon/2 litres cold water	or 2 tsps dried baker's
3 lb/1.25 kg sugar	yeast
juice 1 lemon	¾ pint/375 ml boiling water
½ tsp yeast nutrient	

Wash the blackberries. Put in a bowl with the cold water and mash. Activate the yeast with a little sugar (see page 168) and put it with the lemon juice and yeast nutrient into the blackberry mash. After 5 days, it should have a good froth. Strain the liquid through a jelly bag onto half the sugar and stir until it dissolves. Tip the liquid into a fermentation jar and insert an airlock. For the colour to stay dark, ferment in a dark place or in a pottery or dark-coloured glass jar or wrap the jar in paper. Leave to ferment for 2 weeks. Dissolve the remaining sugar in the boiling water. Add the sugar solution to the wine and make up to 1 gallon/4 litres with cold water. Leave to ferment out – it can take anything from 3 weeks to 9 months.

Siphon off the wine into clean jars, making sure that you leave any sediment behind, and put airlocks or stoppers in them. Store for 3 months in a cool place and then siphon into bottles and cork them. Leave for at least 2 months before drinking.

Beer*

At one time every pub brewed its own beer. Nowadays most of the beer in England is brewed by the six major brewers; gone are many of the regional variations. However, beer can still be brewed on an extremely small scale. One gallon in a (colourless) plastic bucket can produce quite good results. The end product is not only superior to most commercial beers but is much cheaper. And since the major ingredient of beer, by weight, is water, brewing at home could reduce the number of heavy lorries carting what is largely water – and tastes like it – around the country.

Beer is made from malted barley, sugar, hops and yeast. The yeast converts the sugar in the malt to alcohol and during fermentation a gas, carbon dioxide, is given off. The most tedious part of brewing is extracting the sugars from the malted barley grain and most home-brewers find it easier to start from malt extract. Hops are both a flavouring (they give beer a bitter taste) and a preservative.

Cleanliness: By far the most important secret of beer-making is to keep all utensils clean and sterile. Bottles, barrels and the fermenting vat must be sterilized, either with boiling water (which is no good for plastic) or with sodium metabisulphite. To sterilize with sodium metabisulphite, add 1 teaspoon of it to 1 pint/600 ml water and rinse the container thoroughly with this solution; rinse again with clean water. Do not use any cast iron or steel in your brewing, otherwise your beer will have a metallic taste.

Bottling: The best sort of bottles are quart screw-top

*The introduction and recipes for the beer section were compiled by Mick Hamer.

bottles, which are becoming increasingly hard to get. Ordinary beer bottles can be used, but you will need to buy a 'crown corker' to seal them. Plastic barrels can be obtained from home-brewing suppliers.

A *hydrometer* provides a useful, but not essential, check on the fermentation process. In the recipe for bitter, the specific gravity will fall over the first week from about 1.045 to about 1.000.

Bitter

To make 5 gallons/20 litres

4 lb/1.5 kg malt extract (not the sort with added cod-liver oil)	3 oz/75 g Colding's hops
	2 tsps brewer's yeast (not baking yeast or wine yeast)
2 lb/750 g sugar	

These ingredients are available at most branches of Boots the Chemists and home-brewing shops, and from home-brewing suppliers, by mail order. Yeast can also be bought from a local brewer or you can cultivate your own.

Boil three quarters of the hops in 4 pints/2 litres of water for $\frac{3}{4}$ hour. Add the remaining hops 5 minutes before the end of the boiling time. Strain through muslin, use the hops for compost and keep the liquor.

Boil the malt extract in about 4 pints/2 litres of water for about 15 minutes. Stir to make sure that it doesn't stick and make sure that it doesn't boil over (which it does easily). Dissolve the sugar in the hops liquor, add this to the malt extract and make up to 5 gallons/20 litres in a sterile container. Cool to about 75°F (24°C) (just above normal room temperature). Add the yeast and stir vigorously. Do not add yeast at temperatures above 80°F (26°C). Leave covered with a cloth.

After 12 hours there should be a head. After 2 days remove this head – another will form and it may be necessary to skim this off twice.

After about a week the fermentation will have ceased; that is, no more bubbles of gas will be seen. In cold weather, it may take a day or two longer, and in hot weather, a day less. The fermentation can be speeded up by keeping the beer in a warm place during this time.

Siphoning can be done with a plastic tube, but a glass tube with a U-bend (to avoid sucking up sediment), together with plastic tubing and a tap, is more convenient and devices are sold in most places which sell home-brewing supplies. Siphon the beer into bottles (leave the sediment in the bottom of the fermenting vat and use this to start the next brew) or a plastic barrel and add 1 teaspoon of sugar to each quart/1.2 litres of beer. Do not add more sugar or your bottles may explode. If you add less, your beer will be flat. Only use returnable beer bottles – other bottles may not be able to take the pressure. Leave a 1-inch/3-cm gap above the liquid. Keep the beer for at least a week.

A beer of this strength will be at its best about a month after being put in a bottle or barrel, although it will be drinkable sooner.

Other recipes (for 5 gallons/20 litres in each case):

Mild Ale

4 lb/1.5 kg malt extract
2 lb/750 g crystal malt
  grains
3 oz/75 g Fuggle's hops
1 lb/400 g sugar
2 tsps yeast

Follow instructions in the bitter recipe for treatment of malt extract, hops and sugar. For the malt grains: crack them with a rolling pin or grind in a coffee mill and boil them with 4 pints/2.25 litres of water for ½ hour. Leave to settle and strain the liquor through muslin and add to fermenting vat. Then follow bitter instructions.

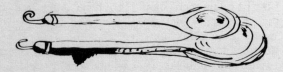

Brown Ale

4 lb/1.5 kg malt extract
2 lb/750 g brown sugar
2 tsps yeast
1½ oz/40 g Fuggle's hops
8 oz/200 g crystal malt
  grains

Follow instructions for Mild Ale.

Stout

4 lb/1.75 kg malt extract
3 lb/1.25 kg dark sugar
1 lb/450 g black malt grains
½ lb/225 g crystal malt
  grains
3 oz/75 g Fuggle's hops
2 tsps yeast

Follow instructions for Mild Ale.

Barley Wine

8 lb/3.75 kg malt extract
6 lb/2.75 kg sugar
4 oz/125 g Colding's hops
2 tsps yeast

This is the strongest beer it is possible to make. It takes longer to ferment (about 10 days) and needs to be kept longer in the bottle or barrel before being drunk – at least 3 months and preferably 6 or more. It will keep for years. Follow the recipe as for bitter.

If you like your beers stronger, add more malt or sugar to the recipes above. If you like weaker beer, reduce the amount of sugar. It is best not to reduce the quantity of malt extract in your beer to below 4 lb/1.5 kg in 5 gallons/20 litres or your beer will lack body. If you do increase the amount of malt or sugar, you will probably find that you prefer to increase the amounts of hops in your recipe. If the recipe is too bitter for your taste, reduce the quantity of hops.

If you live in a part of the country where the water is not permanently hard, bitter and barley wine will benefit from the addition of ½ teaspoon of Epsom salts (magnesium sulphate) per 5 gallons/20 litres and 1 teaspoon of plaster of Paris.

Cider

Wash some apples (any sort will do, but cider or cooking apples are best), crush them up (see page 169) and then compress them, extracting the juice. Leave the juice in a warm place. After a few days, it will ferment – this can be very vigorous and precautions should be taken to allow for overflow. When fermentation has ceased, bottle the liquor.

Ginger Beer

2 oz/50 g baker's yeast
½ pint/300 ml water
9–12 level tsps sugar
9–12 level tsps ground ginger

1 lb/500 g sugar
1 pint/600 ml boiling water
juice of 2 lemons

Mix together the yeast, the ½ pint/300 ml water, 2 level teaspoonfuls of sugar and 2 level teaspoonfuls of ginger and leave for 7 to 10 days. For each day add a further 1 teaspoonful of sugar and 1 teaspoonful of ginger. Strain the mixture through muslin. Add to the liquid the 1 lb/500 g sugar, the 1 pint/600 ml boiling water and the juice of the lemons. Dissolve the sugar and make up to 1 gallon/4 litres with cold water. Bottle, leaving a 3-inch/8-cm gap at the top of each bottle. Leave for 2 hours before corking lightly. Drink after 7 days.

Growingyour...

1.   2.   3.

15.

in a greenhouse

Own

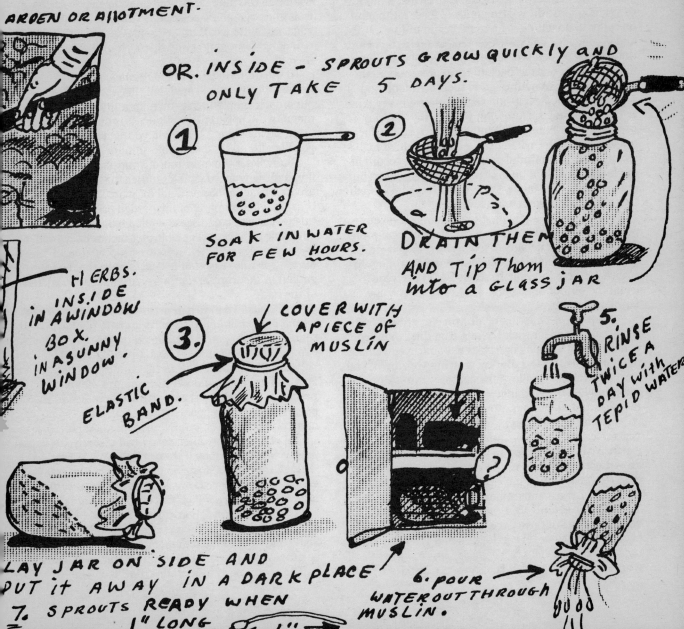

GARDEN OR ALLOTMENT.

OR. INSIDE – SPROUTS GROW QUICKLY AND ONLY TAKE 5 DAYS.

① Soak in water for few hours.

② DRAIN THEM AND TIP THEM into a GLASS JAR

HERBS. INSIDE IN A WINDOW BOX. IN A SUNNY WINDOW.

③ ELASTIC BAND. COVER WITH A PIECE OF MUSLIN

5. RINSE TWICE A DAY WITH TEPID WATER

LAY JAR ON SIDE AND PUT IT AWAY IN A DARK PLACE

6. POUR WATER OUT THROUGH MUSLIN.

7. SPROUTS READY WHEN 1" LONG

The revival of interest in vegetable growing is not just a reaction against the soaring price of food, although this has a lot to do with it. The trend began in the 1960s and it coincided with a widespread desire to be nearer the sources of food production. Some people began to move from large cities back to rural areas where they could be closer to nature, grow their own food and, in some instances, be self-sufficient in almost every way.

The advantages of growing your own fruit and vegetables are numerous. You can eat fresh produce all the year round (providing crops are not ruined by bad weather), avoid harmful pesticides and rest secure in the knowledge that, no matter how little money you may have in your purse, there will always be something to eat from your garden or allotment.

An average-sized town garden can in fact be quite productive. R. H. Best and J. J. Ward noted, some years ago, that the retail value of food grown in private gardens where houses are built at a density of ten to twelve per acre has only to reach £4.00 per year to equal the output of an acre of better-than-average farmland.

Perhaps most tempting of all, you can grow varieties which are noted for their flavour. The thick-skinned, commercial fruit and vegetables which travel well are often quite flavourless. But by growing your own, you can, for example, produce the delicious thin-skinned tomatoes like the Harbinger variety instead of the tasteless and ubiquitous Moneymaker which suits the commercial growers. Also, many of the less common vegetables, like seakale, kohlrabi and salsify, which are expensive or hard to buy in the shops, can be home-grown with very little trouble. The Henry Doubleday Research Association has produced several useful booklets for the amateur gardener; these include *The Vegetable Finder* and *The Fruit Finder*, which list varieties, some of them excellent ones, which are being phased out of the seed catalogues, and *The Good Taste Guide to Garden Fruit and Vegetable Varieties*, the title of which speaks for itself. It is also worth keeping a regular watch on the new seed catalogues, as new varieties of fruit and vegetables, resistant to disease and the vagaries of the weather, are being developed all the time – making gardening a much less chancy affair than it used to be.

To the uninitiated, gardening may seem tremendously complicated, but, like many other pursuits, it simply has its own jargon which helps to magnify the apparent mystique. It is no more daunting than, say, cooking. Above all, you will need good soil, good health and a reasonable amount of time.

You will get the most out of your garden or allotment if you grow your vegetables (other than perennials like asparagus and globe artichokes, which need permanent beds) in different parts of the garden each year, as in this way the risk of disease will be reduced. It is not advisable to have a vegetable plot near a busy road, as the vegetables will get covered with poisonous exhaust fumes. For this reason, it is best to keep the flower garden at the front of the house and hide the vegetables at the back.

Most of us live in urban areas and have to make do with a limited amount of space. A patio garden is better than having no garden at all and quite a few vegetables can be grown in tubs and pots. Growing vegetables in polythene bags filled with fertilized soil is a fairly recent idea and helps to cut down the amount of watering needed in summer as the moisture is retained in the bag. Aubergines, peppers, lettuces, cucumbers, marrows, courgettes, pumpkins, tomatoes, potatoes, spring onions and runner beans will all thrive in bags, pots or tubs, especially if they are put in a sunny, sheltered position. Mushrooms will do well in a well-ventilated shed or cellar as long as the temperature is between 50° and 65°F (10° and 17°C). Vines or any kind of cordon fruits should grow well up a sunny wall. Choose varieties which can be grown out of doors. Some tomatoes and cucumbers, for example, can only be grown in a greenhouse or under frames or cloches.

If your garden is a small one, devoted completely to

flowers, it could be worthwhile interspersing them with at least some vegetables with attractive foliage. Most herbs are suitable for this, as are globe artichokes, beets, runner beans, salsify, curly kale, fennel, ruby chard, asparagus pea and broccoli.

If you would like to grow all your own vegetables but do not have a big enough garden you can, of course, apply for an allotment – or 'leisure garden', as they are called these days. There are usually long waiting lists for allotments so it would be advisable to join one as soon as possible. Under the Smallholdings and Allotment Act of 1908, borough, district or parish councils are obliged 'to provide a sufficient number of allotments to persons... resident in the borough, district or parish and desiring to take same'. If you would like an allotment, ring or write to your local council. In 1944, 10 per cent of our home-grown foods were grown on the $1\frac{1}{2}$ million allotments in use and in private gardens. In 1975, there were only $\frac{3}{4}$ million allotments in England, with a waiting list of 60,000 applicants, 10,000 of whom lived in London. To show that land could be reclaimed for vegetable growing, Friends of the Earth took over a site near Waterloo Station in London which had been derelict since the war and turned it into a thriving allotment. The Friends of the Earth *Allotments Campaign Manual* describes the ways in which derelict land can be put to good, although temporary. use.

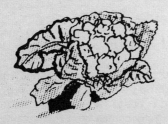

Another way to by-pass a long waiting list for allotments is to join a 'garden sharing scheme'. These are organized by Friends of the Earth and other groups in many parts of the country. The aim is to put people who want gardens in touch with people who have gardens but are unable to use them because of old age, ill health or lack of time to work them. Usually the tenant gardener pays rent in kind by giving some of the produce to the owner of the garden.

Indoor Gardening

Those lacking a garden or allotment can grow at least some produce indoors. A sunny windowsill can support a variety of herbs for use nearly all the year round. Sage, marjoram, basil, thyme, chervil, rosemary, mint, parsley, fennel and chives can all be grown successfully in pots. Make sure your herbs have enough water but don't over-water them as, on the whole, they thrive in somewhat dry climates. Try growing some miniature tomatoes in pots next to a sunny window. Green peppers will also do fairly well indoors in a sunny position.

Another way of gardening indoors is by cultivating sprouting beans; these are rich in protein and are highly nutritious. Sprouting beans are marketed by various seed merchants and wholefood shops and the varieties available include mung beans (Chinese bean sprouts), alfalfa, mixed salad sprouts, aduki beans, fenugreek and triticale. The sprouts grow astonishingly quickly and take only five or six days from start to finish. Soak the seeds in cold water for a few hours, or overnight. Drain them, tip them into a large glass jar and cover the top with a piece of muslin secured with an elastic band. Lay the jar on its side and leave it in a dark place. Rinse the sprouts twice daily with tepid water, pouring the water out through the muslin. The sprouts will be ready when they are about 1 inch/3 cm long. Alternatively, the sprouts can be grown wrapped up in a damp towel.

You can also grow carrot and Hamburg parsley tops by slicing off the top $\frac{1}{2}$ inch or inch (1 to 2 cm) of the vegetable and standing it in a saucer of water. Keep topping up the water, and within a few weeks you will have a few inches of leaves to use when parsley is scarce.

Mustard and cress is also very easy and quick to grow indoors. Scatter the seeds in a shallow tray or seed box containing one of the following: a thin layer of soil, a moistened flannel, or moistened cotton wool or blotting paper. Cover the box to make sure that light is excluded, otherwise the seeds will not germinate. Once they have, remove the cover. Cut the fully grown mustard and cress with scissors after 1 to 2 weeks.

CUCUMBER

Companion Plants

Plants, like people, react to each other. Some plants can tolerate their neighbours and even flourish in their company, whilst others are not only intolerant but will curl up and die if put next to a plant they do not like.

The reasons why plants react to each other are numerous. Plants compete for nutrients in the soil and for light. Some plants, such as the legumes, can fix nitrogen in the soil; the nitrogen produced can then be taken up by other plants. One plant may produce toxic substances which may act as a deterrent to pests feeding on a neighbouring plant.

For example, lettuces are compatible with strawberries, carrots and radishes; spearmint acts as an ant repellent; tomatoes and asparagus grow well together; tomatoes grown next to early brassicas help to ward off the cabbage white butterfly; and roses benefit from the presence of garlic. Many more examples can be found in *Companion Plants* by Helen Philbrick and Richard Gregg (London, Watkins, 1974).

Compost Heaps

Although so many kitchen scraps can be used for cooking, there will be some that no one will be vaguely interested in experimenting with. Even the most imaginative cook would have difficulty inventing new ways with old tea leaves, coffee grounds, eggshells and the tattiest outer leaves of vegetables. Anything organic (and this includes hair and nail clippings) can be used as compost to provide valuable humus for garden fertilizer.

A compost heap is very easy to construct. The aim is to encourage the breakdown of organic material by air, heat and bacteria. The heap needs a sheltered position, but preferably not against a wall. On the base of the heap, place rows of bricks resting on their long edges, with gaps between them, and place some twigs or sticks on top. This base will allow the air to circulate. Build a frame around the base with planks, netting or hardboard measuring roughly 1 square yard/1 square metre. Two layers of netting can be used with cardboard sandwiched between them. Cover the heap to keep out rain and keep in the heat, but be sure to water the heap in dry weather. Autumn heaps are ready to dig in by spring; spring heaps made before midsummer mature in time for autumn digging.

Municipal Compost

Unsorted municipal compost is potentially quite dangerous because it contains so much pulverized glass and plastic and is high in lead and cadmium. The high lead content mainly comes from the coloured inks (especially yellow) from packaging. Better systems for separating rubbish and more recycling schemes will have to operate and a switch to the use of vegetable dyes will have to take place before municipal compost is safe for the gardener. If the 2 million tons of food which we throw away each year were collected from restaurants, hotels, institutions, etc., separately from other rubbish, and sterilized, it could either be fed to pigs or sold to allotment holders, gardeners and market gardeners for compost. Three authorities (Worthing, Leicester and Jersey) are already operating successful schemes of this type and other councils should be encouraged to look into the feasibility of such schemes.

Sewage Sludge

Such an unappealing subject as sewage sludge may not have an obvious place in a cookery book, but it does relate to the fertility of the soil and is a resource which has been used, or rather mis-used, with the utmost stupidity, so it has crept in, appropriately, at the end of the book!

Nothing should be simpler than returning treated sewage sludge to the land where it belongs rather than piping it out to sea to pollute the coastline. Treated dried sewage sludge is seldom used nowadays because the drying process is expensive and because it contains high concentrations of toxic metals, especially lead and cadmium, mainly from industrial effluent and run-off water from roads.

However, the rising cost of artificial fertilizers may act as an incentive to the local authorities to separate domestic sewage from industrial wastes so that sewage sludge can be used more widely. If you are interested in the subject, we would recommend *Fertility without Fertilizers* by Lawrence D. Hills (available from the Henry Doubleday Research Association) and *The Toxic Metals* by Anthony Tucker (published by Earth Island).

Weights And Measures

Solid Measures

British

16 oz = 1 lb

Metric

1000 grams (g) = 1 kilogram (kg)

APPROXIMATE EQUIVALENTS

British	*Metric*
1 lb (16 oz)	450–500 g
$\frac{1}{2}$ lb (8 oz)	225–250 g
$\frac{1}{4}$ lb (4 oz)	100–125 g
1 oz	25 g

Metric	*British*
1 kg (1000 g)	2 lb 3 oz
$\frac{1}{2}$ kg (500 g)	1 lb 2 oz
$\frac{1}{4}$ kg (250 g)	9 oz
100 g	4 oz

Liquid Measures

British

1 quart	=	2 pints	=	40 fl oz
1 pint	=	4 gills	=	20 fl oz
$\frac{1}{2}$ pint	=	2 gills or 1 cup	=	10 fl oz
$\frac{1}{4}$ pint	=	8 tablespoons	=	5 fl oz
		1 tablespoon	=	just over $\frac{1}{2}$ fl oz
		1 dessertspoon	=	$\frac{1}{3}$ fl oz
		1 teaspoon	=	$\frac{1}{6}$ fl oz

Metric

1 litre = 10 decilitres (dl) = 100 centilitres (cl) = 1000 millilitres (ml)

American

1 quart	=	2 pints	=	32 fl oz
1 pint	=	2 cups	=	16 fl oz
		1 cup	=	8 fl oz
		1 tablespoon	=	$\frac{1}{3}$ fl oz
		1 teaspoon	=	$\frac{1}{6}$ fl oz

APPROXIMATE EQUIVALENTS

British	Metric
1 quart	1.1 litre
1 pint	600 ml
$\frac{1}{2}$ pint	300 ml
$\frac{1}{4}$ pint (1 gill)	150 ml
1 tablespoon	15 ml
1 dessertspoon	10 ml
1 teaspoon	5 ml

Metric	British
1 litre	35 fl oz
$\frac{1}{2}$ litre (500 ml)	18 fl oz
$\frac{1}{4}$ litre (250 ml)	9 fl oz
100 ml	4 fl oz

British	American
1 quart	$2\frac{1}{2}$ pints
1 pint	$1\frac{1}{4}$ pints
$\frac{1}{2}$ pint	10 fl oz ($1\frac{1}{4}$ cups)
$\frac{1}{4}$ pint (1 gill)	5 fl oz
1 tablespoon	$1\frac{1}{2}$ tablespoons
1 dessertspoon	1 tablespoon
1 teaspoon	$\frac{1}{3}$ fl oz

American	British
1 quart	$1\frac{1}{2}$ pints plus 3 tbs (32 fl oz)
1 pint	$\frac{3}{4}$ pint plus 2 tbs (16 fl oz)
1 cup	$\frac{1}{2}$ pint minus 2 tbs (8 fl oz)

Temperature Equivalents for Oven Thermostat Markings

Degrees Fahrenheit	Gas Mark	Degrees Centigrade	Heat of Oven
225	$\frac{1}{4}$	110	Very cool
250	$\frac{1}{2}$	120–130	Very cool
275	1	140	Cool
300	2	150	Cool
325	3	160–170	Moderate
350	4	180	Moderate
375	5	190	Fairly hot
400	6	200	Fairly hot
425	7	220	Hot
450	8	230	Very hot
475	9	240	Very hot

Bibliography

Allaby, M., Blyth, C., Hines, C., Wardle, C., *Losing Ground*, Earth Resources Research, 1974

Bender, Arnold E., *The Facts of Food*, Oxford University Press, 1975

Counter Information Service, *Unilever's World*, C.I.S. Anti-Report no. 11, 1975

Friends of the Earth, *The Allotments Campaign Manual*, 1975

Friends of the Earth Southampton, *Eco Cookbook*, Friends of the Earth, Southampton, 1975

Hines, C., *Food Coops*, Friends of the Earth, 1976
Crops and Shares, Friends of the Earth, 1976

Jacobson, M. F., *Eater's Digest, the Consumer Factbook of Food Additives*, Doubleday Anchor, New York, 1972

Lappé, F. Moore, *Diet for a Small Planet*, Ballantine, New York, 1975

Leach, G., *Energy and Food Production*, (International Institute for Environment and Development) I.P.C., 1975

Ministry of Agriculture, Fisheries and Food, *Food from Our Own Resources*, H.M.S.O., 1975
Manual of Nutrition, 8th edn, H.M.S.O., 1977

Roy, Dr Robin, *Wastage in the U.K. Food System*, Earth Resources Research, 1976

United Nations, *The World Food Problem: Proposals for National and International Action*, 1974

Wardle, C., *Britain and the World Food Crisis*, Friends of the Earth, 1974
Changing Food Habits, Earth Resources Research, 1977

ndex